Chosen Peoples

RELIGIOUS CULTURES OF AFRICAN AND AFRICAN DIASPORA PEOPLE

Series editors:
Jacob K. Olupona, Harvard University
Dianne M. Stewart, Emory University
and Terrence L. Johnson, Georgetown University

The book series examines the religious, cultural, and political expressions of African, African American, and African Caribbean traditions. Through transnational, cross-cultural, and multidisciplinary approaches to the study of religion, the series investigates the epistemic boundaries of continental and diasporic religious practices and thought and explores the diverse and distinct ways African-derived religions inform culture and politics. The series aims to establish a forum for imagining the centrality of Black religions in the formation of the "New World."

Chosen Peoples

Christianity and Political Imagination in South Sudan

CHRISTOPHER TOUNSEL

DUKE UNIVERSITY PRESS * DURHAM AND LONDON * 2021

Printed in the United States of America on acid-free paper ∞
Cover designed by Drew Sisk
Typeset in Portrait by Westchester Book Services

Library of Congress Cataloging-in-Publication Data
Names: Tounsel, Christopher, [dates] author.
Title: Chosen peoples : Christianity and political imagination in South
Sudan / Christopher Tounsel.
Other titles: Religious cultures of African and African diaspora people.
Description: Durham : Duke University Press, 2021. | Series:
Religious cultures of African and African diaspora people | Includes
bibliographical references and index.
Identifiers: LCCN 2020036891 (print) | LCCN 2020036892 (ebook) |
ISBN 9781478010630 (hardcover) | ISBN 9781478011767 (paperback) |
ISBN 9781478013105 (ebook)
Subjects: LCSH: Christianity and politics—South Sudan. | South
Sudan—History—21st century. | South Sudan—Politics and
government—2011– | South Sudan—Ethnic relations—Political aspects. |
South Sudan—Relations—Sudan. | Sudan—Relations—South Sudan.
Classification: LCC BR115.P7 T67 2021 (print) | LCC BR115.P7 (ebook) |
DDC 261.709629—dc23
LC record available at https://lccn.loc.gov/2020036891
LC ebook record available at https://lccn.loc.gov/2020036892

ISBN 9781478091707 (ebook/other)
https://doi.org/10.1215/9781478013105

Cover art credit: All Saints Cathedral, Juba, South Sudan.
Photo by Christopher Tounsel. Illustration by Drew Sisk.

This book is freely available in an open access edition thanks to
TOME (Toward an Open Monograph Ecosystem)—a collaboration
of the Association of American Universities, the Association of
University Presses, and the Association of Research Libraries—
and the generous support of the Pennsylvania State University.
Learn more at the TOME website, available at:
openmonographs.org.

For Timeka and Cairo

Contents

Acknowledgments

Timeka, I cannot express how much you mean to me. You were my study partner during those winter nights in the Duderstadt. You were my anchor during restless Juba days. You read countless drafts, engaged me in meaningful discussions, and walked with me as I navigated the joys and pains of this decade-long work. Through it all, you have borne with me in love with humility, gentleness, and patience. Thank you for sticking with this kid from Skokie.

I thank several organizations for the many resources it took to make my research travels. These include the Pennsylvania State University (Department of History, African Studies Program, and College of Liberal Arts), the University of Michigan (Department of History, Department of Afroamerican and African Studies, Horace H. Rackham School of Graduate Studies, and African Studies Center), Macalester College, the Andrew W. Mellon Foundation, the Woodrow Wilson National Fellowship Foundation, the Social Science Research Council, and the Council of American Overseas Research Centers.

At every research site, I was blessed with overwhelming illustrations of hospitality and support. Many thanks to the library and archival staffs in England (Durham University, Oxford University, the School of Oriental and African Studies, Lambeth Palace, and Birmingham University), Italy (particularly Fr. Prandina at the Comboni Mission Archive), Egypt (the American University in Cairo and the All Saints Cathedral, also in Cairo), South Sudan (particularly Youssef Onyalla at the South Sudan National Archives), and the United States (the Billy Graham Center Archives at

Wheaton College, Northwestern University, the Library of Congress, the National Archives, and the Presbyterian Historical Society). Many, many thanks to Derek Peterson, Justin Willis, Douglas Johnson, John Ryle, and everyone at the Rift Valley Institute for allowing me to participate in the 2012 archiving project in Juba.

Portions of chapter 4 and the conclusion appear in "Khartoum Goliath: SPLM/SPLA Update and Martial Theology during the Second Sudanese Civil War," *Journal of Africana Religions* 4, no. 2 (2016): 129–53.

Throughout the past few years, I have had the chance to meet some wonderful people who, in one way or another, provided valuable professional, academic, and emotional support. Many thanks to my Duke University family, which included Susan Thorne, Kerry Haynie, Grant Wacker, Patrick Thompson, and Deborah Wahl. Following my days in Durham, I was grateful for the mentorship of Damon Salesa, Larry Rowley, Matthew Countryman, Derek Peterson, Amal Fadlalla, Brandi Hughes, and Rudolph Ware. Derek, I will always be grateful to you for introducing me, in many respects, to the discipline of African studies. Thank you for challenging me, teaching me, encouraging me, and taking me under your wing. Thanks to the University of Michigan's Black Humanities Collective and Africa History and Anthropology Workshop for stimulating intellectual engagement and pleasant weeknights.

For those who have provided professional support and community during my early years in the professoriate, please accept this statement of gratitude. These include Linda Sturtz, Jay Carney, Alden Young, Noah Salomon, Terrence Johnson, Dianne Stewart, Crystal Sanders, Kevin Thomas, Bryan McDonald, Michael Kulikowski, and so many others at Penn State and in my local church community. Many thanks to Jonathan Brockopp, Alicia Decker, Heather Sharkey, and Daniel Magaziner for the invaluable advice you provided at my manuscript workshop. Combined with anonymous feedback received during the writing and revision process, the study was greatly enhanced by your editorial prowess.

Thank you to all the research participants who volunteered their time to tell me about their stories, those of their families, and those of their nation. A lot of things can be said about South Sudan, and preeminent among them for me is unrivaled hospitality. Members of the Episcopal Church of the Sudan (ECS) extended kindness to me, and the ECS guest house in the shadows of Juba's All Saints Cathedral was my South Sudanese home away from home. You really made me feel like a part of your community and always provided great conversation and home-cooked meals.

Mom and Dad, you have extended to me every resource and opportunity to pursue my love and passion for historical inquiry. Without your sowing, this harvest wouldn't have been possible. I am standing on your shoulders and pray that you are proud. And thank you to all of my family and friends, especially my brother, Decature, for your continued love and support.

Finally, I thank my Lord and Savior Jesus Christ. Before I embarked on this study, I only knew you in part. I have since learned that you are the friend who sticks closer than a brother (Prov. 18:24).

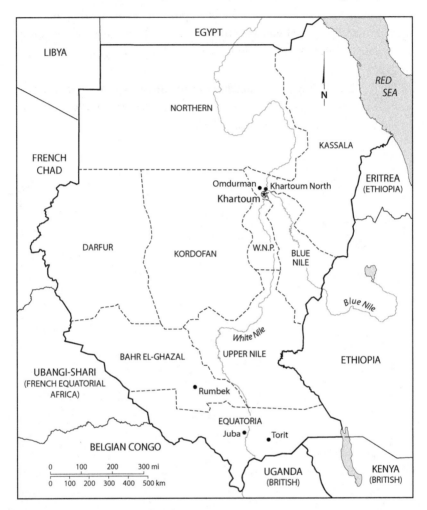

Sudan, ca. 1956. Drawn by Bill Nelson.

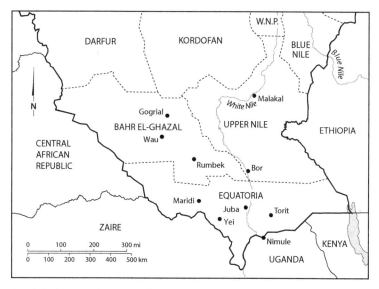

South Sudan, ca. 1983. Drawn by Bill Nelson.

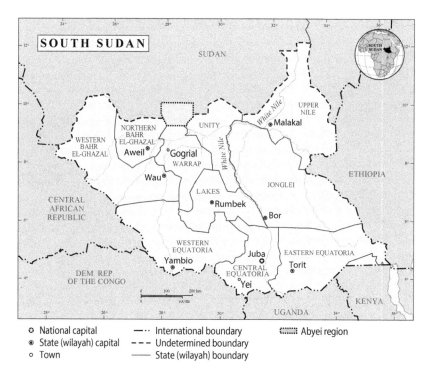

- ⊙ National capital
- ◉ State (wilayah) capital
- ○ Town
- —··— International boundary
- – – – Undetermined boundary
- —— State (wilayah) boundary
- ▥▥▥ Abyei region

South Sudan, 2011. Based on United Nations Map No. 4450 Rev.1.1, October 2011.

Introduction

If there's a book the South Sudanese cannot remove from their lives, it's the Bible. . . . [T]here are books that are very close to the heart of South Sudanese because of our suffering. So if the Bible then is made up of stories of suffering, 50 percent of it, the other 50 percent of the stories is the glory that follows suffering. That's our story. Maybe we are not enjoying the glory now, but we know it's coming.
—Joseph Taban, July 12, 2012

On February 3, 1960, Harold Macmillan stood before the Parliament of South Africa. After a month touring some of Britain's African colonies, the British prime minister opined to the MPs that a "wind of change is blowing through this continent and whether we like it or not, this growth of national consciousness is a political fact."[1] While British-controlled Somalia and Nigeria each obtained independence in 1960, they were not the first in sub-Saharan Africa to wrest free from Her Majesty's encumbrance after World War II. Though Ghana had entered the community of sovereign nations in 1957, Pan-Africanism's shining black star was not the first to achieve independence either. That distinction went to Sudan—formerly the Anglo-Egyptian Condominium—which became independent in 1956.[2]

Seven months after Macmillan's speech, the Anglican bishop of the Sudan referenced other winds of change. In Oliver Allison's address to the Sudan Church Association, he remarked, "We . . . are living under a military regime . . . and the Sudan is a polite police State. The winds of change around and within the Sudan are sometimes not cool refreshing breezes but winds of gale force. The Church is not alone in being the prey of all sorts of forces."[3] Just months before Sudan became independent, the condominium had been almost ripped apart when southern Sudanese soldiers at Torit rejected orders to be transferred to the North. They mutinied, and hundreds were killed in the ensuing violence. The newly independent Sudanese government attempted to unite the country by promoting Arabism and Islam in South Sudan, a region with lengthy experience with Christian missionary work during the colonial era. With the government takeover of mission schools, the elimination of Sunday as a weekly holiday, and restrictions placed on mission work, life for Christians and Christian workers in South Sudan was becoming increasingly precarious by the time Allison made his remarks. In time a full-scale civil war broke out, and the government expelled hundreds of missionaries from the country.[4]

More than a half-century after Allison's speech, another wind of change blew through the country. After decades of civil war, 98.3 percent of participants voted for independence in a January 2011 referendum.[5] As one man remarked before the results were unveiled, "The Northerners have made us their slaves for a long time, and we are ready to show them that we can lead ourselves."[6] This reference to slavery was no mere rhetorical device; rather, it was rooted in real history. During the nineteenth century, Sudan's economy was based in part on the slave trade, an enterprise that practically depopulated some areas of the South. To be sure, the Sudanese slave trade was not novel; Egyptian traders had previously taken enslaved persons from the Funj kingdom. Slavery, according to Jok Madut Jok, was never abolished during the Anglo-Egyptian colonial period or by the independent minority Arab regimes.[7]

On July 9, 2011, South Sudan celebrated its independence as the world's newest nation. More than just a political occasion, independence was also a religious moment. Christian leaders argued that a prophecy concerning Cush from the book of Isaiah had foretold South Sudan's independence, and a draft of the national anthem referred to the country as Cush, Eden, and a land of milk and honey. In February 2012 the *Sudan Tribune* reported that South Sudanese Christians had proposed to Vice President Riek Machar a pilgrimage to Mount Zion to further fulfill Isaiah's prophecy (the Cushites, in the prophet's vision, present gifts to God on Mount Zion after their suffering).[8] I was in the capital city of Juba when the country celebrated its first anniversary of independence. Then a doctoral student working on a cataloging project at the South Sudan National Archives, I was eager to attend commemoration festivities at All Saints Cathedral. As I sat among a throng of attendees, under enormous ornate cloths shielding us from the midday sun, the acting governor spoke. He shared that after John Garang's death in 2005, "God in his mercy [gave] us a Joshua with unique talent and wisdom who took us through the days of difficulty in the administration of . . . South Sudan."[9] Garang had created the Sudan People's Liberation movement (SPLM), the South's dominant political movement and civilian organization. The SPLM paralleled the Sudan People's Liberation Army (SPLA), the southern rebel force that had fought against the northern-based Sudanese government in the Second Sudanese Civil War (1983–2005). After Garang's death, Salva Kiir Mayardit—or Joshua—became the new SPLA commander and future president.[10] Another speaker alluded to the Hebrew captivity in Egypt by thanking God for giving them independence, leading His children across the river, and ending their slavery.[11] It appeared impossible to divorce southern nationalism from biblical vocabulary.

* * *

With the Sudanese state's long history of Islamization policies, it is not surprising that the relationship between religion and political action in Sudan has been the focus of great inquiry.[12] The Sudanese state has attempted to fashion the country as an Islamic state on several occasions, but—as Jok Madut Jok has noted—the presence of a significant population of non-Muslims made such attempts highly problematic and destructive.[13] Despite the prominence of biblical invocations leading up to and through independence, no book-length study focuses on the historical genealogy of such religiously infused political thought in South Sudan. This study shows that modern uses of the Bible are merely the latest iterations in a longer history of religious nationalism. Throughout the second half of the twentieth century and into the twenty-first, Sudanese thinkers transformed Christian thought and theology into spaces where racial identities obtained potent spiritual power. Southern Sudanese used the Bible to provide a lexicon for resistance, a vehicle for defining friends and enemies, and a script for political and often seditious actions in their quest for self-determination and sovereignty. While the political imagination has not been exclusively Christian, some southern thinkers used the Christian Bible to forge a union between theology and nationalism. By doing so, they blurred the lines between secular and sacred in the genealogy of their nation's political thought. Rather than approaching the history of South Sudanese nationalism as mere political history, I show that it is—for many people—a spiritual chronicle. In this vein, *Chosen Peoples* supports Lamin Sanneh's view that religious thought is deeply connected with the roots of the secular state.[14]

Beginning with the end of the Mahdist War (1898) and continuing through the early years of independence, *Chosen Peoples* investigates the ways in which Christian worldviews, organizational work, and theology informed the ideological construction of the South Sudanese nation-state. The Bible provided a critical lexicon of resistance and communal identity formation and was a source with which to levy spiritual critiques against the Arab Other. *Blackness* became an identity marker adopted by southerners of various ethnicities, resulting in a unique case in African Christianity whereby a liberatory, nationalist Christian thought was aimed against non-white and non-Christian co-citizens.

The prevailing context of the struggles against Sudanese governments meant that race (blackness) and religion (Christianity) became dominant identities that southerners of different ethnicities used to distinguish themselves from an enemy that was often framed as Arab and Muslim. Rather than separating race and religion as coexisting elements, I present theology as a crucible of race, a space where racial differences and behaviors were defined. Southerners envisioned themselves as a *chosen* people destined for liberation, while Arabs and Muslims were likened to oppressors in the biblical tradition of Babylon, Egypt, and the Philistines. With the end of the Second Sudanese Civil War (2005) and peace with the traditional northern enemy, however, ethnicity has superseded race as the more politically salient and important identifier in South Sudan's political arena. This reality is critical to understanding the present conflict as a violent referendum on the strengths and limitations of deploying race, religion, and ethnicity as instruments in the construction of a pluralistic democracy.

The racial and religious identity politics at play in this narrative—namely Arabness and Africanness, Christianness and Muslimness—is particularly fascinating when Christian and/or Western nationalism is understood to be about anti-Islamization. Samuel Moyn notes that since "the 1940s . . . Christian human rights have been not so much about the inclusion of the other as about policing the borders and boundaries on which threatening enemies loom." While communism was once feared as the epitome of secularism (and was the target of religious struggle), Moyn contends that the Muslim has replaced the communist in Europe's contemporary imagination (and particularly with respect to religious liberty).[15] While the religious nationalism in this study was created and articulated against the backdrop of state attempts to fashion Sudan as an Islamic nation, some figures levied their critiques against the state, certain individuals, or a particular brand of Islam rather than that religion writ large. Furthermore, the use of scripture after the twentieth-century civil wars and into South Sudanese independence shows that southerners injected biblical language and spiritual thought into public forums long after Islamizing Sudanese governments (based in the northern city of Khartoum) ceased to be the target of their animus. I caution against a limited view of South Sudanese religious nationalism as one based exclusively in anti-Islamization. This notwithstanding, there is room to consider the connections between the rhetoric deployed against Arabs and Muslims in this study and discourses concerning Islam and the war on terror.[16]

Theological knowledge production in South Sudan was not the exclusive domain of clergy; rather, a tapestry of thinkers contributed. Rather than focusing on a specific subset of people or communities in the traditional vein of Sudanese anthropology, I follow in the path of Jonathon Glassman's work on Tanzania and Daniel Magaziner's in South Africa by examining a range of figures, including refugees, soldiers, politicians, students, and clerics, who placed themselves into biblical archetypes.[17] Using circulating print media written by a diversity of authors allows for an examination of religious and political thought that extends beyond ethnicity and toward a more regional and international scope. Building on Steven Feierman's formative study of anthropology and history in Tanzania, I focus on the intellectual labor performed by South Sudanese writers.[18] Intellectuals used print media to interpret their circumstances, define enemies, script action, and define the future through a theological framework—one that conflated spiritual liberation with material political reformation and revolution. Although various Sudanese regimes attempted to create an Islamic state, it is also imperative to recognize the ways in which people in South Sudan—while at war against Khartoum—used religion for their own political purposes.

And yet, after entering "the promised land" of independence, ethnic conflict threatened the nation that religious nationalism envisioned. Division and enmity between southern factions persisted following the end of the Second Sudanese Civil War, and matters came to a head in December 2013, when violence broke out between members of the presidential guard. This action precipitated violence throughout the new South Sudanese nation between forces loyal to President Kiir (of Dinka ethnicity, Sudan's largest ethnic group) and former Vice President Riek Machar (of Nuer ethnicity, the South's second largest ethnic group). Tens of thousands perished in the conflict, which lasted until 2018.[19] Thus, this study can't simply offer a new way of understanding religion's role in South Sudanese political imaginings; it must also consider ethnicity's political relevance in this narrative of religiously infused politics.

DIASPORIC CONNECTIONS: BLACK POLITICS AND THEOLOGY

This book is significantly informed by ideas that emerged from two other contexts in which blacks were socially and politically marginalized: South Africa and the United States. Desmond Tutu was present at the Independence Day ceremonies at All Saints Cathedral that summer day in July 2012. His presence encouraged me to search for the fusion of religious and political rhetoric in South Sudan. Minister of Information Barnaba Marial Benjamin addressed the former archbishop by saying that he (Tutu) had broken racial barriers, and that God had brought him to "your people." Tutu offered congratulatory remarks, pleas for peace, and concluded with a blessing in Xhosa.[20] It was a fraught diasporic moment that linked black South Africa's struggle against white oppression with the South Sudanese fight against Khartoum governments that had tried to create an Arab and Islamic state.

Francis Deng once noted similarities between the Sudan and South Africa: "The Sudan has much in common with South Africa under apartheid. . . . In South Africa, apartheid excluded non-Whites. In the Sudan, Arabism both excludes, in the sense that it discriminates against those who are not Arabized or Islamized, and includes, in the sense that it fosters assimilation, which condescendingly implies rejection of or disregard for the non-Arab and non-Muslim elements."[21] The efflorescence of religiously infused political rhetoric on South Sudanese independence echoed the union between religion and politics during the antiapartheid struggle. White Dutch Reformed clergyman Beyers Naudé founded *Pro Veritate* in 1962. Published in Afrikaans and English, it brought together Christians across racial and denominational lines who were opposed to apartheid. Along with the Christian Institute of Southern Africa, *Pro Veritate* is credited with facilitating the creation of the 1967 Black Theology Conference and the black consciousness movement.[22] Daniel Magaziner writes that South African students, clergy, and activists "donned the prophet's mantle and spoke historical truths to the power of apartheid law" between 1968 and 1977.[23] In

1985 a group of laypeople and clergy (including Tutu) produced the Kairos Document, a theological treatise designed to develop a biblical model that would lead to action. The document argued that scripture condemns states that fail in their God-given duty and referenced Rome, described in the book of Revelation as Satan's servant, as an example. The Kairos authors argued that when regimes become morally illegitimate, theological teaching compels Christians to remove them rather than compromise. God liberated the oppressed, and immoral states are not allowed to rule forever.[24]

As Tutu's appearance at the independence ceremony linked South Africa's experience with South Sudan's, the publication of an essay written by James Cone in *Pro Veritate* linked black theology with Christian antiapartheid opposition. Black theology was a term first used in the United States among a small cadre of African American theologians led by Cone during the second half of the 1960s. Cone's first book, *Black Theology and Black Power*, was published in 1969.[25] "Black Theology and African Theology"—an essay Cone co-authored with Gayraud Wilmore—notes that faith is the encounter between the divine and human in the historical context of oppression. The enslaved community recognizes that its deliverance is the divine's work in history and, therefore, knowing God is "to know the actuality of oppression and the certainty of liberation."[26] They add that God's liberating acts directly inform his people's position and responsibility: "He is the Liberator par excellence, who reveals not only who God is and what he is doing, but also who we are and what we are called to do about human degradation. . . . The free man in Christ is the man who rebels against false authorities by reducing them to their proper status."[27]

Theologian John Mbiti was critical of race's infusion into theology. He criticized black theology and stated that in reading it, "one becomes sated by color consciousness. It is necessary to remind oneself that racial color is not a theological concept in the Scriptures."[28] Importantly, Mbiti acknowledged that southern Africa was to a limited extent similar to the American context that produced black theology.[29] His critique of black theology and nod to southern Africa's similarities to the United States open the door for one to consider how African thinkers elsewhere theologized their racial oppression.

To be sure, the decision within South Sudan to use Christianity to compete with race—or northern Arabism—has been recognized. During the height of the Second Civil War, Francis Deng noted, "the elite circles of the Christian South are promoting the idea that Christianity should be consciously cultivated as a pivotal element in southern identity. Christianity,"

Deng continued, "in combination with such other elements as English and vernacular languages, is the modern model competing with the Arab-Islamic model in the north."[30] He also acknowledged the role of Christian education in creating an antinorthern nationalist sentiment.[31] This study goes beyond the acknowledgment of Christianity's politicization in South Sudan by investigating the discursive processes by which this took place. *Chosen Peoples* is interested in the manner in which southern nationhood was articulated through a biblical lens. By approaching religious thought as a space where racial and political subjectivities were fashioned and harnessed for revolutionary means, my study takes a new approach to South Sudanese social history. Rather than approaching race and religion—the two elements most often used to distinguish North and South Sudan—as separate entities, I analyze religion as a space where race was expressed, defined, and animated with power. South Sudan is an African context in which racial and spiritual identities were combined to argue for political liberation in an environment that was often understood to be made up of Arab rulers and black ruled. While resembling black theology and the ideology expressed in the Kairos document, the South Sudanese variation was aimed against nonwhite and non-Christian co-citizens (in contrast to South Africa). The religious thought under focus in this study, furthermore, was often articulated within the context of civil wars and preceded the creation of a new nation-state.

BEYOND THE NORTH-SOUTH DIVIDE

This study does not aim to perpetuate the general conceptual division of Sudan into an Arab Muslim North and a black, Christian, indigenous theistic South. Douglas Johnson, Cherry Leonardi, Peter Woodward, and Richard Gray have tackled the North-South binary in various ways.[32] The terms *Arab, African,* and *black* are too malleable to be used to argue for firm regional distinctions. Arabism in North Sudan is contested and varied, with "Arabs" commonly identified with the Khartoum government, economically marginalized Arab nomads, and Arabs who live within the South and have long coexisted with southerners. Amal Fadlalla writes that "constructions of 'Arabism' are constantly negotiated, debated, and invented among many Muslim groups, including Darfurians." She concludes that the question of one's Arabness or non-Arabness is "complexly determined by ethnic and racial categories that take into account regionality and skin tone, as well as other bodily attributes."[33]

Nor should *Arab* be used interchangeably with *Islam*. The notion of an *Islam noir*—an Africanized variety of Islam that was somehow diluted from authentic Islam and infused with traditional African beliefs and practices—emerged in French West Africa during the early twentieth century. The colonial French administration was suspicious of Islam after its role in mobilizing anticolonial resistance in Algeria. The administration kept Muslim clerics under surveillance, with files synthesized by Paul Marty, who directed French West Africa's Office of Muslim Affairs in the early twentieth century. These files comprised a series of studies on Islam in French West African colonies, studies that contributed to the conceptual formulation of Islam noir's existence.[34] Robert Launay suggests that though the French may have been comforted by the idea that they did not have to worry about Islamic danger, the idea of Islam noir had damaging consequences for anthropology's study of Islam in French West Africa: "Once 'African Islam' could be reduced to its component parts—Arab Islam and African 'fetishism'—then the study of Islam could be properly left to Orientalists, leaving to anthropologists the task of decoding more 'authentically' African beliefs and practices."[35] Rhetorical distancing between Africa and Islam is evident in Sudan, where an Arab-Muslim North is distinguished from a black African South. Against the historical backdrop of Islam noir, Rudolph Ware notes that Islamic studies have traditionally marginalized Africa, despite its deep Islamic history and African Muslims' demographic strength. The racial elements of this tendency are transparent in the actions of colonial administrator Marty, who was "routinely appealing to the logic of race . . . tapping deeply held stereotypes of black civilizational and intellectual inferiority."[36]

The division of Sudan into two regions comes with an implicit assertion that the South is a uniform entity. It is not. Juba-born journalist and author Steve Paterno once shared with me that a sense of nationhood did not exist until the onset of colonialism. "Otherwise," he continued, "South Sudanese were simply tribes, which . . . to some [extent] still exist today as most cannot [grasp] the idea of nationhood but rather fall to their tribes or clan so as they belong." Paterno added that "the thought of nationhood is for the most part confined within the elites, the so-called educated class. These basically compose of military, politicians, [and] clergy."[37] Jok Madut Jok asserts this sentiment in his *War and Slavery in Sudan*:

> Southerners . . . have always referred to themselves in terms of their ethnic nationalities. . . . Most rural Southerners have linked themselves to

these cultural and ethnic roots and do not even reach the level of the state when talking about their world. They do not identify with a polity called Sudan, nor is there any consciousness or political decision to be part of Africa. The history of the effort to identify with Africa is recent and is confined to the literate. It grew out of the history of unfriendly contact with Northerners.[38]

Throughout the twentieth century, the Sudanese state—along with its political and military opponents—struggled to establish governmental legitimacy. Cherry Leonardi notes that experiences of war, military government, aid, urbanization, local government, and national politics each simultaneously harden and dismantle local identities.[39]

This book does not ignore these realities and makes no attempt to argue that Christianity, blackness, or "southernness" have so enmeshed themselves in the South that they have replaced or eliminated the effects, utility, or meanings of ethnicity. Nor do I attempt to say that all or most southerners, regardless of their ethnicities, ascribe to the religious and racial liberationist thought that rests at the forefront of this analysis. Rather, *Chosen Peoples* shows the ways in which literate elites encouraged indigenous cultures, discouraged "tribalism," posited a shared racial identity, and articulated southern separatism and communal identity through the mediums of Christian work and thought. If nationalism, as Paterno and Jok put forth, has primarily been the work of the literate elite, it is still important to understand how their racial and religious imaginings informed their revolutionary political work and vision.

During the Anglo-Egyptian period, colonial officials sought to shield the South from Arab-Islamic influences and encourage the continuance of indigenous cultures and languages. This was done in various ways but primarily through linguistic work; education was conducted in vernacular languages, missionaries produced vernacular dictionaries, and vernacular newspapers were produced. In this vein, the Christian project not only sponsored African or southern self-identification but also invited people to see themselves as constituents of smaller, ethnic communities. What followed was a tension between the ethnic identities encouraged and buttressed by missionaries (and Africans), an emerging southern consciousness that was grounded in a shared history of slavery, African rather than Arab identification, and political marginalization. In response to specific historical circumstances like midcentury Sudanization, Arabization, and Islamization, *race* became a way of thinking about self and community that superseded others. With changing times, however, race has lost the salience that it had when it was used to distinguish South from North. Given the intimate connection that religion has had with race in Sudan (embodied most often in the division between an Arab Muslim North and a black Christian South), one must consider the ways in which Christians in South Sudan—whether Euro-American or African—have used their faith to inform their approach and use of racial and ethnic identities for political purposes.

Ethnicity's historical realities, debates, and power in the South demand a disavowal of the North-South polarization and an honest recognition of the ways in which the terms *southern*, *black*, and *African*—potent and pervasive as they are—become tenuous when used to describe everyone throughout the region. This study escapes the North-South polarization by showing how ethnic identities in South Sudan continued to be significant in discursive and social spaces that swirled with competing social, racial, religious, and national identities. I employ *the North* rather than *Arab-Islamic North* in my effort to detach the racial and cultural term *Arab* from Islam. I use *the South* to describe the collective regions of Upper Nile, Bahr el-Ghazal, and Equatoria.

RACE AND RELIGION IN MODERN SUDAN

In 2004, Makau Mutua stated that "race—not religion—is the fundamental fault line in Sudan, though religion has certainly added fuel to the fire in the south. Indeed, since independence from the British in 1956, the demon of Sudan has been race."[40] Some have noted that several historical factors inform the importance of Arabism (and race more generally) in the North. Arab-African antagonism can be traced to the Turco-Egyptian period, when Arab nomads allied with the Egyptian army and government to mount raids to find slaves for military and domestic use.[41] Northerners crafted racial ideologies favoring Arabs over Africans, defining who could be free and who could be enslaved, as some developed genealogies that allowed them to claim Arab descent. These stipulations were racially defined, as Arab ancestry defined freedom while those with darker skin or who adhered to indigenous beliefs were connected with servitude. Amir Idris has maintained that racialized states transformed the cultural identities of Arab Muslim North and African Christian indigenous religious South into political identities through precolonial slavery, colonial indirect rule, and postcolonial state-sponsored Arabization and Islamization. Arabism and Islam became foundational to the northern-based nationalism of the postcolonial Sudanese state.[42]

How, then, did race inform South Sudanese understandings of the political circumstances that they had to confront, circumstances largely precipitated by European and Arab actors? This study employs a conceptualization of race most closely aligned with the work of Christopher Lee, who notes that "race is understood to be a marker, as well as a phenomenological schema—a structure of thought for explaining the world. Race is irreducible to any single context or explanation—what Ann Laura Stoler has called its polyvalent mobility—with each of the aforementioned issues carrying historical and pedagogical significance."[43] For many in South Sudan, race—principally Arab and black/African—marked ruler and ruled, favored and marginalized, and, in the spiritual sense, oppressor and oppressed.[44] This study not only shows how racial and religious rhetoric was often blurred but also explores how Sudanese Christians acted as racial architects, fashioning race through a crucible that allied racial with spiritual identity and difference. By looking at the role of African Christians in the formation of racial thought, my focus differs from those who have looked to the role of missions in this regard. Derek Chang once went so far as to note that the mission project "made race" through a language of religion, culture, nation, and transformation, and because of the perceived centrality of the colonial state in the history of race and racism, scholars have noted ways in which missions were involved in the construction and implementation of racial and ethnic projects.[45] While missionaries were involved in maintaining ethnic boundaries, my study shows that Sudanese Christians, long after the condominium period, employed biblical idioms and theology when describing elements of a racial conflict. They were racial and religious thinkers outside the mission context.

In this vein, *Chosen Peoples* builds on studies that have discussed indigenous thinkers fashioning racial thought before, during, and after the colonial period. Africans were innovative in their understanding and navigation of colonial rule's racially fraught environment. Rather than merely receiving imposed ideas, behaviors, and vocabularies from the colonial state, they had precolonial practices of organization and self-identification and were able to transform racial ideologies during and after the colonial period for their own purposes.[46] I examine South Sudanese thinkers who blended racial and religious thought to articulate solidarity and distinction from North Sudanese. While colonialism played a role in institutionalizing and policing the Arab-African divide, I am most concerned with southerners and their differing responses to northerners, Arabs, Islam, and the prospect of political unity with or separation from the North.

Given my argument that southern nationalist thinkers largely perceived the liberation struggle as a racial conflict, the current explosion of ethnic politics demands serious consideration of ethnicity's role in the interplay between race, religion, and politics in South Sudan. The potency of ethnic identity in the South amid a shared black identity suggests a limit to race's ability to bind distinct cultural communities or implies that people believe that ethnicity addresses certain questions, situations, or problems that race does not. In *Citizen and Subject*, Mahmood Mamdani makes the following inquiries concerning the nature of anticolonial nationalism and the roles of ethnicity and racial domination:

> Rather than just uniting diverse ethnic groups in a common predicament, was not racial domination actually mediated through a variety of ethnically organized local powers? If so, is it not too simple even if tempting to think of the anticolonial (nationalist) struggle as just a one-sided repudiation of ethnicity rather than also a series of ethnic revolts against so many ethnically organized and centrally reinforced local powers . . . was not ethnicity a dimension of both power and resistance, of both the problem and the solution?[47]

In one sense, South Sudanese ethnicities are vestiges of colonial power—the condominium government and missionaries were determined to maintain indigenous cultures in the South, which explained their encouragement of vernacular language use in classrooms and for "Native Administration."[48] In another sense, southern ethnicities are symbols of state resistance—the rebel SPLA relied on indigenous chiefs to organize provisions and enlist young men and boys into its forces during the Second Civil War, and ethnicity played a key role in South Sudan's postindependence conflict (one headlined by the Dinka and Nuer).[49]

* * *

"Even if implausible to some," writes David M. Gordon, "the spirits of the invisible world—including ancestors, nature spirits, God, the Holy Spirit, Jesus, and Satan—hold implications for realms of human agency." Rather than setting out to write a history of institutionalized religion in his *Invisible Agents: Spirits in a Central African History*, Gordon frames his text as a history of the spirits understood to have influenced this world.[50] While this study is not principally concerned with ancestors or nature spirits, *Chosen Peoples* supports Gordon's assertion concerning the spiritual implications of human agency and is not an organizational Church history. Rather, it is concerned with how South Sudanese understood Sudan's fractious post-colonial history as a spiritual chronicle: one in which people represented God as an agent working on southerners' behalf, portrayed Satan as working behind the scenes, and invoked biblical precedents to fit contemporary history. From the perspective of many South Sudanese Christians, there was no clean demarcation between the natural and supernatural in the quest for political liberation.

How did southerners use biblical language when describing themselves and their northern neighbors before 2011? How did they use theology to define and augment their efforts to achieve self-determination and separation? Although R. O. Collins and Lilian Sanderson write about missions and education in their general histories of condominium-era Sudan, these questions are largely unaddressed in those studies. While Collins invites readers into the social environment that was Christian mission education, Christianity and missions were only elements, not the primary foci, of his condominium-focused monographs. His *Shadows in the Grass*, furthermore, concludes with 1956, eliminating the space to explore the mission project's postcondominium impact. Conversely, Lilian Sanderson's voluminous study concerns both the condominium and early independence eras, but—like Collins—does not discuss exactly how southerners used the Bible for their own identity politics or sociopolitical action.[51] *Chosen Peoples* is unique in its chronology (beginning in the late nineteenth century and ending in the twenty-first century) and in its primary focus on how biblical literacy and faith informed sociopolitical action. I am interested in how southerners used their faith as a *political technology*. Beth Coleman once encouraged a contemplation of race as technology, an idea that shifted from biological and genetic systems that dominated race's definition toward questions of technological agency (or the ways by which external devices help us navigate the world).[52] I propose that South Sudanese Christians put their religion to practical sociopolitical uses within the contexts of colonialism, independence, and civil wars.

Richard Gray once noted that religion in Africa has long been understood to have political elements; it can legitimate the status quo, possess a prophetic dimension, provide a base from which to levy attacks against those in power, and legitimate revolution.[53] The Bible could be used to provide templates for action that Africans could implement in their particular contexts. David Chidester and Elizabeth Elbourne highlight how Africans wielded agency by reinterpreting the Bible to incorporate it with established beliefs, using Christianity to move within and against colonial regimes.[54] Kikuyu readers and converts in colonial Kenya supplied a grammar and vocabulary for new popular politics; young people, by identifying with biblical subjects, were equipped to articulate anticolonial sentiments.[55] I continue in this vein of confirming the Bible's dissident political utility in Africa by investigating how southerners used Christianity to define themselves in relation to the North, criticize the government, script futures, and forge new identities.

Scholarship on southern political and social history has taken disparate approaches to religion's role in the conflicts between North and South Sudan. Rolandsen notes that anthropological studies on Sudan tend to focus on the local scene, following in Edward Evans-Pritchard's footsteps. As studies from the Second Civil War explore how the conflict has affected local societies, much work on southern religious life and change during that war is consequently localized.[56] Nonetheless, there is a way to examine religious change at the local or ethnic level and link it to organizational uses of theology and the Bible at a wider, regional level. This study moves in this direction by focusing on the ways in which religious thought was and continues to be articulated by a host of actors in a range of print spaces. Rather than limiting my focus to a specific community or ethnic group, the actors in my study include mission students, clergy, politicians, and others from a wide range of ethnicities.

ARGUMENT

Christianity was essential to the southern resistance struggle. A wide swath of South Sudanese actors employed Christian discourses, metaphors, and imageries in various ways. Christian discourse was used to define the Arab Other and black/African Us; Christianity was envisioned as a bond that could unify disparate ethnicities; songs and poems with biblical messages appeared outside devotional contexts within public, circulating print media. Christian print discourse not only provided a lexicon that encouraged an imagined understanding of a South Sudanese nation but also, by positioning God as a God of the black and southern oppressed, Sudanese writers claimed him as being uniquely theirs and themselves as especially his.

And yet, without being confined to the Arab Muslim North versus black Christian South paradigm, religious thought has also been employed to address interethnic relations among southerners. Within the last ten years, the leaders of Sudan's Catholic and Anglican communities have publicly stated that God created diversity and ethnicities.[57] Taken together, the theologies presented in this study have broader relevance for discussions concerning the role of religion in political action and identity formation, the role of religion in the public sphere, and the use of religious thought to encourage inclusion and distinction.

* * *

"Religious identity," wrote Lamin Sanneh, "is one form of self-understanding among many, such as gender, class, or race, and where religion cuts across multiple forms of identity, as it does in Sudan, it can be a mobilizing force for good or for ill."[58] Francis Deng notes that religion has "become a symbol of identity of power sharing, even of the management control of our resources, and certainly, of the culture that gives us our sense of who we are and to whom we relate . . . in the world. . . . It has become the symbolic embodiment of all these other issues we talk about."[59] Building off Sanneh, Deng, and Gray, this study offers an intimate look into just how Sudanese and non-Sudanese figures marshaled Christianity to create and cut across identities, mobilize southerners in their wars against the North, and govern interethnic relationships. During each of the civil wars, South Sudanese lay and ecclesiastical thinkers used the Bible to find historical precedents for their circumstances and a lexicon for resistance. In using the Bible to provide a script for liberation, they came to see themselves as a "chosen people" destined for liberation like Old Testament Israel. While North Sudanese were repeatedly—directly and indirectly—positioned with the biblical Egyptians, Babylonians, and other enemies of Israel, southerners crafted biblical oppressor-oppressed parallels along racial lines, resulting in the demonization of Arabs and the sacralization of black Africans.

The South Sudanese political struggle would have been different without Christianity's injection in several ways. First, an important element of the struggle's righteous moral positioning would have been lost. It is one thing for a group to claim that its politics are superior to those of another group; it is different when the group claims that its opponent is on the wrong side of a spiritual battle between good and evil. As Joseph Taban's quotation at the beginning of this chapter conveys, southerners gravitated to the Bible because of its message of forthcoming glory. The Bible provided scripts at various moments of the struggle that could provide hope when the outcome was uncertain.

The concept of *chosenness* at the core of this study speaks to Christianity's importance for politics. Various scholars have shown how modern nationalist movements adopted the idea of God's chosenness (first experienced by the biblical Israelites). Chosenness has underscored and justified political actions and provided a spark for political and national liberation.[60] South Sudanese appropriations of biblical Israel during the twentieth-century civil wars supports the idea that adopting a sense of *chosenness* remains a viable political stratagem. And yet, South Sudan is a secular state (although, as Noah Salomon has written, the meaning of religious freedom in the new nation is debatable).[61] Nevertheless, this study echoes Sanneh by contending that religious thought is enmeshed with the roots of the world's newest secular state. This reality speaks to the continued power and potential of religious discourse in the political sphere in South Sudan, Africa, and beyond.

This study's relevance for studies of religion and politics beyond Sudan is illustrated by its engagement with certain bigger questions. Ruth Marshall posed important queries in her study on Pentecostalism in Nigeria: Can religious revival be understood primarily as a response to material crises, a response to crisis in moral or symbolic regimes, or some combination of both? Why should solutions to crisis be sought in the religious theater? Marshall contends that if we invoke situations of material crises like social exclusion to explain religious revival, we see such movements in terms of their functionality—as modes of political combat or languages to translate and understand the real, among others. While she acknowledges that religious movements can meet these functions, Marshall asserts that they are insufficient as an explanation for contemporary religious revival and its political meaning.[62] "Born-again Christianity operates in Nigeria within a terribly crowded religious field. What sort of inquiry will enable us to understand why *this* particular form of religious practice develops here and now, and uncover the secret of its remarkable success? What question(s) is Jesus really the answer to?"[63] My study asks similar questions for the Sudanese context. Why did this brand of political theology develop during this time of Sudanese/South Sudanese history?[64] Was it a response to Islamizing government incursions or something else? What did (and does) theology offer to southerners as a solution to experiences of war, exile, and racial-religious oppression?

It is my hope that this book can widen our understanding of how ostensibly secular spaces can be charged with important religious meaning. During the Enlightenment, violent wars and dynastic struggles waged in religion's name contributed to a shift of religion from the public to the private sphere. One argument for this need rested in the belief that religion lives in the domain of passion and faith, a space in which rational argument and interest-guided action could not nor should have a place.[65] During the 1980s, however, religion entered the public sphere in several ways; reasons behind this phenomenon included Iran's Islamic revolution, Poland's solidarity movement, and Protestant fundamentalism as an American political force.[66] When discussing the Sudanese government's efforts to create an Islamic state, Abdullahi A. An-Na'im argues that whenever monotheistic creeds are conflated with government, they make citizens of their adherents but subjects of those who do not follow that faith. Furthermore, efforts to make such creeds the basis of a civil order have resulted in violence throughout history—more recently, in Sudan.[67] Is the union of religious and political thought the friend, enemy, outgrowth, or foundation of secular states? Do religious projects and rhetoric carry empty dreams for forging national community or, conversely, have a legitimate—if not necessary—role in fostering healthy, socially pluralistic states?

On the latter of those questions, the religious discourse concerning ethnicities and ethnic conflict in this study has wider resonance beyond Sudan and Africa. How should one reconcile one priest's comment that there were no longer ethnic separations between Dinka or Nuer—now all were one in Christ—with another by the archbishop of Juba that tribes were "gifts of God"?[68] What does it mean when God is used in one breath to argue for cultural unity and, in another, for cultural diversity? Such a question has particular meaning in global contexts where interracial or interethnic relations are or have been fraught; the multiracial American church's engagement with the Black Lives Matter movement presents an interesting point of contrast, as those who claim that "all lives matter" based on humanity's sharing God's same image and likeness could run up against those who highlight God's creative work in fashioning distinct tribes, tongues, and peoples. Thus, the question of when one can or should reference God or scripture in encouraging unity, diversity, sameness, or difference has broader relevance way beyond South Sudan's borders. Furthermore, the decision made by some condominium mission officials to pose ethnic conflict as a spiritual problem can be placed in conversation with other contexts in which certain social ills like racism, economic inequality, or war have been described or condemned in spiritual terms.[69]

Finally, one of this study's most significant interventions in the field of Sudanese religious history is my contention that South Sudanese religious nationalism was essentially gendered. "One important conceptual problem," write Floya Anthias and Nira Yuval-Davis, "concerns the danger of reifying the 'nation' and the 'ethnic' or 'racial' group, by treating them as totally independent and separate and not considering how they intersect with other modes of differentiation such as class and gender."[70] To be sure, the connection between gender and Sudanese nationalism is evident. In North Sudan, the Anglo-Egyptian administration introduced modern education to develop government administrators and those who could run the cotton schemes. The male educated class led Sudan's nationalist movement (and, along with sectarian leaders, led the postcolonial state), and mostly male elites from Central and North Sudan dominated the military regimes and democratic governments that have ruled the country since 1956. These dominant groups defined the nation's identity as Arab and Islamic, and—given that condominium administrators defined the public sphere as male—the ruling social group was exclusively composed of men. Nada Ali notes that while much has been written on how condominium rule created regional disparities in the country, few have focused on colonialism's gender-specific impact on Sudanese women and men. She contends that the politics and resistance discourses of Sudanese and South Sudanese women's organizations in exile (particularly in Egypt and Kenya in the 1990s and early 2000s) offer the chance to examine how intersections of gender and other identities shape women's and men's experiences of oppression and resistance.[71]

This study of religious thought is largely about men—men who taught at an elite mission school and their male pupils; men who wanted to halt the spread of Islam up the Nile by creating a military regiment; men who fashioned a liberatory theology in exile during the 1960s; men who expressed a martial theology in the SPLA newspaper in the 1990s; male soldiers, clerics, refugees, students, and a host of other intellectuals who infused religion into their racial and regional politics. The rich—though heavily male-authored—print media contained in the archives I visited over the course of this research informs this male focus and, by association, the gendered nature of the thought examined here. As predominantly male contexts must not mean the absence of gender, this book shows that masculinity courses throughout this study, from the militaristic uniform and sporting activities encouraged at the all-male Nugent School (including the Boy Scouts) to the particular biblical figures and narratives that writers referenced and the specific groups tabbed for the purposely un-Islamic Equatorial Corps.

Citing Judith Butler as inspiration, Alicia Decker writes that she sees gender "not only as an intentional act that illuminates the agency of social actors but also as a performative act that creates identity."[72] In her study of women, gender, and militarism in Idi Amin's Uganda, Decker contends that new constructions of masculinity and femininity emerged from militaristic practice and acknowledges that militarism is particularly common within societies that have experienced military coups.[73] This book pivots from Decker by looking at how gender informed religious thought and performance just north of Uganda, in a South Sudan that has been rife with military conflict for the better part of the last half-century. My argument that religious thought was a crucible through which racial identity was defined is coupled with my contention that militarism cannot be separated from the development and substance of southern religious nationalism. The reality that many of the religiously infused political views expressed in circulating print media were not only classed (elite) and raced (black) but also gendered reflects the exclusive nature of who possessed power, public platforms, and privileges.

CHAPTER BREAKDOWN

In the early twentieth century—the infancy of the condominium period—the Church Missionary Society (CMS) established mission schools in South Sudan. Of all the educational institutions it founded, the Nugent School stood out from the rest. Chapter 1, "The Nugent School and the Ethno-Religious Politics of Mission Education," provides insight into the life and legacy of the Nugent School. The school illustrates several important elements of the South Sudanese mission enterprise that relate to the broader narrative of Christian and ethnic politics in the region. First, it was founded to assist in halting the spread of Islam up the Nile. Second, efforts were made at the school to uphold ethnic identities. Third, the presence of ethnic conflict there and at other mission sites highlighted the tension between efforts to protect diverse social identities and encourage a common Christian identity. This dynamic leads to the fourth and final point: the idea that ethnic conflict was a spiritual problem that Christianity could (and should) conquer.

On August 18, 1955, the Equatorial Corps at Torit staged a mutiny. The Torit mutiny was a defining moment in South Sudanese self-determination, an event that has been commonly, albeit inaccurately, used to mark the beginning of the First Civil War. Using sources that include private correspondences, unpublished memoirs, interviews, and court documentation, chapter 2 discusses the causes, conduct, and consequences of the Torit mutiny. The mutiny was not only an emancipatory action to prevent the history of past enslavement from repeating itself; it was also a moment in which members of the corps—a unit created against the backdrop of the Egyptian Army's presence and Islamizing tendencies—rejected an order to be sent North and replaced by northern soldiers. While Christian feeling was not the primary impetus behind the mutiny, Governor General Reginald Wingate had created the corps in an attempt to eliminate the military's Islamic culture. This sentiment is essential for understanding the mutiny as a moment when colonial religious visions had violent, separatist consequences, resulting in a widening chasm between North and South and closer union between a diversity of southerners.

Chapter 3, "Liberation War," examines the liberatory religious thought that emerged during the First Sudanese Civil War. Building off of Cone's black theology and the Kairos document, the chapter explores the ways in which southern activists infused spirituality into the language of racial resistance, an important development in the evolution of South Sudanese political thought. In addition to understanding their struggle against the state as a racial conflict pitting Africans against Arabs, activists also understood it as a spiritual contest. In this vein, figures like soldier Joseph Lagu and priest Paolino Doggale conceptualized southerners as a community defined not only by their racial and cultural identity but also by their favorable position in a narrative of oppression and liberation. These streams of thought encouraged the idea of an imagined community united by race, politics, and spiritual experience; they also provide a lens into how southerners understood their history and national identity at a moment of great trial.[74]

Situated during the Second Sudanese Civil War, chapter 4 shows how editors and contributors to the *SPLM/SPLA Update*—the SPLM's official newspaper medium—were creative intellectuals who sought to organize a unifying account of events amid internal splits and factionalism. The Bible provided a foundation from which people divided by language, politics, and ethnicity could envision themselves as sharing a common heritage through the lens of the ancient (and biblical) Kingdom of Cush. The chapter uses the *Update*, a propaganda form whose content had not been seriously examined until my 2015 article of the same name, as a means to examine the roles of Christianity and theology in SPLM/A ideology and politics.[75] In doing so, it shows the central role that the South Sudanese diaspora had in defining the conflict in spiritual terms.

Chapter 5, "The Troubled Promised Land," is bookended by the end of the Second Civil War (2005) and the end of independent South Sudan's internal conflict (2018). Less than three years into independence, South

Sudan found itself embroiled in an internal conflict drawn along ethnic lines. What became of the liberation theology that was supposed to reach its poetic conclusion with political sovereignty? While the conflict debunked any notion that southerners felt a sense of pan-Christian solidarity strong enough to subsume ethnicity or prevent ethnic tension, it also produced a dynamic crucible of religious thought. While the 2005–18 period was distinct for the efflorescence of ideas that appeared online, the notion that intergroup fighting was a spiritual "evil" and that uniting under God was the solution to this problem recalled a similar train of thought conveyed during the condominium era. Though the traditional enemy from the North was absent, religious thought still functioned as a political technology despite the changed scope of who and what constituted us and them, good and evil, heroes and villains.

The conclusion reexamines the argument and offers implications of how the history presented confirms and challenges understandings of South Sudan's liberation struggle, the role political theology may have for the nation moving forward, and how this narrative may shed light on religion's role in the public sphere internationally.

1

The Nugent School and the Ethno-Religious Politics of Mission Education

O Lord Jesu Christ, Son of the Living God, Who art the brightness of the Father's glory, and the express image of His Person; the chief corner-stone hewn from the mountain without hands . . . Strengthen this stone about to be laid in Thy Name; and . . . be, we beseech Thee, the beginning, the increase, and the consummation of this our work, which is undertaken to the glory of Thy Name, Who, with the Father, and the Holy Ghost liveth and reigneth, ever one God, world without end. AMEN.
—Llewellyn Gwynne, February 7, 1904

Llewellyn Henry Gwynne was born in South Wales on June 11, 1863. His father, Richard, was a village schoolmaster. According to his sister, Llewellyn was ever the family bad boy and mischief maker. Of superior build, Gwynne excelled at sports. Following ordination in 1886, Gwynne held a curacy at St. Chad's, Derby, and stayed in that position until 1890. Particularly proficient at football, he played routinely for Derby County's Association football team and was the team's only amateur. The team was one of England's best eleven at the time, and Gwynne played in an FA Cup semifinal match. Following his curacy at Derby, he served as curate at St. Andrews (Nottingham) and vicar of Nottingham's Emmanuel Church.[1]

Thousands of miles away from England's churches and football fields, epochal events were taking place in the Sudan. In 1885, forces loyal to the Sudanese Mahdi killed Britain's Charles Gordon during the Siege of Khartoum. After an epic campaign, Herbert Kitchener led an Anglo-Egyptian army to the scene of the crime, ready for vengeance. On September 2, 1898, Kitchener's forces bombarded Omdurman. By the end of the afternoon, the Mahdist force commanded by the Khalifa Abdullahi had been decimated. A young war correspondent named Winston Churchill wrote that "thus ended the battle of Omdurman—the most signal triumph ever gained by the arms of science over barbarians. Within the space of five hours the strongest and best-armed savage army yet arrayed against a modern European Power had been destroyed . . . with hardly any difficulty."[2]

A meeting was held at Exeter Hall the following May, where the honorary secretary of the Church Missionary Society alluded to the possibility of evangelizing the Sudan in the near future. "The words," according to W. H. T. Gairdner, "came with a thrill which those who do not remember the events of those former years can hardly understand."[3] The honorary secretary shared that it was hoped that a party would be able to go up the Nile from Cairo in the autumn "to occupy some places in the equatorial provinces of the Eastern Sudan. The Committee anticipate that, in answer to many prayers, the existing interdict on missionary work among the Mohammedans of the Upper Nile will shortly be removed."[4] Llewellyn Gwynne set sail for Sudan as a CMS missionary on November 3, 1899. He arrived in Khartoum just before the dawn of the new century.[5]

Weeks after Gordon's death, the Church Missionary Society in London proposed the Gordon Memorial Mission to Sudan.[6] The project aimed to "perpetuate Gordon's memory . . . through the direct proclamation of the Gospel of Jesus Christ to all the races inhabiting the upper basin of the Nile."[7] The postwar Sudanese—or Anglo-Egyptian—government insisted that for a time no mission station be established north of the tenth parallel or in any other part or district that it recognized as Muslim. Kitchener denied Gwynne the right to perform mission work in the North, and Gwynne ministered instead to British soldiers and the small population of British civilians in Khartoum. In 1904, Lord Cromer—Egypt's consul general and chief architect of the new condominium—wrote to the CMS, inviting the society to extend its work into South Sudan. After an appeal by the CMS Committee, a Gwynne-led party of six men was sent out in October 1905.[8]

Rev. Archibald Shaw was one of the men who departed with Gwynne. In his diary of October 17, 1905, Shaw notes that they left from London's

Charing Cross Station at 9 AM: "A number of people were on the platform to see us off, among my own friends being . . . Miss Nugent . . . The train started suddenly & quite unexpectedly . . . there was an undignified rush for the carriage, one by one we were hauled in, and midst great laughter & cheering, we were finally started on our way."[9] Gwynne's party sailed up the Nile and founded the Gordon Memorial Mission at Malek, in South Sudan. While Gwynne did not stay there for long—he returned to Khartoum and was made its first bishop three years later—one of the most important elements of the work in South Sudan was a school named for one of his well-wishers at Charing Cross: the Sophia Nugent School.[10]

* * *

In the aftermath of the Mahdist War, the Anglo-Egyptian condominium government wanted to transform South Sudan into a buffer zone that could stem the spread of Arabism and Islam up the Nile. Against this backdrop, missionaries entered South Sudan. The CMS quickly established mission stations and schools, and in 1920 the most important school of them all— the Nugent School—was founded. This chapter provides insights into the life and legacy of the Nugent School and the sociopolitical environment in which it operated.

Francis Deng notes that Christian education in the South fostered a new sense of identity that transcended ethnic loyalties and created a deep anti-North nationalist sentiment. He quotes politician and intellectual Bona Malwal, who remarked, "Southerners, at least those who are educated, have come to live together in schools, have worked together and have shared some political objectives for which tribal differences were played down to give an appearance of unity." Malwal further stated that differences with the North "were conceived as differences with Arabs, and were therefore differences with an outsider."[11] Despite the notion that southerners downplayed ethnic differences in favor of a unified anti-Arab sentiment, Christian missions were involved in reinforcing ethnic identities and occasionally became sites of ethnic conflict. This reality showcased an enduring question in South Sudanese society—the appropriate role of the church and Christianity in transcending or reinforcing ethnic identity.

To this end, examining the Nugent School is illustrative of several important elements of the South Sudanese mission enterprise. First, it was founded to assist in halting the spread of Islam up the Nile, a project that was religiously antagonistic, linguistically English, and gendered to produce masculine Christian "warriors." Second, efforts were made at the school to uphold ethnic identities. And yet, the presence of ethnic conflict at the Nugent School and other mission sites highlighted the tension between efforts to protect diverse social identities on one hand and a common Christian identity on the other. This dynamic leads to the final point: the expressed thought that ethnic conflict was a spiritual problem that Christianity could (and should) conquer. Articulated in this chapter by mostly white mission officials, Sudanese actors echoed similar ideas decades later in the Second Sudanese Civil War and South Sudan's internal conflict of the 2010s. Thus, the condominium era represented an early and important moment where state and church/mission officials discussed the relationship between religious and social identity. Was Christianity ultimately compatible with or antithetical to ethnicity? For several Christian officials, it was the very salve to ethnic conflict.

BEFORE THE BRITISH

During the sixteenth and seventeenth centuries, Islam became increasingly allied to Sudanese political power. Political systems with nominal Islamic allegiance were established in regions like Sinnar and Darfur, and a bevy of political shifts and socioeconomic conditions spurred the adoption of Arabic and Islamic culture in northern and western Sudan.[12] Although the influx of Arabism and Islam did not eliminate the North's linguistic, cultural, and ethnic diversity, a cultural unity was established in a manner that was not replicated in the South. In addition to the fact that most northern Muslims claimed patrilineal descent from notable Arab ancestors, "in sharp contrast to Southern Sudan, it was comprehended within a single religious and cultural framework. Most people north of the 13th parallel had by the 19th century become Muslims."[13] In the early nineteenth century, South Sudan had social and political systems ranging from the Shilluk and Azande kingdoms to the more egalitarian Nuer and Dinka structures. In a general sense, *Nilotics*—the Dinka, Nuer, and Shilluk—compose the main group of southerners, along with other ethnic groups such as the Azande, Bari, and Latuko. Although many languages were spoken and religions practiced, there is reason to believe that these conditions did not result in ethnic isolation; on the contrary, groups had frequent contact with one another.[14]

Catholics largely executed pre-Mahdiya Christian missionary work in Sudan. In 1846 Pope Gregory XVI created the Vicariate Apostolic of Central Africa, and Jesuit missionaries began working in the South in 1850. By 1860, however, the Jesuits were compelled to leave their Holy Cross and Gondokoro stations in part because the Bari would only tolerate missionaries if they proved to be sufficient trading partners in firearms and allies in war.[15] The British and Foreign Bible Society started working in the country in 1866, but this proved to be a brief venture that resumed after more than thirty years of inactivity. While only a small number of Muslims were converted during this initial period of mission work, the greatest impact was the establishment of a tangible Christian presence in Sudan (particularly among non-Muslim groups). The rise of Mahdism brought a violent end to this period of mission work.[16]

Bahr el-Ghazal, with its proximity to Kurdufan and Darfur (the epicenter of the Mahdist rebellion), was the first South Sudanese province affected by the revolt. Mahdist agents could encourage groups of people to revolt by capitalizing on lengthy widespread disgruntlement with the government. The Dinka, Nuer, and Shilluk felt no ties with the Arabs and joined the rebellion not for religious reasons or amity with northerners but rather to cast off an unpopular, oppressive government. During Emin Bey's administration, Rumbek reverted to its role as the nucleus of raiding activity in the area, and Egyptian authorities exported ivory, tamarind, and Dinka "conscripts" to Khartoum through Mashra' al-Rek into 1883. The revolt of the Agar Dinka was the first disturbance in Equatoria linked with Mahdist influence. The Agar Dinka, encouraged by the successful uprising of Dinka groups in Bahr el-Ghazal and angry at raids that the mam'ur of Rumbek had made on them for slaves and cattle, attacked the Rumbek garrison in July 1883 and destroyed the station. Throughout 1884–85, as Egyptian garrisons were cut off from Khartoum, more southerners rebelled against the government.[17]

In his study of prophecy and Mahdism in the Upper Nile, Douglas Johnson examined Dinka and Nuer experiences with particular reference to supposed links between Islam and African prophets. Johnson notes that the Dinka were able to incorporate key names and figures from Sudanese Muslim belief and practice into their own experience; one nineteenth-century Dinka hymn referenced the name Mahdi and integrated him into the order of divinities to whom the Dinka already prayed. "The Dinka and Nuer of the nineteenth century," he writes, "were confirmed in their belief in the validity of their own religious life. The impact of the Mahdiyya on the Nilotic heartland of the Upper Nile was far from benign. On the contrary, it left a legacy of conflict and confrontation."[18]

AFTER THE MAHDI

The British and Egyptian governments signed what became known as the Condominium Agreement in 1899. During the early stages, Egypt was for all intents and purposes a British protectorate and could not act unilaterally. While the Egyptian ruler could appoint the governor general, it would be done on the British government's recommendation. The British, in effect, controlled the Sudan. Messianic movements in North Sudan continued to manifest but were forcefully squelched. In southern Sudan, the British reopened the Nile channel and started to establish their control. While Mahdism no longer threatened the condominium by the 1920s, southerners tried to retain their independence, and groups like the Azande, Nuer, and Dinka levied armed resistance. The Nuer and Dinka were led by prophets that claimed direct revelation from divinities. To appease Muslims and discourage nationalistic fervor, the government restricted Christian missionary activity to the South, where there was a sparse Muslim population. The administration saw the utility of sending them South, where it encouraged mission organizations to start mission schools and allowed them the right to evangelize.[19]

* * *

The Roman Catholics, Church Missionary Society, and United Presbyterian Mission (also known as the American Mission) were the most prominent mission organizations in southern Sudan during the condominium period. In 1904 a mission sphere of influence system was adopted to reduce competition. Spaces of operation were designated to each mission: the Roman Catholics worked along the White Nile's western bank, with headquarters at Lul; the CMS operated in the Bahr el-Ghazal district and were headquartered at Malek; the Sobat watershed was given to the Americans, with their first station at Doleib Hill. The Lado Enclave became open for all missions. While mission work entailed Bible translation, education, medicine, and industrial work, evangelization was the overarching and unifying element.[20]

The 1914–19 Annual Report for Egypt and the Sudan stated that though the CMS had established two or three district schools in Mongalla Province, it had not yet opened its central school, which had been planned for several years.[21] One January 1918 report on Mongalla noted that

> the need of a boarding school where the lads who will in the future be the chiefs and subordinate officials under the Government can get an elementary education is very urgent, and C.M.S. has decided to open one with the approval and support of the Government. . . . This should prove a great missionary opening; to give these boys a Christian education should influence the whole district.[22]

ENCOURAGING CHRISTIANITY

In 1919, Rev. C. A. Lea-Wilson was sent to launch a high school for the sons of chiefs and headmen. The Nugent School opened in the Bari village of Juba in 1920. Friends of the deceased Sophia Nugent contributed funds for the original building of Gordon Memorial Mission's first boys' high school. Sophia Nugent of Kensington, with her two sisters, had supported the Gordon Memorial Sudan Mission in the South for many years. Construction work began in January 1920 and comprised the building of a dwelling house, school, church, workshop, and about twelve huts for boys. By August, ten circular huts each capable of housing four to five boys had been built.[23] A 1928 conference decided to move the school to Loka in January 1929, and the move was made the following year. Located 3,000 feet above sea level and sixty miles from Rejaf, Loka contains a massive twin-peaked mountain that reaches a thousand feet high. Initially occupying temporary spaces, the new buildings—a hall, four classrooms, dorms, teachers' houses, and a European house—were completed and occupied in 1933. Numerous improvements and extensions were subsequently made.[24]

"The school will be quite an English one," said Lea-Wilson. "English will be the only language spoken, and all teaching will be in English. The only other language possible would be Arabic, but that would involve the danger of paving the way for Islam. The Government are moreover encouraging us to teach English."[25] Lea-Wilson's statement concerning the dangers of Arabic and the preference for English pointed to the school's central mission. According to one Nugent School pamphlet, the institution was purposed to continue—in English—the education of male students who were selected from each of the mission station schools. The ultimate vision was multifaceted: supplying the schools with teachers, building a Sudanese ministry, educating the sons of chiefs and other indigenous leaders, and providing government departments with superior Sudanese assistants.[26] More than these aims, however, Lea-Wilson noted that the school was founded in an effort to confront Islam and stated as much before the New Alliance Club on December 8, 1922:

> We were sent there three years ago . . . so that we might do what is an intensely important thing—try to forestall Islam. The Government is greatly hampered by the fact that in the Southern Sudan they have no educated people, and they have to get officers for the troops and clerks for the Government officers from Khartoum, all of whom are Moslems. So the Government asked us to start educational work in the Bari village of Juba, and they have given over all the educational work into C.M.S. Hands.[27]

In another instance he clothed this aim in martial Crusade-like imagery: "We hope to send out a flow of Christian young men, who will carry the ideals of Christ wherever they go, & occupy posts some of which are at present filled by Moslems. By such means will we help to Christianize this part of Africa."[28]

The school's Christian mission was executed in several ways. The entire school met for prayers at 6 AM and 6 PM, and each morning's work began with scripture. A short prayer preceded each class. Aside from prayers and scripture, the school's Christian foundation was emblazoned on the school badge: a red Maltese cross.[29] The origins of the eight-pointed Maltese cross have been long debated. The Sovereign Military Hospitaller Order of St. John of Jerusalem of Rhodes and of Malta was founded in 1048 as a monastic order that ran a hospital to treat Christian pilgrims in the Holy Land. At the peak of its power, Rome commanded the order with the military responsibility to defend Christians from the local Muslim population. The cross is famously connected with the knights of Malta, with some believing that it did not appear until after a failed 1565 Turkish siege of Malta. Its eight points represent the Beatitudes, while the four arms were believed to represent the virtues of prudence, temperance, fortitude, and justice.[30]

The selection of the Maltese cross as the school badge is particularly enlightening given that, as Heather Sharkey notes, some Britons in Sudan—particularly CMS missionaries—invoked crusader discourses during the turn of the century. Anthropologist Janice Boddy writes that British officials in Sudan deemed themselves to be "knight administrators" and equated Christianity with civilization.[31] Although it is unclear whether Lea-Wilson knew about the history of the Maltese knights, his comments following his acknowledgment of the Maltese cross clearly took on a Christianity versus

Islam tone: "We should not be ashamed of the Cross of Christ, particularly in this country which is going to be Moslem unless we bestir ourselves. We had to put the letters 'J.H.S.' underneath the Cross (Juba High School) and our hope is that one day these boys will realise that those letters stand also for 'Jesus the Saviour of the World.'"[32]

The Nugent School was home to religious organizations that carried martial symbolism. According to Steven Wöndu, who entered the Loka Intermediate School in 1963, the Boys' Brigade had been one of the Nugent School's attractions during the condominium era. William Alexander Smith conceived of the idea for the brigade in Glasgow in 1883. While Wöndu described the Brigade in Scotland as "a zealous or even militant religious movement," he continued that "its main appeal to us was the uniform, the marching band, and badges."[33] There was also the Crusader Bible class. Revived at the Nugent School in 1948, the Crusader Bible class was voluntary and held on Sunday afternoons. Boys could write letters or read Sunday books, and attendance was noted for growing each week. By May 1949 there were reportedly 110–15 attendees each Sunday.[34]

In addition to the Crusaders, the Boy Scouts also had a presence at the school. When Helena Parry gave a picture of Thursdays—or "Club afternoon"—she described the scouts as spending time on the grass beyond the quad, either playing or sitting under the trees doing patrol work. "They are all smart and clean as Scouts should be—they [wear] a white cotton neckerchief edged with their patrol colour, and this with their badge and shoulder tapes and ribbons, transforms their white school uniforms into 'Scout uniform.'"[35] Southern Sudan's first-ever scoutmasters' training course took place at Loka over the 1948 Christmas holiday. It was a diverse group of attendees, with Europeans, Africans, and those from various Christian and non-Christian backgrounds.[36] J. I. Parry recalled, "We sang carols in English, Italian, Zande, Dinka, Moru, yes, even Welsh! But apart from that we do rejoice that Scouting in the Southern Sudan should have started with a Course which proved from the start the reality of the Scout Brotherhood of Nations based on Christian brotherhood."[37]

General Sir Robert Baden-Powell conceived scouting to reduce Edwardian class tensions and improve the quality of potential military recruits. Transplanted to Africa by British administrators, missionaries, and others, colonial youth experts worked with scout officials and looked to promote docile masculinity. "Baden-Powell and the founders of Scouting," writes Timothy Parsons, "were consciously aware that they were promoting a specific form of masculinity over a range of less desirable masculine identities.

In their eyes, manliness meant physical courage, patriotism, stoicism, chivalry, and sexual continence." In the scout uniform—modeled on that of the South African Constabulary, a paramilitary force Baden-Powell raised and commanded following the Anglo–South African War—he tried to create a strong socializing instrument that would become an attractive recruiting device, establish the scout's elite status, and blur class distinctions. In colonial Africa, where Western styles of dress conveyed respectability and sophistication, the scout uniform had greater impact. While the scout uniform brought prestige, membership was relatively low; by the 1950s, all of Anglophone Africa boasted approximately one hundred thousand registered African Boy Scouts.[38]

The reality of scouting at the Nugent School illuminates several elements of that institution's work. To begin, it illustrated the elite nature of the Nugent School, within not only South Sudan but British Africa. The scout uniform (along with the Nugent uniform) can be read as a visual symbol of social unity, the sublimation of potentially distinct ethnicities under an alternative, more ecumenical identity. Finally, there was the gender dynamic at play that was inseparable from contemporary religious politics. Scouting exposed students to a particular model of masculinity, one linked to martial identity through the uniform. Whether through the scout uniform or the Nugent School's appropriation of the Maltese cross, this gender project was conducted in a Christian educational setting. Given the increasingly martial tone that missionary rhetoric took after World War II—one framing Christian work in Sudan as a race against time against an ensuing Arab Muslim takeover—the Nugent School became, in a sense, an important locus in the "war against Islam" as a site that prepared Christian "soldiers."[39]

Comments from Ian Watts in 1949 illustrate this paradigm. Watts noted that Nugent School boys would no longer go to Ugandan Christian institutions to continue their education but instead went to the new government secondary school in Dinka country and then to Khartoum's Gordon College. In addition to this change, more southern officials were being sent north to receive more training for higher government posts. Watts saw the spiritual potentialities that were being opened up: "What a chance there is for them," he wrote, "to take the Gospel of Jesus Christ to Islam, and what a challenge to us to send boys out from this School who will be convinced, enthusiastic and knowledgeable Christians with a personal faith in the living Christ which will lead them to witness fearlessly in life and speech, cost what it may!"[40]

The gendered—and uneven—mission enterprise in South Sudan during the condominium era is also evident in the demographics and nature of girls' education. At the outbreak of World War I, the Catholics—whom Robert Collins termed "the most aggressive" of the three Christian missionary societies working in the South—had 557 boys in nine elementary schools and 246 girls in four elementary schools (statistics, he claimed, that were clearly inflated).[41] While boys were taught a craft like carpentry or bricklaying (or given clerical training), girls were taught needlework and music. Collins elsewhere noted that girls' education in the South was not central to the South's educational development. In March 1939 the government and CMS appointed a commission, composed of a Miss N. E. Ainley and Mrs. M. C. Warburton, to examine, report, and make recommendations on southern girls' education. The report was apparently not too encouraging: indigenous customs and older missionaries' prejudices posed obstacles. Ainley and Warburton ultimately concluded that given the lack of resources, education should be closely incorporated with the life girls would lead in southern societies.[42]

* * *

Linguistic work—a crucial element of South Sudanese education—was the work of cultural translation. Lamin Sanneh and Andrew Walls have noted that Protestant missionaries' evangelistic strategy was built on the premise that missionaries build on, rather than supplant, the old religion. Driven by Paul's discourse on the "Unknown God" in Acts 17, "Protestant missionaries set out to identify, name, and preach about unknown Gods . . . they established the architecture of the old religion and related the new Christian religion to the vernacular vocabulary."[43] The Dinka had a story of the founding of their religious belief and practice that corresponded with certain elements of Christ's birth, his early career, and the authority that the apostles inherited at his Crucifixion. Understandings of a high god, sin, sacrifice, blood redemption, and God's forgiveness were also central to Dinka religion.[44] *Nhialic* became the Dinka word missionaries translated as "God." The term is often used to refer to the Dinka "supreme being" and comes from a form of *nhial*, which refers to "sky," "above," or "up." Nhialic is considered to be just and all-powerful, with similar attributes to the Christian God. Dinka accepted Nhialic as the creator of all worldly things and a universal being capable of providing blessing and suffering.[45]

Francis Deng contends that Christian missions' primary objective among the Dinka was seen in traditional terms as the pursuit of *wei*, which in its verb form means "to breathe," and as a noun, "breath," and requires supreme moral and physical well-being. The premise was that the Dinka, before

Catholic education, were immersed in darkness or emptiness that was hazardous to wei. Catholic teachings were guaranteed to provide the solution and path to salvation. Dinka ideas of wei, which focused particularly on personal and collective well-being in this world, were combined to entail a new idea that joined the Dinka understanding of health with the Christian principle of ultimate survival in the spiritual sense.[46]

ENCOURAGING ETHNICITY

The first students were admitted to the Nugent School in July 1920. The first four boys arrived in August, and approximately forty boys were enrolled by October. While the Bari were most heavily represented, the early student body was a diverse lot; in November 1920 the school had Acholis, Madis, Dinka, Nyangwara, Kuku, and one Lotuho.[47] At one point thirty-six languages and dialects were spoken at the school. In late 1920, Lea-Wilson reported that each student understood either Bari, Acholi, or Dinka. English was taught through these languages and some Arabic, which was used as little as possible and was hoped, at some point, to be dropped completely. By 1922 the director of education in Khartoum supported the Nugent School's efforts to teach English.[48] The move to Loka did not change the school's diverse demographic. According to one 1949 description,

> There are the tall, slim, jet black Dinka and Nuer boys, whose tribes are great cattle owners . . . there are the Zande boys, short and stocky, and lighter coloured, whose parents live a predominantly agricultural life . . . we have the sturdily-built Moru boys from the Lui district, while the boys from the many Bari speaking tribes around the Juba area are variable in size . . . and their people are both pastoral and agricultural. So the pupils in our School differ very widely in race, language, customs, background and outlook.[49]

After attending village school for two years and primary school for three, about five boys from each ethnic area were chosen each year to attend Loka to be trained to lead their communities as agriculturalists, teachers, administrators, and the like.[50]

The 1928 Rejaf Language Conference spurred several important developments. The conference supported the introduction of vernacular languages in elementary schools. Six languages—Bari, Dinka, Nuer, Lotuho, Shilluk, and Zande—were chosen to be used in southern vernacular education. J. G. Matthew, secretary for education and health (among other areas), announced that English would replace Arabic as the South's official language, while southern colloquial Arabic was rejected in favor of English and local vernaculars as administrative languages.[51] Insulating the South from the proliferation of Arabic was part of the government's stated plan in January 1930 to "build up a series of self contained racial or tribal units with structure and organisation based . . . upon indigenous customs, traditional usage and beliefs."[52] That month the civil secretary wrote a memorandum that explained the "Southern Policy," which aimed to restrict the number of northern and Arab traders and administrators in the South. The ultimate purpose in doing so was to encourage the development of an indigenous administration and leadership in the South, dividing Sudan into northern and southern administrative principalities (native administration was in fact applied in the northern provinces earlier than in the South). Although the continued work of Muslim and Arab traders and British reliance on northern/Egyptian officials mitigated the policy's effectiveness, southern education shifted toward the use of vernacular languages and English as mediums of instruction within a Christian framework.[53]

One of the most intriguing areas in which religious and linguistic projects merged was in the area of naming. By June 1933 A. G. Hickson, resident inspector of education for the southern provinces, had noticed that the Wau Catholic Mission was using the English forms of Christian names "as far as possible." Opining that he did not like many of the Christian names that Catholic converts were given, Hickson continued that "they must, by Mission rule, [be] given saints' names many of which are strange to us." Not limited to the Catholic purview, CMS converts chose a biblical name of their liking; however, the CMS apparently prioritized the vernacularization of Christian names. Hickson opined that the Italian (Catholic) Mission should vernacularize the spelling of Christian names as the CMS did and avoid adopting the English forms. Insisting that official correspondences list indigenous and Christian names, he questioned the utility of addressing "Southern employees by their christian names to the exclusion of their native names."[54] According to this school of thought, conversion to Christianity did not have to mean disavowal of one's cultural heritage.

* * *

Competition was one way unity was encouraged at the diverse Nugent School. In J. B. de Saram's 1945 report from the school, he noted his perception that competing there was beneficial for fostering unity. De Saram wrote that for twenty-five years, Moru had competed against Dinka and Nuer against Zande, resulting in members of those groups liking and understanding one another and forming strong friendships. This kind of rapport, he concluded, laid the foundation for mutual trust and understanding across tribes.[55] There were sports and house/interhouse competitions, and activities like the Table Games Club and Debating Club. On one occasion the school was divided into "tribal groups" and a game organized with the goal of making an illustrated primer in every vernacular language.[56] On occasion the situation devolved into fighting. Interethnic football was organized along house lines "between pupils as different as Greeks and Icelanders," but these matches had to be temporarily abandoned because of their ferocity.[57]

The training of indigenous teachers was seen as a crucial element in ensuring students' connections with their community and culture. Hickson noted that children should be taught to value and enrich their heritage rather than to despise it, and that this could not be done if teachers had lost touch with their people.[58] The Catholic *Messenger* was an educational fortnightly newspaper that was published near Wau, in Bahr el-Ghazal. Founded in 1932, its ethnographic agenda can be gleaned from titles of articles that appeared in the 1930s and 1940s:

Fr. S. Santandrea, "Southern Sudan Folklore—The Bongo in the Central District (Wau) of the B.G.P." (June 1934)
Fr. E. Mason, "Southern Sudan Folklore—A Shilluk Fable" (Feb.–Mar. 1937)
Jerome Bidai, "Tribal Investigation—To the Zande Readers" (Mar. 1942)
Fr. C. Broggini, "The Belanda" (May 1946)
Joseph Ayok, "Dinka Education" (Dec. 1947)
Mathew L. Jambite, "Notes on Moru Customs" (Sept. 1948)[59]

*   *   *

In a May 1946 article, "The Controversy over the Belanda," E. Mason discussed the Belanda language and race: "The two Belandas do not belong to one race; they belong to entirely different racial groups: the Sudanic and the Nilotic."[60] He continued to explain that the Bviri language was akin to the Ndogo but still retained words revealing their Bor origin. The name used for God (or Spirit) was *Joki* (similar to the Luo-Shilluk *Juok*) rather than the Ndogo equivalent *Mbiri*, which is closer to the Zande *Mbori*. In 1946 Mason invited African readers to provide input on a controversy over whether the Bor belonged to the Nilotic race and others to the Sudanic, Ndogo-speaking race. *Messenger's* ethnic-centric focus was coupled with other missionaries' devotion to the study of South Sudanese history, religion, music, and traditions.[61]

Dictionaries produced during the condominium era not only were missionary attempts to transform vernaculars into conduits for Christian revelation but also provide insight into how missionaries sought to fashion political subjectivities.[62] Perhaps the most illustrative dictionary during the condominium period was Father J. Kiggen's 1948 *Nuer-English Dictionary*. A missionary for the St. Joseph's Society for Foreign Missions, Kiggen's definitions provide a compelling view into the way one missionary text sought to define ethnic, racial, and political identities. Defining *rool* as "country," he used ethnic lands (*Rool Naath, TƐat* = Nuer, Shilluk country) as illustrative examples. *Mulki* signified "Arab," and Kiggen often included Arabs in definitions connoting difference and oppression. For example, with *LƐƐiƐ* ("disavow," "disown," or "do not mix") came the phrase "the Arabs and the Nuer don't mix," and with *PƐƐiƐ* (to rob, plunder, take by force, carry off) came "the Turks dragged away the Nuer by force in times gone by."[63] The Dinka also occupy a noteworthy place in Kiggen's illustrative examples. Under the very definition of Dinka (*Jaŋ*) came the phrase *Cì jin a jaŋ* (You are not a Dinka), an unabashed declaration of Nuer-Dinka difference. This presumption of difference was reinforced in the illustration given for the genealogical term *LoƆth* (race, descent, generation, group), which referred to the Dinka race. In the description for *PƐƐiƐ* (to rob, plunder, take by force) the dictionary includes the descriptive phrase "my cattle were stolen by Dinka." Dinka were further placed in an antagonistic position in the description of the word *Mud*, the noun for "spear" (and a war spear in particular), among other definitions. Kiggen's dictionary paired this term with the associated phrase "they went to war with the Dinka."[64] Nuer readers, then, would have been exposed to associations of Arabs and Dinka in definitional descriptions of social/racial difference and predatory behavior. Kiggen's dictionary was a pedagogical resource that defined ethnicities and behaviors. Rather than trying to denounce or minimize the importance of ethnic identities, Kiggen's text went to great lengths to express a calculated understanding and confirmation of them.

ETHNIC CONFLICT, SPIRITUAL SOLUTION

Despite the effort to cultivate unity, there were tangible markers of division at the Nugent School. John Parry, CMS teacher at Yambio, wrote a letter from Loka intimating that lack of a lingua franca was an obstacle to achieving social cohesion among the student body. He noted that their knowledge of English was not strong enough to bind them together as a social unit, leading them to revert to vernaculars once they left the classroom. He also decried the fact that they did not mix and instead broke off to eat, talk, and make friends within their own ethnic groups.[65] Headmaster G. F. Earl opined that ethnic strife at the school was rooted not in the student body but rather in the makeup of the faculty. In 1945 the Sudanese staff consisted of four Moru, one Madi, and one Kakwa, and Earl attributed the imbalanced composition of Moru as "a big disadvantage" during a Dinka-Moru fight, "which might have been averted entirely had there been a Dinka teacher." He continued that the Nuer, who used to be implicated in almost every interethnic fight, were peaceful throughout the year, and that when the aforementioned fight occurred, they acted as peaceful patrols until the tension subsided. He attributed their pacific change to a teacher from Nasir, leading him to conclude that "clearly the solution to the periodic Nilotic outbreaks of fighting is the presence on the staff of respected leaders of their own tribes. Efforts should be made to recruit a properly balanced staff as soon as the teachers are available."[66] According to a 1948 report from Ian Watts, the school's ethnic diversity meant that conflict was not altogether surprising. "This year," he wrote, "all lived, worked and played together in peace. This in itself is remarkable and has not always been true. Tribal divisions and even fights in the school have in the past been serious, but we can thank God that this year has been a happy and successful one."[67] The following year, however, John Parry expressed that helping the boys become Sudanese rather than members of tight-knit tribal entities was a big problem. This had to be overcome, he continued, so that they could be challenged to do more for their own people (as co-nationals).[68]

One quarrel between boys of different ethnicities—though not at Loka—sheds light on how spirituality was injected into conversations concerning ethnic conflict. Writing from Obel in June 1954, Rev. W. B. Adair noted that a fight that had occurred "in spite of the fact that all older boys are living in four 'color' groups irrespective of tribes . . . the matter is not entirely settled after 8 days." The fight, according to Adair, could have been avoided if a teacher had not been drinking. Adair sustained a cut to his leg in his attempt to pry a spear from one of the combatants.[69] The following month, an unnamed writer wrote to Reverend Adair and expressed regret over the incident. Conveying the hope that peace had been restored, the writer added that "if they can learn to live together harmoniously, it will be a real witness to the influence of Christ in their lives."[70]

Another fight occurred at Akot in November 1948, compelling another statement linking spirituality with fighting. Oliver Allison was at the center of the events and provided a detailed account of the scrum. The son of an English clergyman, Allison was ordained in 1932 and, after joining the CMS, arrived in Sudan in 1938. Accepting an assignment in Juba, he had by 1947 been appointed assistant bishop in the Sudan.[71] Allison recounted that he had traveled to Akot, where he had heard that there had been issues with the head teacher. One of the Bor Dinka teachers in training had married a woman that the other teacher—an Agar Dinka—had himself wanted to marry. Conscious of an "underlying unrest" on his arrival, Allison woke up on a Saturday morning and prepared for a confirmation service. It did not happen. "On the evening after prayers," he wrote, "the spiritual germs of evil got the better of the situation, and the devil entered into the head-teacher." The head teacher had words with a Bor teacher, which led to a tussle. Later on he tried to start a massive brawl by leading the Agar schoolboys and others he could find against the Bor. Allison and others were informed in time to prevent the quarrel and took actions, with the assistance of some teachers and others, to prevent another incident. The following morning, Allison decided to have a meeting "of all the Christians on the station" in an attempt to put things in order before deciding whether to continue with the confirmation and other services. "All seemed quiet," he wrote,

> until shortly before the time due the unmistakable clash of clubs was heard. By the time we had arrived on the scene a serious fight had developed, and there was even a threat of spears being used. Young teachers and others who were normally peaceful and happy . . . were "seeing red" and blood was beginning to flow. In the providence of God we were able to intervene and stop the fighting, but not before the ring-leader had a fractured skull and other bad wounds.

Rather than holding the confirmation, Allison had to rush to the nearest hospital with those who had sustained the worst injuries. "If only as a result the Christians can be led to see the sin and folly of such actions," he opined, "and the disgrace that they bring to the Christian Church, good may yet come out of it. Such events are not a good advertisement of the need of the full Gospel of salvation for these people, and of the futility of a nominal adherence to the Christian faith."[72]

Fifteen teachers and teacher trainees were thrown in prison. "Those who assembled in March, 1949," wrote J. B. de Saram, "came very much with their tails between their legs, but not all of them." Before the term had completed a month, two teachers were once again involved in a fight. Each was immediately terminated. After outlining the troubles that Akot had experienced, de Saram framed the recent disturbances through a spiritual lens. "The starting point of a religious revival is a sense of sin," he wrote. "The Abalokole movement in East Africa calls it being 'broken'—broken in spirit. . . . You must be 'broken' before anything can happen. Well, we felt pretty 'broken' at Akot." Noting that remorse was not enough nor the same as a sense of sin, de Saram wrote, "We began, therefore, by realising that Akot's sad plight was due to *sin*. Hatreds and feuds may be part and parcel of normal Dinka life, but for a Christian they are sins."[73]

Allison's and de Saram's framing of the Akot clash in spiritual terms was echoed in some sense at the Nugent School. Parry suggested that only Christ's power could deal with the situations they had encountered at Loka, and that the economic, political, and moral instruction the boys received would be for naught if their hearts were not surrendered to Christ.[74] De Saram described an incident in which a Nuer chief, having compiled an excellent record in school, became the target of a vengeful Dinka. The Dinka eventually brought charges against him in Teacher's Court, and the chief was found guilty on one count and punished. Nonetheless, "the Nuer, after his beating, asked to remain behind, knelt down, and prayed for the Dinka, that he might not hate him but win him for Christ."[75]

The spiritualization of the aforementioned intergroup conflicts marked an important development. For Allison, the fighting was not rooted in jealousy but, rather, could be traced to "spiritual germs of evil" and the devil's influence on the head teacher. Conversely, providence, according to Allison, was responsible for allowing them to stop a fight. Similar to Allison's contentions, for de Saram the conflict was not just wrong but sinful. The solution was deep repentance and a "true" adherence to the faith. De Saram's description of the Nuer chief's desire to convert his Dinka accuser further highlights the positioning of Christianity as a solution to conflict. Taken together, Allison's and de Saram's letters position ethnic conflict as a spiritual dilemma that Christianity could conquer.

While there is no indication that those men believed that ethnicity itself was a problem that had to be done away with, the *Messenger* newspaper published an article—adapted from *Ruru Gene*—that presented Christianity as a community of belonging that should replace ethnicity. Tacisio Migido, a teacher at the Mupoi Normal School, wrote, "You should leave charms altogether. Pagans will find some excuse in their utter ignorance. . . . But what reasonable excuse can a Christian have? The custom of your tribe? . . . now your new tribe is christianity, and unless you are born again . . . you will not be able to enter Heaven."[76] There is the inference that one's ethnicity is as exchangeable as religion; just as one can convert into or out of Christianity, one can just as easily join or leave an ethnicity. Despite his use of the terms *pagan* and *charms*, *tribe* is not employed as antithetical to Christianity; rather, Christianity—as a community of belonging—is itself understood as being tribal. Thus, while Migido establishes an understanding that one must depart from the ignorance of pagans and charms and be born again, he does not associate Christianity as a progression from being "ethnic" or "tribal"; on the contrary, he positions Christianity itself as a tribe.

* * *

C. A. Lea-Wilson and Ian Watts would have been thrilled at the trajectories of Nugent alumni. Paulo Logali, who in 1926 became one of the first three Bari boys to be baptized, was a student at the Nugent School before its move to Loka. A devout Christian, Logali was a founding member of the South Sudan Workers Association (SSWA). Created to represent the interest of southern government employees, it was the first active southern organization and became a political committee in the early 1950s. Joining Logali in cofounding the SSWA was fellow Nugent alum Benjamin Lwoki, who in 1948 was appointed as a member of the legislative assembly.[77] Alum Joseph Lagu led the rebel Anyanya military force during the First Sudanese Civil War, and his political vision, leadership, and military strategies have been noted as being "clearly . . . influenced by his Christian faith."[78] Lagu, Logali, and Lwoki were joined by other alumni who would go on to have a major impact, including (but not limited to) administrator and politician Bullen Alier, MP Dak Dei, MP and Liberal Party member Jon Majak, and Aggrey Jaden—the president of the South Sudan provisional government.[79]

The Nugent School, founded with the hope of stymieing Islam's percolation up the Nile, became a space in which to produce English-speaking, masculine, Christian students. Through the encouragement and codification of several vernacular languages, athletic and nonathletic competition, and the ethnographic nature of the Catholic *Messenger* newspaper, mission and state authorities made efforts at the school and elsewhere to uphold ethnic identities, reflecting a broader condominium push to protect the South from Arabism. And yet, the reality of ethnic conflict highlighted the tension between efforts to encourage indigenous identities and a common

Christianity. Some concluded that ethnic conflict was a spiritual problem that an authentic Christianity could overcome.

There are three reasons why the school (and the mission enterprise in which it operated) is foundational in the narrative of Christian and ethnic politics in South Sudan. First, it provides an early illustration of the converging agendas that state and mission actors had for the Sudanese: namely, maintain one social identity (ethnicity) while encouraging a religious identity (Christianity) and resisting a racial culture (Arabic, Arab culture) and religion (Islam). At a time when Islam was viewed with antagonism, the matter of whether Christianity and ethnicity were compatible with each other was clear, at least to some: "yes." One of the most compelling theological ideas to emerge during the post-2011 years—even after the region had witnessed ethnically driven violence, and the traditional Arab and Islamic enemy from the North had been removed—was the notion that God had created ethnicities and that they should be celebrated. This contemporary thought must be placed in the same genealogy with mission and state actions to uphold ethnicity during the condominium era and, as such, testifies to the notion that there have long been Christians in the Sudan that have not viewed ethnicity as a problem. While it might be fair to question whether the Nugent School failed as a multiethnic site given that ethnic rivalries persisted, doing so would risk giving missions perhaps too much credit if the opposite were true. If there were no fights at the school or other mission sites, what would it mean to attribute such peace primarily to the missionaries rather than the pupils themselves?

The second reason why the condominium-era mission enterprise is so significant when examining the interplay of religious and ethnic politics was the effort by Allison and others to spiritualize the roots of ethnic solidarity and discord. While conflict was "sin," amity reflected authentic Christian influence. This injection of the spiritual into examinations of intra-Sudanese relations is significant considering that for much of the twentieth century, such spiritualization was done within the context of North-South relations. The chapters concerning the First and Second Civil Wars discuss the liberatory theologies that framed various Sudanese regimes as biblical/spiritual evils, while positioning southerners as neo-Israelites destined for freedom. That white mission officials like Allison framed interethnic relations during the condominium necessitates an expanded understanding of political theology in South Sudan from one restricted to interracial and interreligious relations to an interethnic one as well. Sudanese figures like Thomas Attiyah continued to insert theology into discussions about southern ethnicities during the Second Civil War and post-2011 southern conflict, illustrating that for all that can be said about the spiritualization of the Arab Islamic North versus black Christian South rhetoric during the civil wars, there is a tradition of clothing interethnic relations in spiritual terms for an even longer period. This reality can be used to argue that ethnicity, more than race or religion, has been the more stubborn bone of contention in the South.

Finally, the Nugent School illustrates the gendered and martial nature of the Christian project in Sudan. Emblazoned with the Maltese cross and afforded access to the Boy Scouts, Crusader Bible classes, and the Boys' Brigade, Nugent students were surrounded by military idioms. Various Sudanese intellectuals during the twentieth-century civil wars spiritualized those conflicts by referencing relevant biblical passages, invoking a providential God, and at times demonizing Arabs and the government. The fact that various Sudanese regimes attempted to forge the country into an Islamic state further encouraged the notion that the conflicts were inherently religious. And yet, decades before any southern Sudanese Christian Anyanya member or SPLA soldier picked up a gun to fight an Islamizing government, Nugent School founder C. A. Wilson "hope[d] to send out a flow of Christian young men, who will carry the ideals of Christ wherever they go, & occupy posts some of which are at present filled by Moslems." It would not be inaccurate to state that the union of Christianity and militarism among southerners in the twentieth century can be traced to the Nugent School.

The Nugent School was not the only condominium-era institution created to "forestall Islam." The school was joined by the Equatorial Corps, the military unit at the center of the South's most famous rebellion and the subject of the next chapter.

2

The Equatorial Corps
and the Torit Mutiny

No man is sure of his life, the individual is at the mercy of the state,
murdering replaces justice. . . . That any force on earth can shake the
foundations of this pyramid of power and corruption, of human misery
and slavery, seems inconceivable. But thirty years before this day, a miracle
occurred. On the Roman cross in Judea, a Man died to make men free,
to spread the Gospel of love and redemption. Soon that humble cross is
destined to replace the proud eagles that now top the victorious Roman
standards. This is the story of that immortal conflict.
—*Quo Vadis*, 1951

Starring Robert Taylor and Deborah Kerr, the 1951 epic film *Quo Vadis*
focuses on a Roman general, Marcus Vinicius, and a Christian woman,
Lygia, during Nero's reign. Marcus, who embodies Roman power and pa-
ganism, falls in love with Lygia, a member of the suppressed Christian
community. When Nero blames Christians for kindling the Great Fire
of Rome, the matter of religious allegiance becomes an issue of the first
magnitude.[1]

Although the movie had debuted more than two years earlier, *Quo Vadis*
headlined the April 13, 1954, edition of the Sudanese daily newspaper *Morning View*. Despite the film's long-awaited release in the Sudan, the newspaper
reported that the Ministry of the Interior had banned the film. To add insult to injury, the writer reported that to their knowledge, the film had not

been barred anywhere else. Nevertheless, the ministry justified its prohibition amid speculation that its grisly portrayals of Christians being crucified, burned alive, and gored by ravenous lions could have a provocative influence among Sudanese audiences: "The Ministry of the Interior," the article stated, "has been advised by the censor . . . that the facts of the film are presented in such a manner as to be unacceptable . . . and may well have some inciting effects."[2]

The following year the Sudanese government had a far more serious problem on its hands—the mutiny of the Equatorial Corps at Torit. The Torit Mutiny of August 18, 1955, is the kairotic moment of South Sudanese nationalism and has been commonly used to mark the beginning of the First Sudanese Civil War.[3] While some may have considered *Quo Vadis* and its presentation of history to be insignificant in the wake of the mutiny, history's relevance to contemporary political action was undeniable. With historical narratives providing templates for action and important backdrops to the political milieu, the sociopolitical developments of the time could appear like scenes in a larger drama. As Oliver Allison stated in a 1949 edition of the *Sudan Diocesan Review*,

> All the Sudan's a stage, and all the men and women in it players. Whether we like it or not . . . we are actors and not merely passive witnesses on the Sudan stage at this particular moment in its story. The plot is developing rapidly and whether the drama that is being staged will develop into a tragedy, a comedy, or a triumph . . . is hard for us to judge.[4]

For many in the coming years, Sudan became a stage on which dramas from Sudanese and biblical history were reenacted or threatened to do so. The mutiny became one such occasion, when mutineers looked to defend themselves from another chapter of "subjugation" from the North, a history embedded in slavery.

The Torit Mutiny was more than an emancipatory action to prevent this history from repeating itself; rather, it was also a moment in which members of the Equatorial Corps—which was established amid the Egyptian Army's presence and Islamizing tendencies—refused to be transferred and replaced by northern soldiers. Although Christian sentiment was not the mutiny's main catalyst, the British who created the corps saw Christianity as an element of protecting the South from Islam. This sentiment is essential for understanding the mutiny as a moment when colonial religious visions had violent, separatist, material consequences that actualized in a widening chasm between North and South and a closer union between a diversity of southerners.

THE EQUATORIAL CORPS: RELIGIOUS ORIGINS

In many respects, the June 1910 transfer of the Lado Enclave spurred the formation of the Equatorial Corps. Although Charles Gordon had made Lado the capital of Equatoria, the Mahdiya effectively isolated it. Mahdists prevented steamers from reaching the town, and by the time Mahdist forces entered Lado in 1888, the town was empty. After the Congo Free State became a personal possession of Belgium's King Leopold II, he annexed almost half of the southern territory from the Western Nile bank to the Congo. In May 1890 the British recognized Leopold's authority over the enclave in exchange for certain trading rights, but in accordance with a subsequent agreement between the two countries, the Lado Enclave was set to be transferred to the Sudan government on Leopold's death. On June 10, 1910—following his death—the enclave was incorporated into the condominium.[5]

Reginald Wingate did not want to see Islam in the enclave. Wingate began his position as Sudan's governor general on December 23, 1899, and served in that capacity for over sixteen years. He enjoyed a close relationship with Catholic bishop Franz Geyer and in late 1904 urged him to begin work in Wau, a South Sudanese center for the Egyptian Army and a site with a Muslim presence.[6] H. Karl W. Kumm, who after studying Islam's spread in Nigeria played a key role in founding the Sudan United Mission, opined that the British government assisted Islam's transmission among "pagans" in Bahr el-Ghazal through the military. Though the military was recruited from non-Christian, non-Muslim communities, once the men enlisted, they were forced to swear allegiance to the Khedive, received circumcision, and were made Muslims.[7] Other Islamic elements permeated military structure: Friday was the day of rest, soldiers' children were educated by a Muslim *malam*, and the Koran was taught.[8] Rev. Archibald Shaw wrote in his diary from the CMS station at Malek, "It is sad to think that by taking the country under Anglo Egyptian rule we have already begun to force Mohammedanism on the people." Shaw cited several pieces of evidence to support his claim, including the facts that five hundred Muslim soldiers and junior officials had been brought into the country, 150 "natives" had been recruited into Sudanese battalions, and the Koran formed the basis of schooling in the Sudanese battalions. "It is time our hands were strengthened with recruits. . . . At present the natives can only conclude that Mohammedanism is the religion of England."[9]

On March 1, 1911, Wingate wrote a letter to Eldon Gorst, consul general of Egypt from 1907 to 1911. Writing about the Lado Enclave, Wingate shared that when the condominium had first come into possession of the region the previous June, "there was a considerable influx of recruits which we much required to make up the strength of the XIVth Sudanese." But for some unknown reason, he continued, the supply of recruits had virtually disappeared. Wingate opined,

> that the system which prevails in Sudanese Battalions, of turning all recruits into Moslems . . . has something to do with it, and this leads me to the consideration of the desirability of . . . replacing our Regular Troops by some Territorial system . . . reorganization would afford of getting rid of the Moslemizing influence in the shape of Egyptian Officers and fanatical Sudanese N.C.O.'s, and very gradually dropping the Moslem conditions which prevail in all Sudanese Battalions of the Egyptian Army.[10]

Wingate's proposal to create a non-Muslim military unit was a radical one, given Islam's centrality in military culture. Religious impulses aside, locally recruited troops offered several advantages; they would be less expensive, speak the language of their stationed district, and know the country better than outsiders. As Equatoria province bordered Uganda, Kenya, Ethiopia, and the Congo, it was also in the administration's interests to secure the South's borders.[11]

In three years' time the local recruitment policy had been implemented in Yambio and Tembura, where another company took over in 1915. The administration's socializing objectives were clearly reflected in the corps's cultural and linguistic makeup. The unit comprised southern troops and used English as the language of command. Christianity was encouraged, and Islam practically forbidden.[12] When the last batch of northern troops departed from Mongalla on December 7, 1917, the governor reported that he had "removed the more fanatical, super religious Muslim soldiers, jallaba (peddlers) and riff-raffs . . . hoping that the authorities . . . will see that they don't return and . . . keep any old soldiers in Omdurman and generally northern [people] from . . . settling anywhere in the province." His plea to successor C. S. Northcote included an unambiguous reminder of why it was necessary to keep northern merchants out: "if a Jehad [sic] is ever started in the Sudan and northern Africa, it would be a great thing if the countries south of the sudd were free from it and if we could link up with Uganda which is practically entirely Christian and so have an anti-Islam buffer."[13]

THE EQUATORIAL CORPS

The Equatorial Corps was initially created as part of the Egyptian Army and a process in which regular army units were replaced by locally recruited units. The Western Arab Corps replaced the Camel Corps, the mounted infantry replaced the cavalry, and the Eastern Arab Corps was recruited among Kassala's Beja. Following the White Flag Mutiny of 1924, all Sudanese units were detached from the Egyptian Army and combined in the Sudan Defence Force.

The Equatorial Corps were headquartered in Torit, in eastern Equatoria's Latuholand. While the corps was distributed throughout the South, Torit was a prudent location because of its easy accessibility to East Africa and the Lotuho reputation for their military acumen. They had resisted British rule in the early twentieth century, and after their resistance, ethnographic studies indicated their enthusiasm for joining the army. To balance the vast number of people and warrior traditions of the Nilotic Dinka, Nuer, and Shilluk, the British recruited most of the corps from the Lotuho and other small eastern Equatorian ethnic groups. The corps and police were generally recruited from the Lotuho of Equatoria, the Jur of Bahr el-Ghazal, and the Madi, Moru, and Zande.[14]

The recruitment of members from the aforementioned ethnicities points to the connection between religious and gender politics. Farther south in Uganda, military recruitment was linked to martial stereotypes about masculinity and often involved recruits from Lado. In the newly established colonial army, the British divided the Ugandan contingent into an African battalion and an Indian battalion. The African battalion initially had a Sudanese majority. Ethnicity formed the basis of recruitment, with British officers preferring soldiers from groups perceived to have "natural" military qualities. According to Timothy Parsons, a recruit's value was determined solely by his ethnic origins.[15] In Sudan during the nineteenth century, raiding patterns followed those first established by eastern kingdoms. The Ethiopian borderlands, Nuba hills, and lands along the Bahr al-Arab became the first sources for army slaves. Areas that were attacked had a long history of dependency on state peripheries, and Douglas Johnson has noted that the combination of marginality and dependency made them perfect reservoirs for "martial races."[16]

The nineteenth-century *martial race* ideology purported that some groups of men were culturally or biologically predisposed to military prowess.[17] Within the martial race paradigm, initial dependency was used to encourage martial characteristics and fidelity to new masters. Once brought into armies, their ethnic and martial peculiarity was encouraged and emphasized, giving them a "vehicle for gaining respect, legitimacy and protection in the larger social order of which they are now, albeit reluctantly, a part." Thus, argues Johnson, peoples on the Sudanese slave frontier became part of a "martial race," which was identified and maintained by a succession of states.[18]

The British believed that developing strong ethnic imbalances in the army would encourage more politically reliable organizations, and that people would be attracted by opportunities that the army provided. In its early years the corps played an active role in subduing several ethnicities: corps artillery was credited with subduing the Lokoya and Lotuho; the corps was largely responsible for pacifying the Nuer and Dinka in Upper Nile and Bahr el-Ghazal provinces; and district commissioner Jack H. Driberg led his Equatorial Corps (which included Acholi soldiers from Uganda) against the Didinga and Toposa. In 1925, Egyptian mamurs and battalions were withdrawn, and the old Sudanese battalions disbanded, while the responsibility for South Sudan's security was given—under British directions—to the Equatorial Corps and the police. With a British recruitment policy that resulted in an ethnically and territorially divided army, Ahmed El Awad Mohammed has noted, "Each area developed its own politico-military entity."[19]

The aforementioned ethnic dimensions and martial stereotypes cannot be divorced from the religious politics at work in the corps' formation (namely, protecting the South from Islam). While the Nugent School staff may have sought to encourage among their students a martial, Christian consciousness, the Equatorial Corps was a different expression of the same project—a cadre of South Sudanese men purposed to confront the spread of Islam.

* * *

Torit County's Catholic mission was situated in a mountainous region that belonged to Chief Lotila. Fr. Fanti made the first attempt to perform mission work among Acholi soldiers stationed at Torit, and when Bro. Faustin Cosner arrived at Torit, he immediately set about the work of teaching some Sudanese government soldiers in carpentry. By the early 1920s, there were at least a few Catholics in the corps barracks. Protestant missions also targeted southern soldiers. At around the same time the Catholic mission in Torit was getting off the ground, Rev. Archibald Shaw requested prayer for a military school in the Lotuho district and at Loka for soldiers in the new companies.[20] In his address before the Alliance Club on December 8, 1922, Shaw provided an unambiguous explanation as to why his mission was concerned with fostering a connection with the corps:

> We have been anxious to start schools for the garrison Companies of Equatorial troops which have replaced the Moslem Sudanese troops. . . . The Government . . . decided to allow Christian schools to be started for the Equatorial Companies. . . . It will be a great thing if we have a Christian soldiery in the Southern Sudan. If the soldiers are Christians it will make a great difference in the Government centres, which at present are centres of Mohammedanism.[21]

Insulating the South from the proliferation of Arabic was part of the government's stated plan in January 1930 to "build up a series of self contained racial or tribal units with structure and organisation based, to whatever extent the requirements of equity and good government permit, upon indigenous customs, traditional usage and beliefs."[22] By that point English command words had already been introduced into the Equatorial Corps and provincial police forces, but Khartoum's Civil Secretary's Office stated that more was required. More specifically, it was suggested that increased effort be made in ensuring that men used English as their primary mode of communication exclusive of Arabic, which would mean opening English-language classes—for which mission schools were cited as desired instructors—and efforts by authorities to ensure that men used English when local vernaculars could not be used.[23] As a compelling aside, southern governors were informed in 1931 that while English teachers for Equatorial troops could be recruited from mission schools, they were mandated only to teach English—evangelism would have to occur outside their linguistic duties.[24]

By 1949, Torit consistently had about nine hundred soldiers.[25] In a letter dated August 28, 1954, C. M. Lamb—the acting district commissioner and commander of the Equatorial Corps at Torit—alluded to the importance of religious life for soldiers stationed there. Lamb noted that it appeared that the soldiers did not like the new site allocated for the Protestant church because "it is too far from the lines." While he believed it unlikely that permission would be granted to build the church in the military zone, Lamb was shocked at how strongly the soldiers felt about the issue. They appeared to look at the church "as being provided solely for their use. I think this idea has probably grown up due to the [fact] that when it was first built the soldiers of the Equatoria[l] Corps were the only Protestants in Torit and also because they now form the bulk of the congregation."[26]

GROWING UNREST

A series of major developments had occurred since the Southern Policy was instituted in 1930. Egyptian and Sudanese nationalism claims ruled national-ist politics from the 1920s through the 1940s. Sudanese journalism emerged as a force that was free from government control; the issue of whether there was a distinct Sudanese culture (given the country's historical links to the Arab world, Islam, and equatorial African cultures) was debated; and, in North Sudan, an educated class organized for an effective nationalist move-ment. In 1938, graduates of Gordon College founded the Graduates General Congress (or Graduates Congress, for short). Meanwhile, British policies—particularly the 1933 Closed Districts Ordinance—isolated the South.[27]

In 1942 the Graduates Congress petitioned the British for self-government but was rejected. The rejection created a split within the congress. Activists like Ismail al-Azhari demanded a policy of noncooperation with the British and, consequently, became allied with Egyptian nationalism and Nile Val-ley unity. On the other side were moderates who mistrusted Egyptian aims and believed that independence might be more quickly realized by working with the British. In 1944 the British tried to control political developments by creating the North Sudan Advisory Council. Two political parties were organized to contest the first elections for the council; al-Azhari's Ashiqqa Party called for independence with close Egyptian ties, while the Umma Party supported total independence. After Egypt's 1946 effort to assert its sovereignty over Sudan, Britain reversed course and conceded Sudan's right to self-determination and government. Sudan was offered union with Egypt or national independence.[28] At the 1947 Juba Conference, northern and southern attendees agreed on the principle of national unity and southern involvement in the legislative assembly.[29]

In 1948 the legislative assembly, an elected body that included northern and southern representatives, was formed. The following year, representa-tives from Sudan, Egypt, and Britain drafted a new constitution that pro-vided limited autonomy for a united Sudan. The Self-Government Statute was enacted in 1952, providing for self-government after an indefinite period.

The following year, an Anglo-Egyptian agreement was signed that defined the steps toward self-government and self-determination. Northern parties made a deal with Egypt that removed provisions from the Self-Government Statute. The provisions removed from the 1953 agreement were those that southerners believed were necessary to protect their interests in the period leading to self-determination. Following this exclusion, the Liberal Party was formed and ran in the 1953 elections. Despite its intention to attract members from other parts of Sudan, the Liberal Party's leadership was exclusively southern.[30]

The 1954 creation of the first all-Sudanese cabinet under al-Azhari's pro-Egyptian National Union Party (NUP) accelerated southern political thinking toward self-determination and federalism. As self-government became virtually assured, federation emerged as a condition for southern participation in self-determination for a united Sudan. Northern leaders resisted any concession to southern demands. In August 1955 parliament approved a motion for self-determination, and Sudan became independent on January 1, 1956.[31]

* * *

Following World War II, southern officials and mission employees formed the Southern Intellectuals Organisation. While they initially saw an alliance with the North Sudanese–composed Graduates Congress as the best path to Sudanese independence, Leonardi writes that the almost complete exclusion of southerners during Sudanization in the 1950s fueled a growing sense of southern grievances and political identity.[32] A group of educated southerners formed the Southern Party just before the 1953 elections.[33] In 1954 the Southern Party changed its name to the Liberal Party to avoid northern suspicion that the word *Southern* implied separation. The party aimed to secure self-government for the South and fought for equal pay for equally qualified people from the North and South in similar positions. At its 1954 meeting, its delegates condemned the uneven results of Sudanization and called for national federation.[34]

As early as October 1954—the same month Sudanization results were announced—Marko Rume and Daniel Tongun began holding discussions about the possibility of organizing a widespread rebellion throughout the South. Rume was introduced to politics at the Nugent School and later worked as a secretary in the Liberal Party. Born in 1923, Daniel Tongun was a student-teacher at the Nugent School in the early 1940s and became politically active as a government official working in Juba. According to Tongun, there was a general consensus among Equatorial Corps troops in the South that if the region was marginalized in discussions about their political aspirations, they would refuse to be transferred up north.[35] Indeed, Lt. Col. W. B. E. Brown recalled that when the order to Sudanize all British appointments in the corps was received in the middle of June 1954, the handover generated a sense of foreboding: "The news of our impending departure and handover to Northern Sudanese officers caused great shock and dismay among the troops. When I told my Sol Talim, he at first refused to believe it. Eventually having accepted the news he said:—'there will be war down here.'"[36] Rume, assigned to the Equatorial Corps as a cashier, conceptualized the mutiny with Tongun.[37]

In 1955, Saturlino Oboyo of the corps at Torit organized an insurrectional plot. Oboyo, president of the Liberal Party's Equatorial Corps's branch, had spread rumors that northern troops were planning to come South with murderous intentions. In a preemptive move, he tried to organize a massacre of northern officers within the corps. Despite his successful recruitment of noncommissioned officers into the plot, the conspiracy was uncovered on August 6. Oboyo was arrested, and his correspondence and list of coconspirators discovered. In response to the conspiracy northern troops were quickly flown down to Juba. On August 8, amid concerns that southern soldiers were full of anti-northern enmity, the military affirmed its earlier decision to transfer some southern troops to the North and replace them with northern units. Consistent with this order, the No. 2 Company of the Equatorial Corps at Torit was ordered to move to Khartoum on Thursday, August 18. Contrary to the practice of allowing troops' families to move with them, the soldiers were ordered to move without their families or ammunition. This exceptional stipulation exacerbated concerns that the unarmed soldiers could be killed by northern troops on their arrival in Khartoum and that their families would be at the mercy of the newly transferred northern troops.[38]

MUTINY

Rev. Elizabeth Noel, who at the time of our interview was president of the Episcopal Church of Sudan Mothers' Union, had been seven or eight years old in Torit when the mutiny broke out. Her father, who served in the army for eighteen years, was taking tea that morning. According to her account, the order to leave families behind may have provided the critical spark to the ensuing conflagration: "The chief commander was talking that all people should get ready to go to Khartoum. And then one of the soldiers said, 'Okay, but why can we go without our family, our property, the arms?' The chief commander said, 'No, shut up' . . . then after . . . one of the captains shoot one of the soldiers. Immediately and suddenly, things bursted up."[39] The soldiers' fear of leaving their families behind may have been historically rooted. During the Turco-Egyptian period, battalions transferring from one garrison to another often left their wives and families behind. Taking over the wives of the garrison that they were relieving, marriages routinely occurred between incoming conquering Sudanese battalions and the wives of the defeated slave garrisons (or formerly enslaved women).[40] If the casus belli was indeed Torit soldiers' concern over what the incoming troops would do with their wives, the mutiny should be principally read as a masculine defense of the domestic sphere.

On the morning of August 18, troops in the No. 2 Company mutinied. Race, in addition to the possible aforementioned gender dynamic, was also at the epicenter of the violence. Engineer Alberto Marino inferred that a racial slur combined with anti-Muslim angst ignited the uproar. Marino, who was in Wau that evening, asked his substitute whether he had heard of what had taken place in Torit. The substitute shared that the tumult had begun when an Arab officer insulted an elderly black sergeant-major, Latada, by calling him a slave. According to the substitute, this was the worst insult a Muslim could hurl on a southern Negro.[41] After the aspersion, an unspecified shooter fired a pistol, and the unnamed Arab who had spoken the slur fell dead. After the killing, "Negro lieutenants, nearly all Christians, joined Latada leading the insurrection. . . . Latada was very brief in his speech, 'The hour of vengeance against the Moslems has come, do you understand? It is war to the end.'"[42] After rejecting orders to embark on trucks to Juba and be transported to Khartoum, the Torit troops attacked North Sudanese officers. Breaking into the armory to gain arms and ammunition, they killed northern officers and committed arson and looting. Shooting began in Equatoria and spread quickly, with mutinies occurring in Juba, Yei, Terrakeka, Tali Post, Rokon, Kajo Keji, and as far away as Yambio and Meridi. The first wave of violence left 361 northerners and 75 southerners dead. Order was restored by September.[43]

Anti-Arab animus was present in the maelstrom. On August 19, Ismal Gemaa of the Forestry Department drove to Tambechi and "told the villagers that the Mondokoro [Arab] Army killed their relatives in Juba [and] they should kill all the . . . Mondokoro in the area." After he conveyed this message, forest ranger Mohamed Abdel Karim was killed.[44] Anti-Arab sentiment was also exemplified by an episode in which a woman's husband and ten-year-old daughter were killed in her presence. After their deaths, some people directed vitriol toward the new widow by shouting, "Kill her as she would be giving birth to more Mondokoros."[45] Jonathon Glassman has noted that violence against women is a calculated trademark of racial and ethnic violence, as acts like disembowelment and rape are understood as attacks on the enemy's ability to reproduce and an assault on the enemy's manhood.[46] By targeting those capable of producing more members of the race, the aforementioned anecdote suggests an element of racial cleansing from the war's first clash.

Religious identity was also a murderous motivation in the violence. On August 20 a Lotuho man named Airo Ogwana, a muezzin at Torit mosque, speared a northerner to death near Torit's veterinary offices. He was understood as being a Muslim and thus more associated with the northerners under attack. Court documents state that when antinorthern violence commenced, Ogwana "participated by killing one to prove to his people that he was still a Southerner with no sympathy towards his [associates] . . . in the Mosque."[47] His defense was that "he was frightened by the mutineers who told him that unless he killed a Northerner his loyalty to the South would not be proved" was insufficient to prevent Chief Justice Abu Rannat and the governor general from confirming his death sentence.[48] That the Muslim Lotuho Ogwana killed to prove his southernness illustrates that, even at the war's inception, the question of just "how Southern" a Muslim was or could be was debatable and could present an identity crisis of sorts. That the court documents stated that Ogwana was ethnically Lotuho—an identity shared with many of the principal mutineers in Torit's Equatorial Corps—did not appear to prove or reinforce his southernness in the eyes of those who reportedly threatened his life. In this instance, then, Ogwana's Muslim identity superseded his Lotuho ethnicity, revealing the ethnic and religious politics at play during the mutiny. Ogwana's attempt to ensure his acceptance as a southerner by taking a northerner's life was a sanguinary rite of passage.

Alexis Mbali Yangu includes another instance of religion's role in the tumult in his book *The Nile Turns Red*. Arab troops found some Christian boys wearing crucifixes around their necks. The young men were arrested and fastened to trees for execution. One of the soldiers asked his officer why the boys were not blindfolded, to which the officer responded by taking out his pocketknife, extracting their eyes, and giving orders for their death by shooting.[49] To be sure, there is reason to question the veracity of this episode;

how was this story transmitted to Yangu if the witnesses were blinded and subsequently executed? There is a long tradition of martyrology in Christian literature, and though his text was not evangelical, Yangu—a senior figure in the liberation movement during his exile (when he wrote the book)—would have found benefit in framing the soldiers in a persecuting light.[50]

Gabriel Dwatuka was the focus of another incident. A Zande born in the Tombura district, he was ordained a priest in 1953. Dwatuka, who had saved northern officers' lives and their families, was in Maridi during the disturbances. One day, after completing morning Mass, five soldiers arrested the priest. Wanted for routine questioning in connection with a civil disturbance, the soldiers ridiculed Dwatuka as he was led into the prison courtyard. He was stripped, spat on, and hit in the face with his own rosary with such force that the necklace broke. The officer in charge then whipped Dwatuka, and after being led to his cell, his plight went from bad to worse.[51] There a rope was tied around his neck and fixed to the window bars so that he could barely touch the ground with his toes. After the officer beat him all over his body, soldiers roped the bleeding Dwatuka to the floor. The officer continued to beat him to the point of exhaustion. "Then," as Dwatuka was quoted two years later, "they kicked me with their shoes in the mouth and on the head and told me to repeat the Mohammedan credo. . . . I didn't and only gurgled in agony." Revived with kicks, he was again lashed and dragged into a large room. Refusing to proclaim Mohammed, Dwatuka was whipped in the throat and lashed again before other prisoners. Through the intervention of the Verona Fathers' Monsignor Domenico Ferrara, he was released the following day.[52]

Presbyterian missionary Marian Farquhar, who was stationed at Nasir when the mutiny occurred, referenced a powerful sermon made amid the troubles. Born in Iowa, she had attended Missouri's Tarkio College and taken seminary courses in Connecticut and New York. In 1945 the Board of Foreign Missions of the United Presbyterian Church of North America assigned her to southern Sudan, and within four years she was headmistress of a government boarding school in Nasir (located among the Nuer, near the Ethiopian border).[53] Farquhar noted that though trouble in Malakal had only lasted a day, many Nuer fled home to Nasir, 140 miles away. "Then came word," she continued, "that two boats were coming up with northern soldiers to 'subdue' us. Specifically to disarm our unit of southerners. And our unit was going to refuse to give up their arms." The northern soldiers were set to arrive on either Sunday evening or Monday morning. A large crowd gathered at church, no doubt sensing the drama of the moment. A man named Rial preached that evening and borrowed from John 14:9 in addressing his audience. "Am I going to be one of those," he asked, "who says to Him, 'How can we know the way?' I have lived here for many years and heard this word many many times . . . but has it become TRUTH in my heart? Or will He say to me as He did to Philip, 'Have I been so long time with you and yet you have not known me, Rial?'" That night the first boat came in, quietly. Monday, according to Farquhar, "was one of the strangest I have ever lived." Only four out of thirty-one girls came to school, along with one teacher. "NO ONE was anywhere and you heard no noises of any kind. . . . Breathlessly the few faithful-at-work were saying, 'Wait. . . . Wait until they ask for the key to the guns and you'll hear the shooting.'" However, no shooting came. "We had a good District Commissioner, a northerner, and he handled the situation VERY well, and the people in time came to trust us."[54]

After the governor general told mutineers to surrender, terms were offered, and the army entered Torit with scant opposition. Many who surrendered were executed, and others were imprisoned despite many people's expectation that their cases would be heard. Many were packed into boats and carried to different prisons in the North.[55] "These supreme trials," wrote Yangu, "were the cause of an unprecedented unity among the Southern tribes."[56] And yet, writes Scopas Poggo, interethnic rivalries persisted because earlier officials had not attempted to encourage ethnic groups to move across territorial spaces. To this end, he posits that southern ethnicities did not have a shared position concerning an independent South by the time of the mutiny.[57]

Made over a decade after the mutiny, Yangu's comment was a romantic attempt to frame the mutiny as something that it was not: unified. Presbyterian missionary Dorothy Rankin shared her feeling in November 1955 that "the people in our area, the school boys who have been in school in the South, seemed to have a rather detached attitude toward the situation. As if they don't exactly classify themselves with those who started the trouble—one way or the other."[58] The conduct of the Torit Mutiny illustrated that there was no pervasive social or political ideology uniting southerners at the time. The plan to mutiny at Torit was conceived primarily by Latuko soldiers, and though some soldiers from ethnic groups from the Nile's East Bank participated in the operation, the Latuko were more active. Soldiers stationed at Wau and Malakal were not initially part of the plan to revolt, and though news of the mutiny quickly reached Equatorial soldiers at those two locations, it was thought to be a problem between the Latuko and Arabs. No violence was reported in Bahr el-Ghazal province, and in Wau the southern garrison there—along with police and prison wardens—remained loyal to the government and maintained order. Part of a local conspiracy among some soldiers, the mutiny had very little planning for a general revolt. Other mutinies that occurred in the army, police, and prison service (across the South) were made in response to news from Torit and did not comprise a single coordinated uprising. While some mutineers wanted to delay the British exit and others wanted union with Egypt, no one was calling for southern separation yet. Equatoria—where most of the mutineers were based and originated—was most devastated by the violence, while in Upper Nile and Bahr el-Ghazal, the Nilotic Dinka and Nuer did not hold Equatorian police and soldiers in warm regard.[59]

THE LEGACY OF SLAVERY

Although the mutiny entailed the aforementioned racial, religious, and ethnic elements, it also brought forward the history of Sudanese slavery. R. O. Collins once noted that the Sudanese slave trade was as ancient as recorded history. It is probable that Muhammad Ali, longtime Ottoman ruler of Egypt during the first half of the nineteenth century, wanted to add Sudan to his dominions principally because of slaves. In the early 1820s, he resorted to building a new army by gathering slaves from Sudan. During Turco-Egyptian rule (1821–85), the Turks turned to the recruitment of military slaves from South and Central Sudan. The Shilluk, Dinka, and Nuba were targeted as the three principal ethnic groups.[60] The slave trade became massive when the Egyptian government opened the Bahr el-Ghazal and Equatoria provinces. The trade was initially in ivory; traders, often in league with a local chief, raided neighboring tribes for grain and cattle to trade for tusks. Prisoners taken in these raids became enslaved to the merchants, and the traders' zaribas became staging posts for slaves bound for the North.[61]

By the mid-1840s a significant amount of ivory was flowing from South Sudan to the North, and by the following decade thousands of southerners were being transported to Khartoum and Cairo. Private slave armies led by ivory and slave merchants began to appear in the South by the 1850s, and soldiers from these armies and the Egyptian Army went on to form the nucleus of Mahdist forces in the late nineteenth century. Lacking comparable access to firearms, vulnerable southern groups were unable to provide meaningful resistance to the traders' raids. The Dinka were the most valued slaves during the Turco-Egyptian period, with constant penetration into their northwest Dinkaland villages. John Dunn once noted that the Sudan garrison's soldiers were among the best in the army. In 1863 they totaled seven thousand regulars and five thousand irregulars.[62]

Western nations began to apply pressure on Egyptian and Ottoman rulers to eliminate the slave trade in the Upper Nile. Under Khedive Ismail—who had a public relations campaign with western Europe—a suppression effort was made in response to British pressure. Ismail ended large government-sponsored raids and ordered selective intervention against the slave trade. Ottoman rulers sought help from Europeans like Samuel Baker and Charles Gordon to bring order and establish legitimate trade. These men had little success. In the 1860s and 1870s there were an estimated five to six thousand slave traders in the South.[63]

Upon General Kitchener's appointment as the Anglo-Egyptian Sudan's first governor general, he instructed his provincial governors to move cautiously concerning slavery:

> Slavery is not recognized in the Sudan, but as long as service is willingly rendered by servants to masters it is unnecessary to interfere in the conditions existing between them. . . . I leave it to your discretion to adopt the best methods of gradually eradicating the habit of depending upon the slave labour which has so long been part of the religious creed and customs of this country, and which it is impossible to remove at once without doing great violence to the feelings and injuring the prosperity of the inhabitants. Without proclaiming any intention of abruptly doing away with all slave-holding, much can be done in the way of discouraging it and teaching the people to get on without it.

Wingate and Cromer shared Kitchener's views. More than merely believing that the social and economic situation demanded the toleration of domestic slavery, they feared that their interference could lead to a resurgence of fanatical Islam.[64]

Slavery's enduring impact on southern Sudanese attitudes toward northerners in the years leading up to the mutiny was evidenced in several ways. Andrew Wieu, a Dinka from Upper Nile province, stated that the British "kept reminding them [southerners] of the Mahdi, the slavery, and all that. They . . . said they came to help the southerners out of slavery . . . this fanned something in the minds of southerners. Therefore, there remained some hatred."[65] In April 1947, southern staff in Aweil wrote a statement claiming that it was too early for southerners to join with northerners "in any form of Community or Parliament." Asserting that northerners would not properly look after southern matters, the staff referenced the early history of slavery by noting that "most Northerners . . . still have the habit of saying 'Habbid' [*abid*, or slave] to their southern employees or those who may have some contact with them."[66] An Arab soldier's use of the term *abid* toward a southern soldier was, at least according to Marino's account, the very spark that ignited the mutiny. The salience of slavery in the mutiny was inferred by another observer, who directly identified it as a primary impetus behind the maelstrom:

> It seemed as though the whole Southern Corps was on a man hunt. Their hear[t]s were so filled with bitterness and hatred toward all the northerners. Vengeance, not only for present grievances but that which has been stored up down through the past half century, was now running wild. . . . Many of the tribesmen of Central Africa have the proverbial "elephant's memory," especially when it comes to the Arab atrocities of 50 years ago. Even the youth of today know of relatives who had suffered at their hands.[67]

According to Scopas Poggo, the Kuku viewed rebellion as an attempt to wrest free of Arab subjugation.[68] One story emerged about an old woman who, when rebel escapees had come to Kajo-Kajo with news of the uprising, left her house and called together "her children." Saying that they should run for safety, she spontaneously sang the following words:

> The Turks came in my days
> The Kuturiya came in my days. Many invaders of Kuku came in
> my days
> And found me still alive.
> I am too tired to run.
> All the fighting has come in my days . . .
> Let my children run.[69]

The woman's mention of the "Turks," which no doubt referred to the history of external predation dating back to the nineteenth century, evinced the enduring impact of that period on southern conceptions of the North. For this Kuku woman, the mutiny was an occasion to recall past abuses by outsiders and to place the rebellion in the same genealogy.

* * *

"For a complete month," said Benjamin Odomiyanf Loful, "we were carried out from the prison every night to a foothill, some three miles outside Juba Township." At that location, said the mutiny survivor, "we were brutally beaten, abused, and humiliated. The Arab officers trod on us while we were on the ground tied up, legs and hands in heavy iron chains. There they screamed at us in order to make us say that the Northern Arabs were our masters and we Southerners were slaves." According to Loful, several died inside the cells as a result of the ever-increasing punishments.[70]

Many of those imprisoned after the mutiny were housed at locations with connections to the history of Sudanese slavery, establishing a stronger association between that legacy and the events of 1955. Situated on a coral island off the Red Sea coast, Suakin was at one point an important merchant harbor that connected the Nile region and the hinterland savannahs with neighboring Egypt, Ethiopia, and Arabia and with regions as far east as China. Beginning in the fifteenth century, it became Africa's most important Red Sea harbor. In the seventeenth century, however, it declined as a result of navigation around the African continent. Largely in ruins at the beginning of the nineteenth century, Suakin entered a new period of prosperity with the extension of Egyptian influence to the Upper Nile district. The introduction of steamers in the 1860s enhanced access to the equatorial regions, and trading in slaves and ivory became the bedrock of Suakin's success. Slave ships transported South Sudanese from Suakin to the Arabian Peninsula, and after the Egyptian slave market closed in the 1870s, Suakin became the hub of this traffic. The island's fortunes ebbed and flowed during the Mahdist and early condominium years, and after World War I, the development of Port Sudan hastened. Suakin's population declined to roughly six thousand by 1929.[71]

Emedio Tafeng—who received a ten-year sentence after the mutiny—spent seven years in the prisons off the Red Sea, in the old port of Suakin. Of Lotuho ethnicity, the Torit-born Tafeng was recruited into the army in 1930. Trained at Sudan's Military College, he served as a sergeant in the Ethiopian campaign in World War II and was known at the time as the country's best marksman. Among the first southerners to achieve the rank of second lieutenant, Tafeng was sent to Juba by senior northern officers during the disarmament of the Equatorial Corps to collect the salaries for August 1955. Believed to have been one of the ringleaders behind the plot, he was arrested in Juba and imprisoned there without charge. His time in prison not only is said to have strengthened his will to fight for South Sudan's liberation but also had a spiritual influence. It was in prison that Tafeng converted to Christianity and received the Christian name Emedio (Emilio).[72]

Tafeng's conversion, along with comments made by Allison in his memoir, suggest that prison may have been a thriving spiritual space for incarcerated ex-mutineers. Bishop Allison records that one of the most memorable confirmation services he could recall was held in a large Suakin prison, where men who had been confined after the mutiny and uprising were held. The commissioner of prisons granted Allison special permission to hold services there during his annual visits to Port Sudan. On one occasion, 120 men belonging to four ethnicities were baptized at Suakin's harbor entrance. On Easter Monday 1958, those who had been baptized were presented to Allison for confirmation and Holy Communion. Following the service, the prison governor remarked with astonishment that he could not "understand how these men could have committed any crime. I have never known prisoners [to] behave so well. They are always singing and often reading their Bibles and praying together." He allowed vernacular New Testaments, prayer books, hymn books, and other Christian literature to be distributed.[73]

Like Suakin sixty kilometers to the south, Port Sudan had connections to slavery. Construction of the port started in 1905, and the first ships began using it two years later. Rather than hindering the economic recovery that was largely predicated on enslaved persons, the condominium government had ignored slavery's pervasive endurance until after World War I. Red Sea province officials acknowledged that nomads who temporarily settled in Port Sudan brought their "servants" with them, and runaway enslaved persons who sought official help were typically placed in the care of sheikhs. Those without jobs resorted to crime and prostitution. Between November 1924 and May 1925, nearly 1,800 enslaved and ex-enslaved refugees from Jidda arrived in Port Sudan and Suakin as a result of the Saudi force's increasing control on the Hijaz. The League of Nations condemned the condominium's feeble position on slavery, and in response, the government ordered that an asylum for manumitted persons be built at Port Sudan.[74] Following the mutiny, Lotuho soldiers of the Equatorial Corps were among those confined in Port Sudan. Jacob Sebit translated and transcribed lyrics that the soldiers sang in prison:

Iyati hohoi Port Sudan
Laduri Lotuho odihi naye
Laduri Lotuho odihi naye
Etongo hohoi iko Arabi togele
Ettu adi edou tubana

Take us to Port Sudan
Sons of Latuka endure death
Sons of Latuka endure death

We stay separate from the Arabs
The heavens will amalgamate us (×2)[75]

Rumbek, along with Suakin and Port Sudan, was another location with connections to slavery where South Sudanese were jailed after the mutiny. After Mehmed Said, the Ottoman ruler of Egypt from 1854 to 1863, abolished government raids, private merchants quickly assumed control of the slave trade. Slave and ivory traders established zaribas across large parts of South Sudan and fortified enclosures that were used, among other purposes, as temporary holding camps from which to launch slave raids. At least one zariba was located in Rumbek in the days of nineteenth-century Italian soldier Romolo Gessi, and in one instance, Emin Pasha released 567 slaves from Rumbek in a single day. Alexis Yangu connected the experience of his post-mutiny imprisonment at Rumbek to the history of Arab slavery. Yangu was one of three South Sudanese recruited into Juba's police force in 1946 and served in western Bahr el-Ghazal for nearly a decade. In 1955 he was dismissed from the force after being accused of involvement in political activities. Arrested in Wau, he was sentenced to five years' imprisonment there in May 1956 (this was commuted to six months).[76] According to Yangu, all prisoners in Bahr el-Ghazal who did not receive death sentences were gathered in Rumbek prison after mutiny-related trials were completed. He described his prison experience:

> In all, we were 1,114 prisoners crammed like sardines in small barracks. . . . In the dark we recalled all the horrible episodes of Arab barbarism of which we had heard or read. . . . I looked at all these tortures [in the prison] with the eyes of a 33-year-old whose father was once captured in an Arab slave raid. I was brought up in the traditional Arab slave-raid history, and I was optimistic about a better future for the Southern Sudanese people.[77]

THE COMMISSION OF ENQUIRY

On August 18—the day the mutiny began—the Sudanese Parliament voted unanimously to accelerate the independence process, and on August 30 it approved a measure mandating that Sudan should determine its political future through a plebiscite. On December 19 the legislative assembly and senate unanimously approved the resolution declaring Sudan's independence. Though southern MPs had been reluctant to vote for the Independence Resolution without the guarantee that the nation's constitution would be a federal one, the assembly resolved that federation for the southern provinces would receive full consideration. On January 1, 1956, the Republic of the Sudan became independent.[78]

A Commission of Enquiry was formed with the responsibility of identifying the mutiny's causes. The three-member committee was established under Judge Tawfiq Cotran, a Palestinian Christian who served as a police magistrate in Khartoum. Northern Sudanese Khalifa Mahjoub, a general manager in the Equatoria Scheme Board, also worked on the commission. The third member and sole southern representative was chief and MP Lolik Lado. Considered a model government chief, the illiterate Lado had purchased grain for the Sudan Defence Force in Juba during World War II and was recognized by private traders as a broker. He participated in the 1947 Juba Conference, where he famously opined that southerners' dilemma was akin to a girl who, being asked to marry a young man, needed to know more about her suitor before consenting.[79]

While the commission was instructed to carry out its investigation in Juba and in any areas Cotran deemed appropriate, it was restricted from looking into the mutiny's political or social aspects. Meetings and hearings were to be public or secret based on circumstance. With the defense minister's approval, the commission was authorized to appoint two advisers.[80] Southern politicians contributed little evidence to the commission, though much of it was—according to Peter Woodward—contradictory. Nevertheless, the commission gathered evidence that included letters along the lines of one written by Chief Lako Logono to the governor of Equatoria, which stated, "If the Northerners and the Egyptians want to join with the South let them bring our grandfathers and grandmothers, and all our brethren whom they carried as slaves long ago, then we can link with them."[81] The commission submitted its report on February 18, 1956, and the government published the *Report of the Commission of Enquiry* into the mutiny in October.[82] The commission concluded that five foundational elements were behind the disturbances:

1. Northerners and southerners had little in common.
2. For historical reasons, southerners regarded northerners as foes.
3. The British policy encouraging southerners to "progress on African and Negroid lines" prevented northerners and southerners from knowing each other. Missionaries favored and influenced this policy.
4. The North had progressed far ahead of the South, creating "a feeling in the underdeveloped people . . . that they are being cheated, exploited and dominated."

5. These factors discouraged a feeling of common citizenship; "the average Southerner is becoming politically conscious, but this political consciousness . . . is regional and not national."[83]

Given the government's religious policies in the coming years, it is important to note that the report's section on "Education and Religion" stated that religious differences had not played a part in the disturbances. On the contrary, it found "that the real trouble in the South is political and not religious. . . . In the extensive disturbances that took place in Equatoria, Christians, Pagans, as well as Muslims, took part . . . some of the leaders of the anti-northern propagandists are southern moslims [sic]." The report also stated that the slave trade was not a contributing element: "the historical fact of the slave trade was used by different people for different purposes."[84]

Despite the commission's findings regarding slavery's relevance, Sudan ambassador E. Chapman-Andrews noted in his reflections on the commission's report that memories of the slave trade had long been a source of antinorthern resentment in the South. He hinted at the Southern Policy's necessity in a milieu where this animus was so strong: "Southerners were so suspicious of the North and had such indelible memories of the slave trade that it was essential to keep them apart. . . . The slave trade . . . must be regarded as a major cause of trouble between Arab and Negro."[85] Daniel Tongun, who was arrested and imprisoned in Juba after the mutiny, alluded to the historical roots of southern antipathy in his exhaustive testimony: "We don't like you. My plan would have been to order the Southern Sudanese soldiers to capture the airstrips . . . the steamer, and then declare our intention to secede from you [northerners] . . . we cannot forget the atrocities that you committed against our ancestors."[86]

* * *

The Equatorial Corps was a distinctly South Sudanese, multiethnic military force that was birthed out of the British concern for protecting the South from Islam. While arguably the most "southern" of condominium institutions, it was heavily and intentionally divided along ethnic lines. The religious crucible from which the Equatorial Corps emerged and the ethnic politics that drove its recruitment each manifested themselves in August 1955. Just months after the mutiny had ended, Sudan entered independence in January 1956 as a fractured nation. In one personal account of the mutiny, a missionary opined that "the Sudan is engulfed in the birth-pangs similar to those that have been experience[d] by other nations of the world and history is repeating itself."[87] In 1957, President Abdallah Khalil noted, "We thought we could take independence, but we discovered that we must build it."[88] In the coming years, several Sudanese regimes attempted to build the divided country under the banners of Arabism and Islam. Thousands of southerners fled, fought, protested, and died resisting Khartoum's agenda. South Sudan's labor of liberation proved difficult indeed.

More than simply representing a significant point in South Sudan's military struggle against Khartoum, the Torit Mutiny is an important moment in the genealogy of southern Christian nationalism. As mutineers looked to protect themselves from another instance of northern "subjugation," the mutiny foreshadowed the way in which history—whether Sudanese or biblical—would be used to inspire and comfort southerners during the ensuing civil wars against the government. While it would be inaccurate to claim that Christianity was the primary engine driving the violence, the religious vision that inspired the British to create the corps in the early twentieth century should not be ignored when assessing the mutiny. Created as an element of protecting the South from Islam, the Equatorial Corps and CMS Nugent School were two elements of the same anti-Islamic vision. Thus, the mutiny was a moment when earlier religious visions had violent, material consequences.

* * *

In a *Le Figaro* piece published in 1966, three Christian guerrillas informed correspondent Jean-Marie Garraud that "our struggle is not a religious one. . . . Although it is for the Arabs, who have raised the banner of a Holy War against us and want to convert us to Islamism. . . . We are nationalists, we don't want to become Arabs. For centuries they have hunted us down in order to make slaves of us."[89] Despite their sentiment that this was not a religious war, many were indeed translating the events of the First Sudanese Civil War in theological terms. Those years would see more than Sudanese state efforts to Islamize the new nation; rather, the period also saw southerners using their faith and scripture for their own designs. It is to these religious ideations that we now turn.

3

Liberation War

Our inheritance has been turned over to strangers,
Our home to foreigners.
We have become orphans, fatherless,
Our mothers are widows.
With our lives at gun point we are cruelly beaten with fire,
    we are weary, we are given no rest.
Arabs rule over us; there is none to deliver us from their hands.
Our skin is hot as an oven with the burning heat of famine.
Women are vanishing in the South, virgins in the towns of the South.
Southerners are just shot dead, young men are compelled to murder their
    brothers, and boys stagger under loads of wood.
The joy of our hearts has ceased; our dancing has been turned to moarning
    [*sic*].
The crown has fallen from our head; woe to us, for we have sinned!
For this our heart has become sick; for these things our eyes have grown
    dim; for the South is devastated; Arabs roam over it.
But thou, O lord, dost reign for ever; thy crown endure to all generations.
Why dost thou forget us for ever; why dost thou so long forsake us!
Restore us thyself, O'lord, that we may be restored!
—P. K. Mabuong, 1967

The prophet Jeremiah composed the book of Lamentations six centuries
before the birth of Christ. The Weeping Prophet bemoaned Israel's trans-
gressions, God's righteous indignation that had wrought Jerusalem's

destruction, and the Jewish exile to Babylon. Despite Israel's claim to being God's peculiar nation, its sins would not go unpunished. This truth notwithstanding, Jeremiah's underlying theme was that God had not forsaken his people; on the contrary, providence was working amid their suffering.[1]

The First Sudanese Civil War (1955–72) produced rippling effects throughout the South's physical, ideological, and spiritual landscapes. According to Ali Mazrui, the conflict "was widely regarded as a religious confrontation between a Muslim government in Khartoum and its armies, and Christian liberation fighters in the South."[2] Against this backdrop, P. K. Mabuong used the Bible to transform South Sudan into a new Zion. In an article published in *SANU Youth Organ Monthly Bulletin*, Mabuong replaced the words "Judah," "Zion," and "Mount Zion" from Lamentations chapter 3 with "the South."[3] And yet, more than merely being a confrontation between members of different religions, the *Bulletin* piece is illustrative of two critical ways in which some intellectuals framed the war: first, in the blending of racial and religious identities in framings of the Sudanese state and state actors; and second, in the transformation of the conflict into a spiritual war with biblical antecedents. These developments mark the war as a critical chapter in the history of South Sudanese political theology.

Mabuong was not alone in linking Arabs to spiritual or biblical oppression, as others expressed that the conflict was spiritual warfare being waged in the physical realm. Religious thought provided an important spiritual hue to the racial dynamics of the war, becoming a space for southerners to articulate the extent of racial division and hostility. Some positioned Arabs as inhuman evil agents being used by Satan to war against God's people. Through a series of calculated insertions, Christians in South Sudan likened their circumstances to biblical Israel's history with Egypt and Babylon. While the Sudanese government and its soldiers were linked with Egypt and Babylon, southerners—like their Israelite predecessors—were marked as God's beloved, destined for national liberation.[4]

This chapter pushes against one recent contention that despite "incendiary religious restrictions, the frame of the conflict hinged on elite choices regarding land and resources, which inspired an ethno-racial perspective rather than a religious one."[5] The war witnessed the creation of a theology that maintained that providence was leading southerners to victory. Southern intellectuals framed the conflict as a liberation war in which racial and religious identities became increasingly interwoven. Southerners could claim to share not only a racial and cultural identity but also the spiritual experience of oppression. These streams of thought encouraged the idea of an imagined community united by race, politics, and spiritual experience and provide a lens into how southerners understood their history and national identity.

The Christian thought that emerged in this period developed from a context of state-sponsored Arabization and Islamization. The government's Arab and Islamic policies began to emerge during the early independence period. In 1956 the Ministry of Foreign Affairs stated that "Sudan is in the main a cognate part of the Arab world. Our policy towards the Arab League is to support it, to strengthen it and draw strength from it."[6] This policy manifested itself in the Arab-Israeli conflict that year, when Sudan sent volunteers to assist the Egyptians after Anglo-French-Israeli forces invaded the Suez Canal. While the condominium government had regulated major Islamic institutions, one of the models advanced at independence was an Islamic parliamentary republic, which the Umma and Khatimiya camps supported. In July of that year the Mahdist Umma Party and Khatimiya People's Democratic Party (PDP) replaced the al-Azhari government and elected Abdallah Khalil as prime minister. The publicly financed Department of Religious Affairs (DRA) was founded in 1956 and was purposed to promote Islam among non-Muslim, non-Arab Sudanese communities (particularly in the South). The DRA's establishment ushered in the government's targeting of education, and Ziada Arbab was one of the leading figures in this process. In February 1957, Arbab announced government intentions to take over mission schools. Implementation began two months later. In 1958 Arbab was appointed minister of education and justice.[7]

The government's Arab and Islamic push initiated a major parliamentary crisis. In 1956 a national committee was appointed to draft a constitution that would be presented to the Constituent Assembly. The proposed constitution included Islam as the religion of state and Arabic as the national language. The Arab-Islamic push was coupled with northern resistance to federation, an opposition partially rooted in a fear that it would mean eventual separation. In March 1958 the first parliamentary elections were held, and another Umma-PDP coalition government was formed. While the Umma government appointed three South Sudanese ministers, the Liberal Party had its nominations ignored. In response, southerners sought support from non-Arab MPs. The government was unable to pass the constitution, leading to a stalemate. On June 16, 1958, all southern MPs walked out when the Constituent Assembly rejected the federation proposal. Unable to handle southern demands and economic problems, the coalition government was in a precarious position. On November 17, 1958, the army conducted a coup. Parliament was dissolved, and General Ibrahim Abboud assumed control. The new Sudanese leader tried to eliminate unrest in the South with Islam and Arabic.[8]

School programs were soon Arabized, and missionaries were removed from the educational system over a five-year period, until their final expulsion in 1963–64. By September 1958, church schools had to provide Islamic instruction for Muslim students. Those who embraced Islam were given advantages in school recruiting. The gradual transferal of Christian teachers to the North meant a reduction in religious training for southern Christian students.[9] In Ziada Arbab's speech published in the December 27, 1958, issue of the *Bahr El Ghazal Daily*, he suggested that the education question (and Islam's role in it) was crucial to establishing national unity. Claiming that "our growing Sudanese nation is rich with its spiritual potentialities," he stated that national understanding could be reached through the study of Arabic in southern village and elementary schools. "We cannot build a good community and a sound Sudanese nationality," Arbab argued, "unless we take aid of the religious doctrine and quote from the philosophy of the Islamic Sharia."[10]

In February 1960, the Friday Law replaced South Sudan's Sunday holiday.[11] This decree—which allowed Christians free time to attend church services—was confronted by students at the forefront of the "Sunday Protest."[12] Missions (particularly Protestant missions) had stressed the importance of their students needing rest on Sundays, and secondary students were aware of the state's Islamizing intentions toward them. Protest from the Rumbek Secondary School was particularly virulent. After Fr. Paolino Doggale printed protest papers, he and the Rumbek student leaders were arrested and sentenced to prison. Perhaps the pinnacle of antigovernment angst occurred in the wake of the 1962 Missionary Societies Act. It demanded that Sudanese pastors be registered and licensed by the Ministry of Religious Affairs and Endowment and that registered church workers be paid by this ministry, aiming to allow the government unlimited interference with missionaries. Section 3 stipulated that no missionary society or member do any mission work outside the terms of a license granted by the council of ministers. The act's ultimate intention was clarified in 1964, when the government ordered the expulsion of all foreign missionaries from South Sudan.[13]

As the Sunday Protest demonstrated, many southerners were not content to stand idly by while the government enacted its policies. In 1962 Fr. Saturnino Lohure, William Deng, Clement Mboro, and Joseph Oduho formed the Sudan African Closed Districts National Union. When the headquarters moved to Kampala, the name was shortened to the Sudan African National Union (SANU). Consisting primarily of southerners, the organization pushed for complete separation. In 1963 the SANU founded *Voice of Southern Sudan*, a magazine published from Britain with missionary assistance.[14]

In July 1963, Saturnino and Oduho visited Europe to procure financial assistance and support. In Rome they formulated the idea of a guerrilla movement that would need propaganda to rouse the support of exiled southern intellectuals, former Equatorial Corps members, southern students, and others. Saturnino proposed that this military wing be named the Sudan Pan-African Freedom Fighters to attract Pan-African sympathizers throughout the continent. SANU members opposed his suggestion, preferring a name with local meaning. In the end, administrative secretary Severino Fuli suggested the indigenous name Inyanya. The Inyanya borrowed its name from the poison of the Gabon viper. Joseph Lagu—who was commissioned as a lieutenant in the Sudanese Army before joining the resistance movement—suggested that the spelling begin with *A* (which he believed would be easier to pronounce). A policy paper dated July 31, 1963, outlined a program based on two foundational aims—to wage a liberation war against Arab imperialism for complete southern independence and to fight another war against illiteracy.[15] It is useful to note that people in the Upper Nile disdained and rejected the term Anyanya, choosing instead their own names reflecting the Anyanya's goals but with greater appeal to their own culture. The Dinka of Bahr el-Ghazal, for example, named the southern military Koc Roor.[16] A loose phrase used by the Dinka to describe the Anyanya, it means "people of the forest" or "guerrilla fighters" in Dinka—those who fought with hit-and-run tactics. The Anyanya fighters were also deemed Koc Roor because they were considered to be living in the forest or bush, not having a permanent home.[17]

On September 30, 1964, the first seminar on the southern problem was held at the University of Khartoum. Being hitherto unable to crush the southern rebellion, the government was forced to appease its critics and improve its image. In mid-October 1964 it announced that University of Khartoum students would be allowed to publicly discuss the southern dilemma. On the evening of October 21, the student union held a meeting to discuss the Southern Problem and concluded that the situation would never be resolved as long as the regime remained in power. The government then reversed its decision and banned future meetings. The following evening, students defied the ban by holding another meeting on campus. This decision led to a clash between students and police. Known as the October Revolution, the uprising led to Abboud's overthrow and replacement by a transitional government responsible for supervising elections.[18]

While the October Revolution may have given southerners reason to hope that change was on the horizon, internal divisions loomed. When the Abboud regime was unseated, William Deng wrote to the new civilian prime minister, Sirr el Khatim el Khalifa. Deng stated that, for all intents and purposes, the SANU was ready to return to the February 1958 circumstance, when the first Constituent Assembly was elected (provided that there be a clear northern commitment to federation this time). The SANU exiles in Kampala, however, did not support this position. A national convention to reorganize the SANU was held in Kampala in November 1964. While Oduho hoped to be reaffirmed as president, Joseph Lagu solicited SANU deputy secretary general Aggrey Jaden to challenge Oduho so that he would not run unopposed. Nugent School alum Jaden defeated Oduho by a single vote and won the presidency. Oduho subsequently formed his own faction (the Azanian Liberation Front), and Deng refused to accept his demotion. Deng's former colleagues announced that they had suspended him from occupying any office.[19]

The SANU was beset with personality, factional, and ethnic differences over policy. R. O. Collins once noted that the organization's most public failure was its incapacity to establish a viable SANU organization outside Sudan's borders. And yet, underground southern cells developed outside the SANU fold. One of them—the Southern Front—was a rival southern political organization in Khartoum. In March 1965 the Round Table Conference in Khartoum was the first meeting to directly address the South's future within the country since independence. While all the northern parties there refused to accept separation as a solution, the southern parties—including the SANU—were divided. Santino Deng's Sudan Unity Party stood for national unity, while the Southern Front, Anyanya, and SANU wanted secession. No resolution was achieved. William Deng backed away from self-determination and stayed as leader of SANU "inside" to work for a federal solution, while Oduho and Jaden returned to Uganda as leaders of the separatist SANU "outside." The new government pursued military action against the Anyanya and worked with southerners who favored unity.[20]

A CHANGING CHURCH

While the war years saw major changes within the national political fold, significant evolutions were also in store for the Sudanese church. Sudanese Christian communities at independence were prototypical mission station communities that depended on non-Sudanese individuals for major leadership (though locals provided limited leadership).[21] The Dinka church primarily comprised students, former students, and those who had moved to towns or near mission stations. It was smaller in comparison to other groups like the Moru, who—though a smaller ethnicity—had nearly the same amount of people confirmed during Bishop Oliver Allison's 1960 tour of the South as the Dinka did. Before the 1960s the Nuer church was also small, with Christianity limited to three mission schools that few Nuer attended, even following the government's 1947 effort to begin encouraging education. While South Sudan's population around independence was approximately 2.8 million, this number dwarfed the number of Christians in the South that the Roman Catholic Church, Church Missionary Society (CMS), and American Presbyterian Mission collectively tallied in 1956: 206,751, or approximately 7.4 percent of the South's estimated 1955 population. Most of these Christians were located in Equatoria province and, perhaps as a direct consequence, were singled out for Islamization and Arabization.[22]

After the nationalization of mission schools, evangelizing became difficult for churches, and with the foreign missionary expulsion of 1963–64, the military government intended to end Christian proselytizing in the South. And yet, the expulsion encouraged an opposite result: South Sudanese rather than Europeans or Americans directed Sudanese churches. To be sure, decreasing Western missionary influence during the period was evidenced long before the expulsion. In 1944, the Catholic Church ordained its first Sudanese priest (Guido Akou) since 1887. Eight years later Daniel Deng Atong was consecrated the first Sudanese Anglican bishop, and Ireneo Dud became the first Sudanese Catholic bishop. Dinka clergy officially took the reins of Anglican missionary work among the Dinka when missionary

Leonard Sharland returned to England in 1959 and was not replaced by a European. Though the CMS mourned the missionary expulsion, it boasted just six missionaries in the South at the time. By 1964 the Episcopal Church had fifty-seven Sudanese pastors, while the Catholic Church ordained twenty-eight Sudanese between 1955 and 1964.[23]

In addition to the changing demographics of Christian leadership, the lay demographic was also changing. Conversions started to rise in the late 1950s, and Catholic baptisms at Isoke and Torit increased significantly from 1960 to 1964. In 1961, Roman Catholic missionaries in eastern Equatoria mobilized clergy and catechists and campaigned to bring people into the church. More than seven thousand people were baptized that year. No random initiative, the campaign was done in response to the approaching enactment of the Missionary Societies Act.[24] In late February 1964 the *New York Times* reproduced a Reuters report that—statistical accuracy notwithstanding—indicated growth in the South Sudanese Church since the national census a decade before. Listing the South's population at approximately three million, it stated that "Roman Catholic missions from countries other than the United States claim 400,000 to 500,000, the Church of England 120,000 and the American Mission of the Upper Nile (Presbyterian and Reformed), about 3,000."[25] Conversion to the local evangelical church in the southern Blue Nile also increased after the expulsion. The Sudan Interior Mission had secured a foothold to work among the Uduk at Chali in 1938. Chali district had belonged to the Upper Nile province (in the South) until July 1953, when it became part of Blue Nile province (in the North).[26]

Among the Nuer there were hitherto few Christian converts outside the small, literate, and missionary-trained elite. Nonetheless, many viewed the burning of a southern church in Khartoum and the expulsion as crucial turning points in their attitudes toward the government and, consequently, their willingness to rebel. While early Nuer converts appeared on the Ethiopian frontier during the war, western Nuer regions were spared some of the war's worst effects because of unusually high floods that restricted troop movements. Consequently, western Nuer did not experience the move toward Christianity as those in the East did. Nevertheless, Nuer now exposed other Nuer in rural areas to Christianity, and the Christian teachings so presented appeared less foreign than missionary instruction.[27] References were made throughout the war to the songs and prophecies of Nuer prophet Ngundeng Bong, a late nineteenth-century figure who emerged as a leader around the time that condominium authority was starting to assert itself in the South. Southern Nilotic peoples have a long tradition of religious leadership by inspired figures, and anthropologist E. E. Evans-Pritchard termed these figures "prophets." Douglas Johnson has noted that many Nuer have drawn parallels between the teachings of Christ and Ngundeng.[28]

The civil war era was a period of significant religious change for the Dinka. A combination of factors generated new displacement and migration. Some young men went to North Sudanese cities to pursue different livelihoods, while the war forced others into refuge outside the country. Both movements led to a greater openness to Christianity, an attraction rooted in exposure to a world beyond cattle camps and recognition of the need for new resources that education provided.[29] During the 1960s many Jieng boys and young men left the South for North Sudanese urban centers, and as black youth sought opportunities in largely Muslim and Arab settings, many found a sense of solidarity in Catholic and Protestant "clubs."[30] Club attendance meant learning to read the vernacular language and studying the Bible. The majority converted to Christianity, a faith that provided a foundation for a new communal identity. The Anglican congregation in Khartoum North became a primary gathering point for young Dinka migrants. While an indigenous African church started to emerge among the Dinka during the sixties and seventies, and Christian adherence grew, these developments were principally driven by Dinka movement from their cattle camps and villages. In this vein, the geographic expanse of Christian belief was what it had long been: Christian growth during the sixties still happened in towns, cities, and now refugee camps.[31] "To be a Christian," writes Jesse Zink, "still meant that Dinka had to leave the landscape in which they had been raised."[32]

BLACK CHRISTIAN LIBERATION

Government attempts to inculcate the South with Islam and Arab culture gave way to violent military operations and atrocities that drove thousands to flee to neighboring countries. Many churches, schools, and villages were destroyed in the summer of 1965, forcing many to flee into the bush or take exile in Zaire or Uganda. Northern troops destroyed Sudan's Anglican theological college (Bishop Gwynne College), compelling students and staff to leave with their families to Uganda. In October 1969 the Ecumenical Programme for Emergency in Africa reported that approximately 180,000 Sudanese refugees were spread throughout several East African countries, West Cameroon, Europe, and the United States.[33] Amid massive southern flight after 1963, Andrew Wheeler has noted, "in the insecurity and deprivation of these years great numerical growth took place, as well as a profound spiritual deepening."[34]

Within a milieu of violence, rebellion, and exile, various individuals from several segments of society—including refugees, clerics, Anyanya, and others—spiritualized their circumstances in extraordinary ways. Within this discourse, God was positioned as being concerned about the southern plight and working out their deliverance. This rhetoric was racialized in that southerners demonized Arabs and the Arab regime while framing themselves as God's special people analogous to the Israelites. The dissemination of this thought in personal and public spaces suggests a link between private religious views and the political goal of national independence; it represents a defining moment in the narrative of Sudanese political theology.

* * *

To begin, Arabs were demonized in varying ways. Southerners driven to prevent a new chapter in the history of Sudanese slavery cited Arab intentions to enslave blacks as a motivation driving government policies. Slavery, as a result, became a central element to an articulated paradigm of racial war. In 1963, exile Zacharia Duot de Atem wrote to his former teacher that "the Northern Sudanese . . . are actually attempting to transform the Southerners into a servile people who will always be the servants of the muslims. . . . They are determined to convert us into an abundant source of slaves for the Arab World."[35] Another example comes from President Ibrahim Nyigilo of the Southern Sudan Christian Association. In January 1962, refugees in East Africa established a sister organization called the Sudanese Christian Association in East Africa (SCAEA). Headquartered in Kampala, members sought support from Christian organizations and communities in East Africa and farther abroad, wanting to draw global attention to the persecution in Sudan. Although it took on the appearance of an organization aimed at assisting refugees, it was actually a front organization for the SANU. The financing body of the liberation movement, it secretly raised funds, facilitated contacts, provided accommodations for members, and promoted SANU and Anyanya political and military goals. The association's scholarship program was perhaps its greatest legacy, producing most of the southern leadership after the war (including a young student named John Garang).[36] In Nyigilo's letter to the UN secretary general, African heads of state, and church leaders, he remarked,

We would not accept unity based on our national degradation, cultural and political slavery. The African everywhere, is rediscovering the African image and personality, you would not ask us to suffer the fate of Arab racialism and colonialism. In such a nation as the Sudan is constituted today, the African shall remain nothing but a slave . . . at the best a second rate citizen. We have no choice but to fight for freedom.[37]

The SACNU (the acronym occasionally used by the exile movement in 1962) implored Milton Obote to recognize that liberated African nations were responsible for helping to free Africans still struggling under a foreign yoke. Arguing that Sudanese nationalism was part of the Pan-Arab movement and had never positioned itself with Africanism, southerners were suffering under a yoke akin to their ancestral bondage: "in the Sudan the Arab invaders are holding the four million Negroes in chains, who[se] grandparents they had in the last century raided and sold into slavery. [Arabs] call the great nilotics and nilo-hamites, verily the Negroes here, slaves."[38]

After witnessing atrocities caused by security forces in Juba and Wau, Bishop Ireneo Dud expressed to the minister of interior that this "inhuman behaviour" could not secure God's protection.[39] The perception that southerners were struggling against people who were operating outside the confines of humanity and God's grace embellished the seemingly ingrained nature of northern Arab cruelty. As an unnamed writer expressed to a priest in 1965, "I do not trust an Arab in my life even when an Arab says he has seen GOD I would not believe so."[40] The notion that one's actions could expel people—and Arab soldiers specifically—from God's grace was also expressed in poetic verse by J. M. Deng in the April 1971 issue of *Grass Curtain*. *Grass Curtain* was published from London by the Southern Sudan Association, an organization formed in 1970. Directed by Mading de Garang, at one point the Anyanya High Command revised and adopted a plan to use the *Curtain* as an effective medium for the movement.[41] Invoking the legacy of past invasions and fifteen years of war, Deng lamented, "They feel free now / To lay you waste. . . . / Defying the Almighty's great hands / In their reckless disregard of humanity."[42] Joseph Lagu similarly levied the "inhuman" label on the government when in a 1971 issue he exclaimed that Khartoum's response to Anyanya development programs in the countryside had "always been inhuman, brutal and barbaric."[43]

Some clerics inferred that the troubles they faced were nothing short of devilish, claims implying that policies that stifled the church and wrought suffering were essentially evil. An October 1965 letter written by Eduardo Mason, Sisto Mazzoldi, Domenico Ferrara, and Herman te Riele to Bishop Dud and all southern clergy and laity expressed such sentiments. Each author occupied positions in Sudanese Catholic leadership: Mason had been the vicar apostolic of Bahr el-Ghazal before his appointment as vicar apostolic of El Obeid; Ferrara was the prefect of Mupoi; Mazzoldi was the prefect apostolic of Bahr el-Gebel; and Riele, the prefect of Malakal.[44] Expressing sorrow at the violent deaths of priests Barnaba Deng and Arkangelo Ali, they cited Matthew 5:11 ("blessed are those that are persecuted for Christ's sake") and acknowledged that the southern church "carried on valiantly as faithful disciples of Jesus, in the midst of trials and difficulties which were meant by the devil to take the faith from you and to take you out of the Church."[45] A Comboni priest of Dinka Malwal background, Barnaba Deng had the distinction of being ordained by Cardinal Giovanni Montini—the future Pope Paul VI—in 1959. Police mounted a deadly search for him after he was accused of assisting the rebels. Fleeing to Wau, Deng was eventually arrested and killed. Arkangelo Ali was ordained into the Catholic priesthood in 1946. On the morning of July 21, 1965, military trucks burst into the Rumbek mission compound. The two fathers stationed there were ordered to walk in front of the soldiers. After being taken under the veranda, Fr. Ali was killed. The soldiers hid his body.[46] Later that year Fr. Avellino Wani started a letter to Bishop Dud by echoing the belief that spiritual warfare was operating in the conflict: "Before greeting you, I would insul[t] the devil! . . . How much it tries to destroy and wickedly demoralize and despairingly disperse us! But in vain."[47]

An anecdote from William Levi sheds further light on the perception that spiritual forces were operating in Sudan. Born in 1964 to Messianic Jewish parents, Levi's family lived in the village of Moli, in Equatoria. In his autobiography *The Bible or the Axe*, Levi notes that the situation in Sudan had become increasingly tenuous in 1965. "No one was safe. . . . Churches were burned, schools closed, and crops destroyed. . . . Later that year [1965], my parents decided that the time had come to leave their beloved homeland. With heavy hearts, they set about the difficult task of moving to Uganda."[48] He recalls one religion class from his days as a grade two student in Nyakaningwa. Although the anecdote took place during the postwar period of the 1970s, it illustrates how the people and events of the day were perceived through a spiritual point of view. Ephesians 6:10–13 was the topic of study, and as the class contemplated the meaning of the scripture, the teacher—Levi's grandfather—stated:

"There is an enemy . . . one who would erase the name of Yeshua from our country, and would gladly shed our blood to gain his ground. Who can name our enemy?" . . . A hand went up. "The Muslims of Khartoum are our enemies. They would like to drive Christians from this country." A murmur of agreement filled the room, until my grandfather silenced it. . . . "No. . . . We do not struggle against flesh and blood. . . . Satan is our enemy. He blinds the eyes of the Muslims to the gospel message."[49]

Amid accusations that Arabs were "inhuman" in their cruelty and fighting on the wrong side of spiritual warfare, southern clerics and laity requested God's help in dealing with such foes. These sentiments were often expressed in private correspondences. Michael Maror Liec reacted to the missionary expulsion by praying that peace could be achieved peacefully: "All the priests of ours . . . are deported back by the Arabs, but nevertheless God is great. Let us pray to God so that we achieve our country without blood(shed)."[50] Former mission student Elia Seng Majok, writing as a political refugee in the Central African Republic, prayed that through God's help the Arabs could be chased out and defeated despite their strength. For this Majok asked former teacher Fr. Matordes to help "by praying for us to get our freedom."[51] Refugee Juliano Kita, writing from the Congo, closed one letter to a Catholic brother with the hope that "God help us from Arbation [Arabization]."[52]

In the midst of travails with the government, southerners invoked specific moments from biblical Israel's history. One such instance occurred after the expulsion of American Presbyterian missionary Dorothy Rankin. Rankin found herself in the government's crosshairs in early 1961. Charged with "causing ill feeling and hatred towards the Government of the Sudan" at her Doleib Hill station, Rankin was summoned to appear before the police investigator at Malakal on April 25, 1961.[53] Two incidents were in question: one in which she reportedly criticized the quality of the food (in reference to school regulations) and another in which she reportedly punished workers who had worked on Sunday by lowering their pay. Even though permanent undersecretary of the interior Hassan Abdulla stated that the evidence was not sufficient or reliable enough to warrant legal action in courts, there was enough evidence to warrant administrative action. In an irreversible decision, Rankin was ordered out of the country on August 20, 1961.[54] The following month, one of Rankin's students wrote a letter to her that likened her situation with that of biblical Joseph:

God will help us. There was a man named Joseph. That man was . . . sold to the Arabs and was taken away by the Arabs. There was a famine in their land. When he interpreted the king of Egypt's dream he was made chief of the dura store. And when his brothers came he recognized them but he didn't tell them who he was, because he wasn't angry at them and even gave them grain. Now don't you be upset, for God doesn't hold any hard feeling, and He loves all, except those who refuse His Word He punishes.[55]

While the biblical narrative describes the group that enslaved Joseph and brought him into Egypt as "Ishmaelites"—people who perhaps came from east of the Jordan River—the student's decision to describe them as "Arabs" is significant, given the government's Arabization policies at the time.[56] While not as direct as Mabuong's insertion of Arabs into Lamentations 3, this student's letter reads as an attempt to place the missionary expulsion in an older narrative of Arab mistreatments of God's people.

Fr. Jerome Siri, writing from the Congo, related his contemporary experiences with biblical Israel's exile to Babylon. Siri had been ordained a Catholic priest in December 1948. He worked among the Zande for seven years and subsequently worked in the new Rumbek Vicariate. Siri was with Arkangelo Ali the day he was killed by government soldiers. Narrowly escaping, he reached Doruma in Zaire and translated and revised Christian texts into Zande.[57] Writing to Monsignor Domenico Ferrara, Siri expressed hope that God would quickly answer their prayers if he did not intend for them to suffer as long as their Israelite forebears: "Here we feel out of place and homesick. If God does not intend to have our captivity as . . . long as that of Babilon [sic], let Him listen to our sighs."[58]

In Severino Fuli Boki Tombe Ga'le's 2002 autobiography, he references how Old Testament narratives were applied to contemporary circumstances. Born in Nimule in 1922, he was baptized in 1934 and eventually joined Juba's Province Headquarters Training School. After his training had concluded, Severino became a junior accountant in Juba and became politically active in Khartoum. With the likes of Abel Alier and Hilary Logali, he created a network of underground cells that gathered funds inside Sudan to support the armed liberation struggle. Severino joined the liberation movement in Uganda in July 1963.[59] As God had offered providential aid to the Israelites in their journey to the promised land, Severino offers an elaborate description of God's assistance after reaching Uganda. After advancing fifty meters past the Ugandan border, he relates that he called a halt. Kneeling down and facing Sudan, he prayed the following:

> Lord Jesus Christ . . . I thank you for the wonderful assistance you have accorded us in our flight . . . guide my kids and indeed the entire family-members who have been thrown into destitution in Defence of your Christian faith and our cultural identity and origin . . . which are being annihilated by the Arab North Government. . . . Help me, Lord, to stand up like a man and like a man die, if necessary, in defence of our Christian Religion and Faith.[60]

Once in Uganda, he framed a fortuitous development with another moment in biblical history—Israel's journey to the promised land. In 1967 the Parliament of Uganda passed a Trophy Act, which allowed Ugandans to sell an unlimited number of tusks, rhino horns, and reptile hides. One day, Ga'le was shown a particular batch of trophies that "was to be known from then on as the ANYANYA MANNA. Like in the case of Israel's Manna which maintained the Jews until they reached the promised land, the ANYANYA MANNA also sustained and indeed saved the ANYANYA-Eastern Command from collapse until . . . 1969."[61] The decision of Rankin's student to reference Joseph, Fr. Siri's mention of the Babylonian exile, and the labeling of Ugandan trophies as manna each illustrate the ways in which Sudanese used biblical history to encourage themselves and understand their circumstances.

Some refugees and those who remained in the South used songs to express their hopes and fears. In some lyrics, God was approached and described as the providential agent that could change their lot. Several Kuku-Balokole songs written in the mid-1960s were mixed with expectation for God's deliverance and pleas for pity. Before the Torit Mutiny, most of the Kuku people who lived in southwestern Equatoria believed in their ancestral spirits. Their well-being was largely attributed to their relations with these spirits. An abundant harvest, for example, reflected happy spirits, while natural disasters were attributed to their societal neglect.[62] Christianity's arrival—and particularly the Church Missionary Society—marked a new era in Kuku religious belief systems, and after the mutiny, many Kuku fled to Uganda, where during funerals "youth sang hymns, emotionally-laden songs, and beat drums all day and night to alleviate psychological pain."[63]

Balokole connections to South Sudan can be inferred in part from the travels of Sosthenes Dronyi, a teacher who converted to Christianity amid the East African Revival and became an evangelist. By the 1960s he resolved to undertake itinerant lay preaching throughout the region, and it is estimated that through him thousands in Uganda, Kenya, the Congo, and Sudan accepted Christ. As he is remembered in part for advocating African church music, it is possible that some of these Kuku-Balokole songs were indirectly inspired by or connected to Dronyi (or written by Kuku refugees in Uganda).[64] Durham University's Sudan Archive contains manuscripts of three songs that were translated and transcribed by Enoch Lobiya, including one that contains the lyrics:

> Ti yi moronic ko to'diri
> Anyen yi tete'ya
> Kujön kune a ti Sudan nikan
> Nun wone konyen
> Ko yi i döru kata ni
> Let us in reality struggle
> That we may win.
> The soil of the Sudan is ours
> God pity us
> Here in the grass[65]

Another Kuku-Balokole song expressed a similar message, though with more of a tone of dread:

> Jur likan lo
> Lunasirik kuwe kulo rite ko Merok
> Sudan 'du'dudyö
> Lunasirik Nun wone konyen
> My brothers!
> Our land is occupied by enemies
> The Sudan is ending
> Brothers, let God pity us.[66]

One song expressed hope in the following lines:

> Momo'yi ta Nun
> Talo juwe i boro kata
> Yesu ko rinit duma lwögu
> Na nutu
> You who are driven to
> The bush—pray to God.
> Jesus has great power
> To save people.[67]

The Comboni Archives in Rome are flush with letters written by those who acknowledged God's providence in the inexplicable ways their lives had been spared. Several cited God as directly intervening in their encounters with Arab soldiers. Fr. Adelino Fuli, rector of St. Augustine's Minor Seminary at Tore, recounted an attack from Arab soldiers in which he expressed that God had helped them escape with the effect of bullets passing over their heads.[68] Athian Joseph shared with Fr. Arthur Nebel a similar story of God's saving action in the lives of three men who were heading to Juba despite shooting and house burning in the area. "The Arab soldiers . . . began firing [at] them across the Nile," Joseph wrote. "One of the soldiers said: 'Dak Abuna Kabir; be human edrib' (shoot him), but God had put an unseen shiled [sic] behind which H. Lorship stood with his flock. Three-four bullets passed by them but none of them so far was touched."[69] Felix Kule stated that God assisted Anyanya forces in a clash against Arab soldiers. After stating that the Anyanya had shot down a plane in Maridi, Kule wrote, "The Almighty God punished them that day by confusing them thus shooting each other while the tactful Anya-Nya made their way off without any losses."[70]

Just as clerics noted God's work in their encounters with Arab soldiers, exilic stories regularly featured recognitions of divine intervention. A letter written by "D. Paul" (Fr. Paolino Doggale) recounts a tale in which priests at Tore Minor Seminary accused of harboring Anyanya soldiers were pursued by government troops. These troops had orders to arrest them and destroy a nearby mission. After mentioning that physical destruction had occurred, Doggale noted that "through God's Providence the Priests and the Seminarists managed to escape and fled to Congo."[71] Writing from the Central African Republic, Alfredo Akot Bak wrote to an Italian priest that God had assisted his trek to the Congo. Despite sadness on hearing that missionaries had been expelled, he expressed that only God knew when the South would be delivered from the Arabs' hands.[72] Bro. Gabriel Ngor similarly recognized God's hand in his passage to Uganda. After stating that the towns of Juba, Torit, Maridi, and others were nearly empty because of widespread killings done by government forces, Ngor explained to Fr. Giuseppe Gusmini that after eight days roaming in the bush in adverse conditions, his well-being could only be attributed to God's help.[73]

Finally, there was the confidence that southerners were special in God's sight and that he was concerned with their success and freedom—as his children. This sense of national destiny provided a sense that God would reward southern efforts in the face of uncertainty, an important spiritual undercurrent to the struggle. As one anonymous writer asserted in 1965,

"The present conflict . . . is not only a Political, social, Economical, but also a Religious and [Racial] . . . issue. How it is going to be solved, and when, the answer rests with God and his abandoned children of the South, who are beseeching Him to bring peace."[74] While the imagery of God's children praying for peace was perhaps meant to evoke sympathy, *Nouvel Observateur* reported Anyanya dances that included the line "We the children of Mary will kill the Arabs," words that illustrated the union of spiritual identity and racial warfare.[75]

One war song read as follows:

> The war is hot: Enemies are strong;
> But Lord's people will not be defeated at all.
> If we are with him, he would save us,
> He who can't change, we shall defeat . . .
> he had agreed you, to be his people;
> In the work of the King let us [trust],
> Let us be strong in his power.[76]

One Kuku political song expressed the author's request of God for deliverance:

> Yi kwkwaddu nun lo
> Yi kwkwaddu nun lo gweja yi
> Yi kwkwadou lepen ti yne tiki yi
> Toliyen nikay na Southern Sudan
> We pray to God
> We pray to you who created us
> We pray let Him give us
> Our freedom of Southern Sudan[77]

In Rodolfo Deng's letter to Fr. Nebel, he expresses his conviction that victory was assured because of their special relationship to God. Despite the recent deaths of priests Arkangelo Ali and Barnaba Deng at the hands of Arab soldiers, Deng was convinced that the righteousness of their cause and divine assistance would ensure their eventual success: "We shall not surrender . . . the road to Liberty is 'de facto' one of bloodshed. We shall win because the truth is on our side . . . Confident in God's Providence, of History and in our . . . Mother Mary we shall fight on . . . we have the mightiest of all weapons—Prayer."[78] When Pope Paul VI visited Africa in 1969, Emedio Tafeng conjectured that the papal visit was a sign from God meant specifically for southern Sudan. Tafeng, chairman of the Revolutionary Council and president of the Anyidi government, addressed a letter to the Pontiff and conjectured that "perhaps Your visit is a God sent occasion to mark the beginning of our human recognition and eventual Liberation from the hands of our destryers [sic]."[79]

PEACE WITHOUT FREEDOM: THE ADDIS ABABA AGREEMENT

General Ja'afar al-Nimeiri seized power in Sudan on May 25, 1969, ending the period of parliamentary politics that the 1964 October Revolution had begun. Public opinion generally accepted the new government, as party politics had been unable to solve the Southern Problem. Nimeiri, despite an attempted coup in 1971, regained his position, and the May Revolution continued. In March 1972 it achieved what no Sudanese government had done yet: ending the civil war.[80]

Negotiations commenced at the Addis Ababa Hilton Hotel on February 16, 1972. Conducted with Haile Selassie's blessing, there was a basic understanding that the talks would produce a plan for regional autonomy rather than a separate southern state. Though the Southern Sudan Liberation Movement originally demanded a southern state, African governments in the 1970s were opposed to secessionist movements. Selassie, himself fighting secessionists in Eritrea, was among this number. The long conflict reached its conclusion when Nimeiri announced the following month that a peace settlement had been reached. The specifics of the Addis Ababa Agreement were multilayered, but the key component was that it granted regional autonomy to the South under the governing umbrella of the national government. The World Council of Churches, All Africa Council of Churches, and Sudan Council of Churches worked as intermediaries and messengers for both sides.[81]

William Levi attended a ribbon-cutting ceremony in Chinyaquia, where Lagu and Nimeiri commemorated the agreement. "As the fragments of the delicate ribbon fluttered to the ground," he noted, "a great roar erupted . . . southern Sudan would have the authority to govern her own affairs without interference from the North. For millions of Sudanese refugees, it was a chance to go home at long last."[82] One group of exiles employed the theme of Babylonian exile to memorialize the refugee return. A sign carried between bamboo poles was adorned with a quotation from Jeremiah 23:3: "Then I will gather the remnant of my flock out of all the countries where I have driven them. The returnees."[83] Given P. K. Mabuong's earlier borrowing from Jeremiah's Lamentations to decry the South's situation, the recognition that God was now bringing the refugees back to the South brought the situation full circle. While those people evoked an Old Testament prophet, others hearkened to Nuer prophet Ngundeng. Peter Gatkuoth Gual was a deputy for Abel Alier, minister for southern affairs and leader of the government negotiating team at Addis Ababa. Following the agreement, Gatkuoth met with Lou chiefs, who told him that Ngundeng had predicted that peace would come from the east (Ethiopia's direction); a Nuer with a left-handed mother (which Gatkuoth's mother was); and a slim left-handed stranger (which described Alier).[84] Thus, people placed the Addis Ababa Agreement within longer prophetic traditions.

The changes experienced by the Sudanese Church during the war continued into the postwar era. In 1976 the Episcopal Church of the Sudan (ECS) became an independent province within the Anglican Communion. Within the Catholic Church, the vicariates and prefectures were elevated in 1974 to metropolitan sees in Khartoum and Juba and five suffragan sees. The Sudan Council of Churches conducted development projects in both North and South Sudan, and other Christian agencies like Norwegian Church Aid worked with various medical, government, and educational programs throughout the South. These agencies were involved in the arrival of Ugandan refugees into Sudan following Idi Amin's first demise and then Obote. "Only someone who experienced these years in southern Sudan," Wheeler wrote, "can adequately appreciate how the Churches grew in size, in their evangelistic and developmental endeavors, and in their institutional complexity."[85]

* * *

During the First Sudanese Civil War, activists infused spirituality into their language of racial resistance, marking an important development in the evolution of South Sudanese political thought. Several understood the war as a spiritual contest, and in this vein, figures like Joseph Lagu and Paolino Doggale conceptualized southerners as a community defined not only by their racial and cultural identity but by their favorable position in a narrative of oppression and liberation.

The public and private spaces in which southerners theologized their circumstances speaks to the fact that this theology was not aimed exclusively at non-Sudanese audiences for self-serving, sympathy-conjuring purposes. Personal religious views or thoughts expressed in private correspondences are different from public prophetic affirmations of faith. And yet, while this book is principally concerned with what happens when politico-religious views are announced, the similarities found in public and private articulations speak to a theology that was not confined to the public sphere. One must conclude, then, that the thoughts examined in this chapter were not artificial or intended primarily to generate support from outside supporters (even if they did, in fact, help to render such support).

The circumstances in which this rhetoric emerged—during the infancy of decolonization, in sub-Saharan Africa's first postcolonial state, and among this religious minority—invite the South Sudanese case to be placed in conversation with other contemporary instances of revolutionary movements in which race or religion were primary points of division (Zanzibar and South Africa come to mind).[86] The South Sudanese case provides a provocative lens into race and religion as public and policed political identities. Southern intellectuals, rather than approaching race and religion as mutually exclusive subjectivities, used theology as a crucible with which to define race. Finally, the Christian discourse highlights the ways in which biblical metaphors and imageries shaped the thought of a diverse cadre of southern thinkers. Religious messages were carried outside traditionally devotional contexts by clerics, laypeople, civilians, and soldiers. This reality points to the importance of expanding the scope of sources used to trace the influence of religious thought on early postcolonial political imaginaries.

Chapter 4 examines another theology that emerged in another war against Khartoum: the longer Second Sudanese Civil War.

4

Khartoum Goliath

THE MARTIAL THEOLOGY OF *SPLM/SPLA UPDATE*

Like Biblical Philistine Goliath
The NIF enemy looks giant and great
tricky and treacherous all the time . . .
Says thousands of mega-ton lies
In the name of false Arabism and
distorted Islam . . .
The NIF bitter enemy gives terror and destruction
To the people of Southern Sudan, Nuba and Ingessena
But Alas! The brave furious confident SPLA
Like Biblical small David with stone and sling
The SPLA keeps Goliath at bay
The stone and sling of our SPLA will smash and mash the skull of NIF
Falling dead face downward
Marking the beginning of the end
Like Goliath defeated by little David
The NIF brutal enemy is doomed . . .
With sure triumphant victory
We shall shout SPLA Oyee
—Isaac D. Malith, 1995

The Philistines and Israelites were gathered for war. While the Philistines occupied one hill, King Saul and his Israelites were camped on another. A valley lay between them. Goliath, a Philistine champion and mountain of a man, donned the regalia of war—a bronze helmet, a bronze coat of armor, bronze greaves on his legs, a bronze javelin on his back, a spear, and a shield. "Choose a man," he taunted, "and have him come down to me. If he is able to fight and kill me, we will become your subjects; but if I overcome him and kill him, you will become our subjects and serve us." Goliath took his stand every morning and evening for forty days. Now David, son of Jesse, had been anointed by the prophet Samuel to rule as Israel's future king. Jesse asked his son to take grain and bread to his brothers in the camp. Early one morning, David left his flock in a shepherd's care, loaded up, and set out. He reached the camp just as the army was moving into its battle positions and shouting the war cry. Leaving his items, David ran to the battle lines and asked how his brothers were doing. As he was speaking to them, Goliath shouted his habitual message. The shepherd boy asked those standing near him, "What will be done for the man who kills this Philistine and removes this disgrace from Israel? Who is this uncircumcised Philistine that he should defy the armies of the living God?" David informed Saul that he would fight the giant. Saul conceded, and David warned Goliath that "the whole world will know that there is a God in Israel. All those gathered here will know that it is not by sword or spear that the Lord saves; for the battle is the Lord's and he will give all of you into our hands." With stone and sling David stunned Goliath, decapitated him with his own sword, and became a legend.[1]

Goliath's physical and sartorial description represented the reality of superior Philistine wealth, militancy, and technology. Despite these advantages, the Israelites had God on their side. As Goliath and David represented each of their respective armies, their tête-à-tête was a struggle not only between two men but also between lifestyles and gods, with the dominant position in a master-slave hierarchy at stake.[2] It has also been surmised that while modern racial understandings had no real basis in 1 Samuel or its ancient contexts, biblical tradition often cast the Philistines as an Other to Israel in a higher degree than its other neighbors. For example, Philistines were castigated for being uncircumcised while Israel and most of its neighbors practiced circumcision. Matthew Arnold states that based on the German use of the word *Philistine*, the term "must have originally meant . . . a strong, dogged, unenlightened opponent of the chosen people. . . . They regarded [the Philistines] as . . . enemies to light; stupid and oppressive, but at the same time very strong."[3] In the mid-1990s, South Sudanese in the midst of the Second Sudanese Civil War wanted the Bible to address them so that their place in the world could be recognized. Apart from the Bible, few other sources were available with which to interpret their position.[4] Episodes from biblical Israel's history, like David's clash with Goliath, became popular narratives to fit the modern situation.

The Sudanese government framed its fight against rebel forces as a jihad to recruit more Muslims into the ranks of the Popular Defense Force (PDF). The theme of Islamic martyrdom obscured the war's high level of casualties sustained by ill-trained PDF members. In a similar fashion, southern leaders infused religious themes into their thought and action. Churches and other Christian institutions and communities fashioned theological responses to the war, and many understood their struggle in terms of biblical themes, especially that of suffering. Though the Sudan People's Liberation Movement (SPLM) never officially affiliated with any religion and maintained a policy of religious toleration, it manipulated religion to mobilize and garner support at home and abroad. The Sudan People's Liberation Army (SPLA) was transformed into a largely Christian force that explicitly used Christian themes and language as propaganda.[5]

The *SPLM/SPLA Update* is important to the genealogy of religious politics through its contribution to the Second Civil War's framing in spiritual terms and the significance of circulating print media in the dissemination of political theology. Published by the SPLM and SPLA, the *Update* published content that constituted a martial theology pitting the SPLA against the National Islamic Front (NIF). Founded by Hasan al-Turabi, the Islamist NIF co-ruled the country under his political guidance.[6] After the war's 2005 conclusion, SPLA leader John Garang became "Moses," and Isaiah's prophecy concerning Cush was referenced as foretelling southern independence. Paralleling themes that could be heard over Radio SPLA, *Update* contributors fashioned new theories of conflict and identity and attempted to lend a unified theory of divine "chosenness" and victory over an evil enemy.[7] By featuring David, Moses, and Isaiah, this martial theology was gendered masculine.

Rather than acting as proselytizers, contributors were creative intellectuals who organized a spiritual, liberatory account of the war. These authors interpreted events inside biblical and ancient Israelite templates, placed circumstances in a narrative trajectory, and transformed political history into a spiritual chronicle. That chronicle attracted readers beyond Sudan's political borders, situating itself within a global Sudanese diaspora and reaching into the ancient past to locate the struggles of Sudanese Christians in an older story of divine chosenness. That the *Update* was a secular medium illustrates the importance of diversifying the sources in which we search and analyze the percolation of religious thought in the diaspora. Though it may be natural to zero in on religious spaces like churches, religious organizations, and media, secular arenas are also significant spaces to explore contours of religious ideology. The danger of marginalizing those spaces in such investigations is to ignore important ways that religion shapes and cuts across the totality of lived experiences in the Sudanese diaspora and, more broadly, the Africana world.

THE SPLA AND GLOBAL CHRISTENDOM

Repeated violations of the 1972 Addis Ababa peace agreement led to a Second Civil War, which began in 1983. The Regional Self-Government Act worked in concert with the 1973 constitution to establish power-sharing arrangements formed between the government and a unified southern region. A decade after these establishments, President Ja'afar al-Nimeiri enacted Sharia law (he realized that he could no longer fend off opposition from the religious right). Nimeiri also repealed the Addis Ababa Agreement and divided the South into regions based on the old Equatoria, Upper Nile, and Bahr el-Ghazal provinces. In May 1983, an army mutiny in the Upper Nile marked the beginning of the Sudan People's Liberation Movement and Army (SPLM/A).[8]

Before the Second Civil War, Christianity in South Sudan was more closely linked with educated and formally employed people living in towns rather than those in rural areas. Southerners saw Christian missions as bases to learn skills like literacy rather than resources for spiritual direction. Christian conversions in the East increased after the conclusion of the First Civil War. Sharon Hutchinson explains that this development represented a Nuer attempt to resist a coercive government increasingly stirred by Islamic fundamentalist principles. In addition to such conversions, Nuer labor migration to northern cities after the hostilities transformed many northern churches into social and educational centers in scattered, estranging urban landscapes. The Second Civil War destroyed the southern urban life that had been connected with Christianity, and against the backdrop of the government's politicization of Islam, many southerners began to view churches as political allies. Churches, particularly in northern cities, offered displaced southerners clubs that provided religious teaching, literacy classes, and other social services—resources that, according to Francis Deng, allowed them to build broader relationships and a sense of unity.[9] The 2005 *CIA World Factbook* reported that Sudan's population was 70 percent Muslim and 5 percent Christian, while 25 percent adhered to indigenous religions. Christian leaders, however, put their numbers quite higher. One report, published in 2007, noted that the Episcopal and Catholic churches were strongest among the Dinka, while the Presbyterians were foremost among the Nuer.[10]

Two events had major repercussions on the SPLM/SPLA's trajectory and the politicization of Christianity in the war. The first was the NIF's rise to power and General Omer al-Bashir's ascendance to national leadership. Organized after Nimeiri's 1985 ouster, the NIF was an outgrowth of the Muslim Brotherhood. Its program underscored national unity and, as a consequence, presented federalism as an answer to civil war. Perhaps most significant was the policy that Islamic law is the only enforceable law. In 1989 al-Bashir came to power in a June coup that unseated Prime Minister Sadiq al-Mahdi's coalition government. Al-Bashir instituted a host of measures centralizing national power and silencing opposition: all political parties were banned, government leaders and scores of military leaders were arrested, and the constitution, national assembly, and trade unions were abolished. The Revolutionary Command Council for National Salvation was established as the ruling body, and Hasan al-Turabi—the NIF's founder and ideologue—was considered the regime's main theorist. Southern reactions to al-Bashir's coup were generally negative. A year into the new regime, it had still not had any direct peace talks with the SPLM, and the issue of Islamic law was, generally speaking, non-negotiable for southerners.[11]

An SPLM/SPLA radio broadcast after al-Mahdi's overthrow indicated its sentiment moving forward. Citing the SPLM manifesto's statement concerning the ideal separation between mosque and state, the broadcast stated that "we advise El Bashir not to take the position taken by fundamentalists for that position is dangerous, unhistorical and alien to the Sudan and to Africa. . . . Sharia, or any other religious law pertaining to other religions, is personal law, a relationship between the believer and his God."[12] However, the National Islamic Front had come to power in 1989 with the express aim of establishing an Islamic political order throughout the country.[13]

The fall of Ethiopia's Mengistu regime was the second formative event, signaling important shifts for the SPLA from an operational standpoint and in relation to Christian bodies. The SPLA lost its main supply lines and military bases in southwestern Ethiopia, and 350,000 South Sudanese were forced to flee from their refugee camps. The regime's collapse meant that major changes were in store for Radio SPLA. *Radio SPLA: The Voice of Revolutionary Armed Struggle* had been established after the SPLM/SPLA was urged to create a revolutionary radio station. Located in suburban Addis Ababa, Radio SPLA made its first long-range broadcast in October 1984 and became a medium for broadcasting SPLM/A policy and changes, battles with the Sudanese government, news, commentaries, war songs, and poems that celebrated the SPLA.[14] Despite Radio SPLA's popularity, the fall of the Mengistu regime spelled doom for the SPLM/A in Ethiopia. Radio SPLA went off the air in 1991, and though the movement had plans to use Upper Talanga as a new radio base, it was unstable. The movement needed to find another foreign communications base and turned to print media as a means to disseminate information.[15]

Without the benefit of Ethiopia and cut off from its Marxist supporters, the SPLA's relations with the church warmed. The evacuation of refugee camps—former arenas for evangelism—meant that many trained ministers and new Christians reentered the country. Military leaders began to show increasing respect for the church, and Christian spirituality appeared among the soldiery. Combatants, for example, created makeshift chapels, and the cross was worn around necks and sewn into uniforms. After al-Bashir's coup the SPLA allowed church leaders more freedom of activity within SPLA-controlled areas. Church leaders were also allowed to form the New Sudan Council of Churches (NSCC), which was joined by all southern churches in 1989 (Khartoum's Sudan Council of Churches could no longer maintain contacts with churches in SPLA-controlled areas). This tightening of SPLA-church relations resulted in improved credentials with industrialized countries by suggesting religious freedom and Christian identity. The movement hoped that the West could be encouraged to give aid to the South, with the NSCC providing channels for assistance from Christian organizations abroad. The council's advocacy visits to England, the World Council of Churches, and the Vatican successfully showcased South Sudanese needs. George Carey, the archbishop of Canterbury, repaid these visits with one of his own in 1994.[16]

Amid the ethnic and organizational factionalism of the period, the church tried to rein in the military and reconcile ethnic groups. In August 1991 the SPLA split into two warring factions, a division spurred by an unsuccessful coup led by the Nuer Riek Machar (along with other senior officers) against commander-in-chief John Garang, a Dinka. The coup leaders rejected the SPLA's stated political agenda and instead advocated South Sudanese political independence. This rift eventually led to outright military conflict between the Dinka and the Nuer, the South's largest ethnic groups. Following the split, the church called for reconciliation and brought the factional leaders together for negotiation.[17]

Within the context of tensions between the SPLA and NSCC, the dialogue at the Anglican parish center of Kejiko in July 1997 was intended to allow wounds and misunderstandings to be discussed and to establish a mutual agreement. The meeting resulted in the Yei Declaration, in which the SPLA and NSCC committed to closer cooperation in factional reconciliation, national peacemaking, human rights promotion, and reconstructing "New Sudan" through activities like demining and demobilization. In 1998 the NSCC's Peace Department responded to cries for peace from Dinka and Nuer civilians in Upper Nile and Bahr el-Ghazal. Thirty-five people met at Lokichoggio, where Nuer and Dinka shared stories of suffering they had experienced because of their interethnic conflict. The Lokichoggio Conference demanded an end to abductions, cattle raiding, and killing, and that all commanders halt hostile actions. Following this conference the Nuer and Dinka participants, along with NSCC staff, prepared for the first reconciliation conference. More than two thousand people witnessed the Wunlit Dinka-Nuer Conference in early 1999, where people gained "release from their pain . . . whilst at the same time identifying the issues that would have to be confronted and solved." More than three hundred Nuer and Dinka leaders signed a covenant.[18] Rev. William Lowrey, who during the 1960s had founded the first multiracial Christian organization at the University of Southern Mississippi, played no small part in reconciliation efforts. Arriving in Sudan as a mission worker among the Nuer in 1991, Rev. Lowrey returned in 1998 as the peace consultant for the NSCC. Through the NSCC, Lowrey developed a People-to-People Peace Process among the Nuer and the Dinka. In June 1998 he convened the Nuer-Dinka Chiefs and Church Leaders Reconciliation Conference in Loki, Kenya.[19]

Lowrey's actions point to the role of international activism. Following the SPLM/A split in 1991, the NSCC found religious activists in the United States who were eager to pressure the American government to get involved in the war. This effort to link with American activists led to a coalition of religious and antislavery human rights organizations, which looked to pressure the government to work toward ending the war. The war, in its view, was between Arabs and Africans, Christianity and Islam, and—particularly important—masters and slaves.[20] Modern Sudanese slavery was first reported in American and British newspapers in the late 1980s, when raiders from the North started attacking southern villages. Christian Solidarity International (CSI) pioneered "slave redemptions," paying traders from North Sudan to purchase captives and return them to their southern homes. A CSI representative would work with SPLA members during the redemption trips, and the Christians who redeemed the freed Sudanese typically addressed them. The American Anti-Slavery Group (AASG) joined CSI in highlighting the issue of modern slavery in the South. American human rights groups like CSI and AASG linked the southern plight with that of Christians, blacks, and Jewish minorities in America. Their work and humanitarian rhetoric influenced the manner in which the conflict was represented in mainstream Western media. The ritualized slave redemptions resonated with slavery's US history and marked the American and Sudanese participants in the redemptions as liberators.[21]

In 2000, Joe Madison—a civil rights activist, talk show host, and board member of the National Association for the Advancement of Colored People (NAACP)—went with CSI on a redemption trip. The following year Gloria White-Hammond, an African American co-pastor of Jamaica Plain's (Boston) Bethel AME Church, similarly set off on a CSI-organized redemption trip. Perceiving the abductions as modern slavery, White-Hammond and her group saw slave redemption as a way for them—as black American Christians—to address the weights they shouldered concerning slavery and Africa. Black pastors occupied a special position because they could speak to race and religion. Activist ministers like Rev. Walter Fauntroy and Rev. Al Sharpton traveled to South Sudan, gave media interviews, and spoke at rallies and their churches. One cadre of black American pastors wrote to the Congressional Black Caucus demanding greater leadership on the Sudanese slavery issue. During White-Hammond's 2001 trip, CSI informed Sudanese captives that they were freed because there were people in America (i.e., Christians, black Americans) who had been touched by their suffering.[22]

Beginning in the 1990s, Sudan entered the American evangelical mind as a site of Christian persecution. Samuel Moyn once noted that the Muslim has taken the place of the Communist in the contemporary European imagination (with particular respect to the matter of religious liberty), and in this respect, the post–Cold War context cannot be divorced from America's turn to Sudan. Only a decade after divisions over antiapartheid activism had showcased racial and political ruptures among theologically conservative believers, black and white Americans rallied around South Sudanese moral claims. More than being a mere evangelical fixation, the Sudan campaign became one of the most broad-based political coalitions on international matters since apartheid's demise. Conservative pro-Israel groups listed Sudan—behind Osama bin Laden and Hamas—as principal elements in the fight against the danger posed by "militant Islam."[23]

SPLA UPDATE: ORIGINS, COMPOSITION, AND CONTEXT

Many southern Christians viewed Christianity as a unifying mechanism that could curtail ethnic strife and bind the region together against the North. Against the backdrop of ethnic conflict, some thought that since Muslims were not fighting one another, a Christian South could be similarly united.[24] Some elites in the South promoted the notion that Christianity be fostered as an important element of southern identity, a religion that—in league with factors like English and indigenous languages—competed against North Sudan's Arab and Islamic framework. Francis Deng called this "an essential ingredient in the hidden agendas of the war of visions," even though, in his estimation, those in the SPLM/SPLA leadership may not have openly supported that model.[25] By the late 1980s, however, Machar recognized the potential for Christian conversion to galvanize southern resistance and encouraged conversion among civilians.[26] One civil official in Bahr el-Ghazal explained, "Christianity is needed to stand firm against encroaching civilisations. We need a Christian Fundamentalism."[27] With Radio SPLA off the air and a renewed emphasis on Christianity's position in the war, *SPLM/SPLA Update* became a medium with which to disseminate a martial theology of political dissent.

Created after the SPLA fled Ethiopia, the *Update* was designed to keep accurate records and reach those who could not be reached through traditional communication. Alternate commander George Akol was appointed as its first director. Based in Nairobi, it was disseminated throughout East Africa free of charge. Between 1992 and 2004 it was published almost every week and was a channel of communication between the national leadership, diaspora, and Sudanese public. Most issues included commentaries, field updates, official reports, and poetry. A main media outlet on organizational policy and activities, the *Update* was one of several publications issued by SPLA factions from Nairobi.[28]

The *Update* was a global forum. In addition to being distributed to liberated areas within Sudan, it was distributed to all international SPLM chapters and countries that included the United Kingdom, Norway, Denmark, and the United States. Atem Yaak Atem noted that Nairobi's non-Sudanese expatriate community was attracted to his column, and he further noted that Sudanese SPLM sympathizers from the Gulf and Khartoum-controlled areas secretly read the *Update* and sent letters praising his column.[29] Elhag Paul, who received the *Update* in the UK, remembers first becoming aware of the newspaper when he was posted a copy by the SPLM/A London office. He would receive copies by mail or collect it when he was near their offices: "Many South Sudanese in the UK also read it."[30] The *Update* was also international in its content and in the distribution of its contributors: there was coverage of apartheid's demise, Archbishop Benjamin Yugusuk's visit to Kakuma refugee camp, and a post-9/11 condolence letter to George W. Bush. Contributions came from Nairobi, Lesotho, Germany, New Jersey, London, and Harare.[31]

The *Update*'s global reach may have reflected the movement's attempt to involve the Sudanese diaspora—and Africans more generally—in its liberationist project. The war separated children from their families, and the SPLA convinced the Ethiopian government to accept southern refugees. The Lost Boys entered Ethiopia in 1987, and SPLA-appointed caretakers in the Panyidu refugee camps organized them into groups.[32] Abraham Nhial's story is emblematic of the hardships Lost Boys faced in their flight from Sudan. As he shared with me, his walk from Aweil to Ethiopia took over three months and included many hardships: "People were eating young boys and girl[s] were eaten by wild animals, thrown in the rivers, eaten by crocodiles, died because there's no water." Nhial—who by the time of our interview was the Anglican bishop of Aweil—credited God's power in keeping some of them alive as the reason he became a Christian. By 1991 more than 400,000 South Sudanese were living in refugee camps in western Ethiopia, but after Mengistu's fall, the SPLA facilitated the Lost Boy resettlement in Kenya.[33]

In the late 1990s and early 2000s many southern refugees arrived in Western nations. Nearly four thousand resettled in the United States. The Lost Boys raised the visibility of southern suffering to American Christians who were interested in their struggle against Islam, an interest that seriously influenced US-Sudan relations. The media focused close attention on the Lost Boys' stories, testimonies sponsored by church groups that directed attention to America's policy toward Sudan. In March 2001, Secretary of State Colin Powell declared before the House Subcommittee on Africa that the world's greatest tragedy was occurring in Sudan, and two months later, President Bush highlighted Sudan's religious freedom violations. He appointed Senator John Danforth—an ordained Episcopal minster—as his special envoy on the Sudan. Nhial, who went on to attend college in Georgia and seminary in Pennsylvania, is among those who have raised awareness about the Lost Boys and broader South Sudanese plight to American audiences.[34] It should be noted, however, that the Lost Boy moniker is misleading; many were entire families on a secondary resettlement scheme adopted by Australia, Canada, and the United States.

Members of the diaspora wrote letters to the Intergovernmental Authority on Development (IGAD) and to the United States, UK, and Norway demanding the right to self-determination. Diaspora organizations also drew attention to South Sudanese wishes to secede. The UK-based Sudan Christian Fellowship (SCF) and Sudanese in Diaspora (SID) each spoke about the South's wishes. Run by Josephine Lagu, the SID worked with the House of Commons' All-Party Parliamentary Group for Sudan and South Sudan. Among other services, it aimed to raise awareness of the refugee plight among policy makers and agencies and to provide assistance for asylum applications.[35] Diasporic support was not lost on John Garang, who "constantly wooed" the diaspora "because he wanted to be the sole leader of South Sudan. . . . Members of the Diaspora used their connections with senior members of the SPLM to influence the agenda."[36] In Garang's 2004 meeting with Lost Boys in Phoenix, he referred to them as "freedom fighters" and, in recognition of their role in strengthening relations between the United States and South Sudan, claimed "that he had 3,800 ambassadors to the United States."[37]

MARTIAL THEOLOGY OF *SPLM/SPLA UPDATE*

Writing from Nairobi, Kong Chang used the example of biblical David to argue that southern youth carried great responsibility: "David, the Israelite youth who was quite religious not only killed Goliath . . . but was also deemed fit to be King . . . our elders . . . did fight in many parts of the country . . . the torch is with you. History will judge you harshly if it burns out in your hands."[38] In many ways, the *Update*'s martial brand of Christian thought adopted the theological and racial themes and arguments from the David and Goliath story. As David represented God's chosen people and Goliath an evil Other bent on subjugation, contributors made similar distinctions between themselves and Khartoum. Following the First Abuja Conference, the *Update* published a commentary that likened the regime to "the Biblical Goliath." The conference, convened in May 1992, was intended as a space where the SPLM and Sudanese government could attempt to resolve issues of division. The government argued that the Muslim majority had a right to establish an Islamic constitutional system, that the South could be exempt from Islamic punishments (but not Islamic laws), and that Sudan would be transformed into an Arab-Islamic country. Both SPLM wings rejected the government's position in favor of a secular democratic system.[39] One writer expressed discontent at Khartoum's position: "Like the Biblical Goliath, the enemy went to Abuja . . . told the SPLM/SPLA to cave in or die . . . the South stood its ground . . . and chose to be free or dead. . . . The Abuja Declaration sent Goliath reading [reeling]."[40] Years later Isaac Malith appropriated David and Goliath to argue that SPLA victory was certain: "Like Biblical Philistine Goliath / The NIF enemy looks giant. . . . / But Alas! . . . / The stone and sling of our SPLA will smash and mash the skull of NIF. . . . / With sure triumphant victory / We shall shout SPLA Oyee."[41] This framing of the SPLA, though evocative, contradicted reality. With arms and support from the Ethiopian government, the SPLA could by the early 1990s mobilize fifty thousand soldiers that could attack in concert with northern allies. The army had at least twelve battalions and weaponry that included antiaircraft missiles, AK-47s, and mines.[42] While the sense of destiny and righteousness that the David and Goliath parallel imparted was significant, the David appropriation nevertheless covered up the structural realities of the SPLA's war machine.

While the David narrative scripted a victorious outcome, the most famous biblical tale of liberation—Exodus—was also featured to convey a similar message. In this paradigm John Garang was Moses, called to lead Sudan into a new promised land. In 1994 the *Update* published perhaps its first Garang-Moses comparison when Fr. Thomas Attiyah opined that slavery united New Sudan with the historical Jews. Born in eastern Equatoria in 1941, Attiyah was ordained as a priest in the Congregation of the Apostles of Jesus in 1969 in Kenya. During his lengthy clerical career, he served as a rector at several East African seminaries. During the Second Sudanese Civil War, South Sudanese members of the Apostles of Jesus worked primarily in Kenya and liberated areas controlled by the SPLA. Attiyah worked mostly in Juba. Written under the heading "Let my people go," Attiyah acknowledged that God worked through history and suggested that Garang could fill Moses's position in leading his people to an independent state: "He is 'our Moses' . . . Dr John. . . . Be courageous! . . . be humble like Moses of old, full of trust . . . in the Lord and lead the people to their total freedom."[43]

The *Update* published content that used scripture to decry tribalism and political factionalism—realities that, throughout the war, threatened to upend the liberation project. In Fr. Attiyah's published homily, he stated that the Sudanese shared the Israelite experience of suffering and suggested that they "get united like the Israelites . . . and confront the beast in unity and solidarity."[44] Benjamin Izale echoed the belief that the Israelites represented a model of unity in his poem against tribalism: "We fight the divisive policy, / Divide and rule, / No Madi No Latuko . . . / 'Moses' at Sudan echoes, / A joint front, / Unity, / Equality."[45] While some used the Jewish scriptures to convey the belief that unity was required for victory, the Christian New Testament was employed for the same purpose. Fr. Attiyah used Colossians to express the harmony that different ethnicities had in Christ: "Every ethnic group in the South has the Christian responsibility to unite with fellow men and women. . . . Today our unity . . . is a matter of life and death." Paraphrasing Paul, Attiyah stated, "As Christians, we have put on the image of Christ . . . there is no room for distinction between Dinka and Nuer, Shilluk and Zande. . . . There is only Christ."[46]

A contemporary statement recorded in Wendy James's *War and Survival* shows both the connection some had with the Exodus narrative outside the *Update* and the different applications that people could glean from it. Itang was a refugee site near Gambela for people from South Sudan. In May 1988, the *New York Times* reported that approximately 182,000 had crowded into the camp. Suske, the first wife of Pastor Paul Sol (a senior elder in Chali's Christian community), referenced Itang in her following statement to James in early October 1991:

> Yes, we are living like the people of old.—*What people?*—The Israelite people . . . we shall wait and eventually believe, as the Israelites did. And when everyone believes, our God will lead us, to look after us in our home where we shall one day live . . . we are like the Israelite people, from crying in the wilderness. They strayed, and they went into a cave in the mountains. Moses led them, he went to help them . . . as we came from Itang, I began to really believe again, as we came through the water. And it was raining, and we were really like the Israelites of old, and I wanted to believe like them, and go on with a good will.[47]

In addition to claims that the Sudanese government could be likened to Goliath, other writers in the *Update* demonized al-Bashir, the NIF, and Arabs in general. Latio Lo Jaden participated in this trend. Born in 1947, Latio Jaden was the son of Aggrey Jaden, the prominent South Sudanese leader who distinguished himself during the First Civil War. Latio Jaden finished primary school as one of the top twenty students in Juba, allowing him entry into secondary school. To his surprise, however, he was rejected and admitted instead to a *mahad* (a Muslim training center that would have prepared him to become a Muslim teacher for Islamic *khalwa* schools). When his father found out, he advised his son to stay out of school, which he did until the age of fifteen. By 1958 Aggrey Jaden had fallen into disfavor with the Sudanese government, been placed under house arrest, and been informed that none of his children would be educated. Fleeing to Uganda in 1960, Aggrey sent for his family to join him in 1961. Latio resumed his education in Kampala and began learning English. In 1983 he became involved in a movement that advocated for South Sudan's liberation, which led to his final exiling to Zaire and later Uganda.[48] The *Update* published his poem "Khartoum by Night" in its February 27, 1994, issue. Written from Nairobi, it included the following lines:

Oh! Khartoum
Holy Khartoum
Sodomy
possessed souls
Drinking at the
Brothels and bars
And in the open play
Grounds at night
And in the dark . . .
Man to man
Man with a donkey . . .
Sinful nights
Devils wear
Angels faces
Behaving like saints
Oh! Khartoum
Holy Khartoum
You devilish city.[49]

Latio Jaden's decision to link Khartoum with sodomy hearkened back to similar references made to Khartoum and the adjacent city of Omdurman during earlier periods in Sudanese history. On seeing the carnage and destruction of Omdurman following Kitchener's decisive victory in September 1898, Owen S. Watkins—a Wesleyan chaplain attached to his forces—reflected, "His wrath came to our minds, for this was a veritable African Sodom. . . . Never in my whole life has sin appeared so evil and disgusting as on that day when viewed in its brutal native ugliness."[50] In Andrew Wheeler's description of nineteenth-century mission work in the Sudan, he writes that Khartoum came to be known as the "Capital of Hell."[51] Thus, Jaden's description of Khartoum as a city with souls possessed by sodomy not only aimed to soil its reputation but also echoed other instances of framing North Sudan's biggest cities as paragons of wickedness.

Jaden was joined in his aspersions by Nyandeng Malek Deliech. Born in 1964, Malek moved with her aunt to Juba to pursue her education at the age of thirteen, a decision that protected her from early nuptials. After completing secondary school, she received a scholarship to attend Egypt's Zagazig University, and in Egypt, she became politically active and joined the SPLM. Graduating in 1991, she eventually received another scholarship to continue her studies in England, where she earned a master's degree from the University of Wolverhampton in 2003.[52] It was perhaps during her stint in England that Malek, shortly after the 9/11 attacks, made a Crucifixion analogy when lamenting that southerners had suffered from the same enemy that had just struck America:

> We, the survivors of the suffering civil society of South Sudan . . . share the grief with the American leadership and the relatives and friends of the victims of the barbaric attack. . . . We strongly condemn all sorts of violence and wanton massacre of innocent human beings. . . . This has been the plea of South Sudan civilians during the last half century of unmatched brutal atrocities by the same enemies of civilization and democratization. . . . We are being forced . . . to drink from the same cup of the deadly liquid served to Jesus on the Cross.[53]

Malek's reference to the "same enemies" is revealing when considering the NIF's ties to Osama bin Laden. In 1991 bin Laden moved from Afghanistan to Khartoum, where he was nominally involved in development projects but actually engaged in furthering his Islamic causes. During his stint in Sudan, he was implicated in several terrorist attacks and accused by the United States of running militant camps in the country. The United States charged Sudan as a "state sponsor of terrorism" after the 1993 World Trade Center bombing. The Sudanese foreign minister asked American diplomats what his country needed to do to shed the terrorist label, and after US ambassador Tim Carney applied pressure, bin Laden was forced out in May 1996.[54]

Malek's involvement with the SPLM and the *Update*'s inclusion of her article is one illustration of women's involvement in the movement. According to Nhial, "They [women] were the one[s] running the church in most cases. They were the one[s] taking care of the children of our soldiers. Our soldiers were not having salaries, so they were the one[s] cooking for them and provid[ing] food for them."[55] To be sure, women's involvement went beyond simply taking care of soldiers. In 1984 John Garang created Ketiba Banat, the SPLA's only girls' battalion. Many left school or home to join the SPLA, including Elizabeth Anei—a member of the University of Juba's student union, who joined the SPLA and trained others in military tactics. Oftentimes the military life offered women the chance to further their education while gaining job skills on an equal plane with men. Many trained for such positions as armed patrol, radio communications, the medical corps, and participation on the front with men. All told, the SPLA incorporated more women than the Anyanya force in the 1960s. And yet, Clémence Pinaud writes, the SPLA differed from other socialist guerrilla groups through its exclusion of women from its political agenda (a reality that dated to the beginning). Some groups of women in Equatoria, the Nuba Mountains, Ethiopia, and Cuba were militarily trained and stayed in the SPLA longer than most Ketiba Banat recruits, who were speedily married off to SPLA dignitaries and departed the front lines.[56]

Along with Malek's post-9/11 reference to the Crucifixion came antigovernment vilifications that Khartoum was evil. In Amosa Michael's "Weapons to Defeat the NIF in the Bible: Letter to All Freedom Fighters," he used several scriptures to encourage readers to hold fast and resist al-Bashir:

> Satan has legions of . . . wicked spirits waging war against you. . . . Their base of operation is . . . Khartoum and other countries that sponsor Islamic fundamentalism . . . the devil is devising this devastating mission of Christian cleansing of which Omer Beshir is one of the field commanders. . . . Let us come together, plan our warfare and fight the enemy of the children of God.

Michael comforted readers by pointing to Luke 7, where Jesus heals a centurion's servant. In that passage, according to Michael, "we see a classical example of long range missile in the battlefield." "I challenge you in the name of Jesus," he continued, "stand up and start bombing any satanic targets in the Sudan."[57] Father Attiyah similarly adopted the theme of good versus evil when he coupled the assertion that Khartoum's political system was "evil" with the claim that "social justice requires that evil system be destroyed and replaced with the just one."[58] Another example of demonization included assistant commander Gabriel Riak's assertion that the Sudanese were suffering from "blood sucking Lucifers/devils. . . . / Fighting our way out means your liberation / From feisty hands."[59]

Despite such excoriations, the SPLM/A did not look to completely suppress or distance itself from Islam. On the contrary, the movement—on the battlefield and in the *Update*—made efforts to show respect for Islam. Within the newspaper, some contributors made sure to separate Islam from the SPLA's Muslim opponents. One such figure was Steven Wöndu, who reserved his disdain for individuals rather than Islam entirely: "The moral and ethical decadence of the Turabi-Beshir syndicate is beyond human understanding. . . . Allah and Islam, I thought, represent purity. . . . The Turabi-Beshir regime . . . portray the characters of Lucifer."[60] His decision to associate Islam with goodness represents the fact that the *Update* rarely if ever directed angst against Islam writ large but instead targeted the NIF's fundamentalist Islam. Latio Jaden expressed this distinction in poetic verse: "Ours is not hatred of Arabism or Islam / But this type of Islam."[61] Nine clerics who participated in the 1993 NSCC General Assembly in Kaya wrote a letter on behalf of South Sudan's Christian community, expressing pacific sentiments toward North Sudanese Muslims. The *Update* published this letter, with one portion reading: "We do not hate the Arabs and Muslims of Northern Sudan . . . among them there are many who are tired of this senseless war . . . we have still hope that those whose hearts have hardened may . . . recognise that brotherhood and sisterhood is our common call."[62]

Several of my research participants who were (and still are) active in the church acknowledged the presence of Muslims in the SPLM/SPLA. Rev. John Daau, founder of the Good Shepherd College and Seminary as well as founder and editor of the *Christian Times*, expressed that the SPLA allowed soldiers to follow their religion of choice. Muslims "were given their own opportunities to worship and to preach to their own fellow Muslims . . . on Fridays, Muslims were allowed to do their own thing."[63] The Rt. Rev. Bismark Avokaya, Anglican bishop of Mundri, referenced the fact that some SPLA senior commanders were Muslim.[64] Angelo Lokoyome, who at the time of our interview was working as the justice and peace coordinator in the Catholic Archdiocese of Juba, similarly acknowledged the Muslim presence in the war: "This war was not fought by Christians alone. We had Muslims . . . in the bush. . . . Even this SPLA war, and even with all our struggles now, we have Muslims also who behave as South Sudanese because for them, they are saying before they became Muslims they were first South Sudanese."[65] In the words of Mahmoud E. Yousif, former chairman of the New Sudan Islamic Council and South Sudan Islamic Council, "the role played by Muslims in SPLM/A (from South Sudan, Nuba Mountains, Blue Nile and Darfur), can't be underestimated, and without them South Sudan wouldn't be as it is today." One illustration he used to support his argument occurred after Riek Machar formed the Nasir faction in 1992. Yousif explained to me that after Machar destroyed several SPLA forces up to Mongalla, Salva Kiir led three SPLM/A battalions from Nuba. These forces—which were more than 65 percent Muslim—repulsed Machar.[66]

The final component of religious thought stipulated that God would protect New Sudan and ensure its liberation. Amosa Michael lent a sense of confidence by borrowing from 2 Corinthians: "Let us stand alongside our brethren who are in combat with the demon possessed Omer Beshir and his followers. All of us are soldiers in Christ. . . . Our weapons have a divine power for the pulling down [of] strongholds."[67] This New Testament example notwithstanding, a prophecy concerning Cush from the book of Isaiah was the foundational element of the belief in ultimate victory. The Kingdom of Cush was an ancient civilization located south of Egypt. As it controlled the Nile cataracts—barriers to river transportation—it occupied a strategic location with respect to regional trade. In around 650 BCE, a garrison of Jewish mercenary soldiers that had been brought to Egypt to defend the southern border with Cush was established on Elephantine Island. Reputed in ancient art and literature as soldiers, Cush and Cushites are referenced in the Bible fifty-four times.[68] In Isaiah 18, the Old Testament prophet outlined the following "Prophesy against Cush":

Woe to the land of whirring wings
      along the rivers of Cush,
      which sends envoys by sea
in papyrus boats over the water.
Go, swift messengers,
to a people tall and smooth-skinned,
      to a people feared far and wide,
an aggressive nation of strange speech,
      whose land is divided by rivers.
All you people of the world,
      you who live on the earth,
when a banner is raised on the mountains,
      you will see it,
and when a trumpet sounds,
      you will hear it.

Isaiah states that the Lord would "cut off the shoots with pruning knives, and cut down and take away the spreading branches," and the Cushites would be left to become the food of preying mountain birds and wild animals. "At that time," however,

> gifts will be brought to the Lord Almighty
> from a people tall and smooth-skinned,
>> from a people feared far and wide,
> an aggressive nation of strange speech,
>> whose land is divided by rivers—
> the gifts will be brought to Mount Zion, the place of the Name of the
> Lord Almighty.[69]

Prophecy interpretation is relevant to any discussion concerning Isaiah 18 and South Sudan. Douglas Johnson has analyzed interpretations of the prophecies of Ngundeng, noting that his songs became quite popular with SPLA soldiers who were originally recruited mainly from Dinka and Nuer from Upper Nile and Bahr el-Ghazal. During the 1980s, the SPLA reinterpreted his songs to create military unity among its soldiery and to strengthen its claim to establish bases in Gajaak areas (the Gajaak are the largest Nuer group in Ethiopian territory). Songs that mentioned *Kartum hari* were understood to foretell military and political victory in Khartoum. Increasingly prominent during the war as a symbol of antigovernment resistance, as Christiane Falge has noted, Ngundeng's post-1991 fame was linked to the fragmentation of southern political and military unity and Nuer society's ethnic, religious, and political fragmentation.[70]

By the early 1990s, one Nuer evangelist had already begun to invoke Isaiah's prophecy as an argument to encourage Christian conversion. In James Mut Kueth's interview with journalist Deborah Scroggins, the Presbyterian minister at Nasir argued that Isaiah 18 foretold Sudan's future.[71] The *Update* published invocations to Cush as a foundation for Sudanese nationalism, Pan-Africanism, and the belief that liberation was at hand through the realization of Isaiah's prophecy. A special edition published a paper conveying that "we" were the land of Cush, the dark-skinned people noted for their martial prowess. Cush, the writer maintained, provided the example for New Sudan from which "we must re-trace our cultural roots . . . to evolve a concept of Sudanese nationalism, which is capable of rallying all the present Sudanese peoples around 'nation-formation,' 'nation-building' and 'national unity.'"[72] Kwarnyikiir Abdelilah Zion addressed a poem to "Cushites everywhere," admonishing readers to trust God for victory: "March with hopes and do not despair. / For the God of Isaiah is quite aware. . . . / The present war by all means shall be won. . . . / You have been named by Zion."[73] Perhaps the most compelling reference to Cush appeared in Ater Deng Abuk's poem "The Sudan Laugh." Referring to the quip that God laughed when he created Sudan, Abuk rejoiced that the curse on Cush was no more:

> Yes! Comes a voice from beyond Isaiah 18. . . . Cush is uncursed! Lam, Riek, Nyuon, Kuanyin *Achan's sons of Jericho* have removed the curse at *Ngundeang's* Sobat Valley of *An-chor*. . . . Cush lost, now regained! You, tall smooth-skinned people feared far and wide! . . . Your Hour has come! . . . the New Sudan![74]

To grasp the full meaning of Abuk's allusions, political developments in South Sudan in 1994 (when the poem was published) warrant elucidation. Divisions within the SPLA-United resulted in fighting between the two largest Nuer groups. The conference purposed to end the Nuer civil war rededicated the SPLA-United to achieving southern independence and dismissed those accused of collaborating with the government (including Nyuon, Kuanyin, and Lam). This move appeared to pave the way for a truce with the SPLA.[75] Abuk must have interpreted their dismissal as strengthening by subtraction. In the book of Joshua, the Israelite Achan is punished for taking spoils from Jericho that should have been devoted to the Lord's treasury. God turns his anger from Israel after Achan is stoned. Thus, Abuk adopted the biblical narrative by conflating Achan's stoning with the "stoning" of the Khartoum collaborators.

The SPLA leadership also referenced biblical Cush outside the pages of the *Update*. In "Vision, Perspective, and Position of the SPLM," secretary for education and religious affairs Samson L. Kwaje stated that Isaiah's mention of Cush was a clear description of contemporary South Sudan.[76] Garang, a secularist at the beginning of the war, saw utility in including Cush in his politics. He began combing the Bible "in the hope of divining the future outcome of this war."[77] In a paper delivered on his behalf to the All Africa Students Conference in 2005, Garang mentioned Cush in his attempt to link the SPLM project with Pan-Africanism. Connecting Sudan to the Pan-African movement's struggle, Sudanese fights against oppression were "aimed and are aimed at regaining African dignity and nationhood that has been mutilated over the centuries." He contextualized the liberation struggle by referencing civilizations that had appeared and disappeared in South Sudan (including Cush). For Garang such precedents spoke to Sudan's critical role in history and provided a counterargument for those wishing to remove Sudanese from history.[78] In these ways the SPLM/A adopted Cush as a means to add a sense of heritage and prophetic destiny.

And yet, one of my research participants, whom I have given the pseudonym "Faith," explained that borrowing Cush may have been related to the SPLA's heavily Dinka membership. She noted that just as many northerners trace their genealogy to Muhammad, the Dinka have an affinity for tracing "their ancestry to ancient Cush and therefore Jewish ancestry." The Dinka, in her view, conceptualized themselves as being like the Cushites—modern warriors who likely dreamed of creating a kingdom as their imagined predecessors had.[79] Thus, appropriating Cush may have been used to support two objectives: first, to invite people to perform ethnic and gender identities; and second, to justify the organization's objective of a united Sudan (Elhag Paul opined that using Cush may have related to Garang's attempt to sell his united objective to people in the North and South).[80] Such a desire would contradict the references to Cush and Isaiah leading up to and through independence, when they were linked to the prospect of political separation.

African religionists have long identified with the history of ancient Israel. Tudor Parfitt notes that Israelite racial identities were widely suggested and imposed throughout the world during colonialism. Often imbued with area- or group-specific genealogies and justifications, adopting an Israelite faith "was a way of creating . . . independence from colonial authority, of establishing a measure of racial superiority, of saying 'this is *our* religion.'" Olaudah Equiano suggested in his slave narrative that the Igbo might be related to the ancient Jews and that Igbo religion may have been a modern vestige of ancient Jewish faith. Recent Igbo history—namely, being a scattered minority in Nigeria's cities and experiencing the Biafran genocide—has drawn comparisons between their experiences and those of the Jews.[81] In the first Zulu history written by a Zulu author, Magema Fuze—who was cognizant of colonial analogies between Zulu practices and Israel's rituals—claimed that his people did not originate in southern Africa and agreed with the notion that "we black people came from the people of Israel."[82] In addition to the Igbo and Zulu, other African claims to links with biblical Israel include the Malian Inadan, who claim descent from David; Ethiopian claims that trace back to Solomon; and Ugandan traditions that claim a lineage of thirty-three kings tracing back to David.[83]

Finally, Salim C. Wilson was the first Dinka to publish the claim that they were descended from the ancient Israelites, an assertion he made in his circa 1939 *I Was a Slave*.[84] Decades later, Professor M. M. Ninan of Juba University wrote a comparative study of Kuku and Hebrew culture, suggesting that "a historical common contact theory or information exchange theory could not possibly explain such close similarity. We are thus led to the only alternative of common source . . . God did reveal himself to Kukus in a way similar to the Hebrews."[85]

COMPREHENSIVE PEACE AND THE DEATH OF MOSES

The SPLA Update illustrates that political theology did not end with the First Civil War; on the contrary, this newspaper produced by the revolutionary SPLM/SPLA disseminated content during the subsequent war that spiritualized the conflict in creative ways. Wendy James notes that the influence of old ideas about suffering, loss, and wandering in the bush may have joined with the concept of a war against evil, a combination that perhaps led to strange and novel visions, dreams, and enactments. "But through dreams and memories," she writes, "both strong Christian believers and others can find meaningful ways of connecting present experience with the past, and somehow rationalizing the world by looking back to . . . kinds of self-understanding which refer back to times long before the advent of the missionaries."[86] The religious references found throughout the Update reveal the SPLA's newspaper as a space where contributors creatively used theology to fashion a sense of self that was historical, spiritual, and divinely favored in the midst of war.

The Update's biblical references suggest that its editors wanted to use scripture to broadcast a narrative in which oppressed Sudanese obtain victory and liberation from the Khartoum government. Facing the reality of factionalism, invocations of Cush and ancient Israel not only provided a common heritage and reading of history but also invited readers to turn their gaze from challenges to a narrative of assured victory. Theology performed the political work of defining enemies and reinterpreting circumstances into biblical templates so that a trajectory ending with SPLM/A victory could be established and disseminated. While the Update's use of theology mirrored Khartoum's use of Islam in framing the war as a jihad, the SPLA's use of Christianity was not comparable in scale. Nevertheless, the Update's religious thought was similarly intended to transform the war into a spiritual contest for its readership within and outside Sudan.

There is room to consider how Sudanese invocations of Cush may parallel those by other African or diasporic religionists. The Africa Bible Commentary's coverage of Cush/Cushites offers insight into the meaning of Cush for African theologians. Edouard Nsiku, a Congolese Baptist, used the Isaiah prophecy to both argue that blacks and whites have been oppressive and that Africans have reason to hope: "Africa will turn to god in its misery . . . and its former glory will be restored (18:7). What a message of hope for our continent!"[87] Congolese Nupanga Weanzana noted that Cush could be considered Africa's ancestors, thereby widening the scope of the term to infer all Africans (and not just Sudanese).[88] In another instance Weanzana, along with the Kenyan Samuel Ngewa, Eritrean Tewoldemedhin Habtu, and Nigerian Zamani Kafang, used Cush's appearance in Psalm 7 to note that the psalmist speaks to the African Church "and reminds it of the role it should play in promoting justice."[89] In these ways, then, the *Commentary* frames Cush as being representative of Africa and, consequently, a reference point by which Africans can see themselves in scripture. Furthermore, there is the added assurance that Africans can look to Cush to provide hope for the present day. This perspective is consistent with Garang's use of the Cush marker to link the SPLM project with Pan-Africanism. Identifying Cush with Sudan not only provided Sudanese with historical legitimacy but also situated the nation in an African framework despite Khartoum's historical efforts to align itself with the Arab world. Cush, therefore, provided a biblical, African, and liberationist heritage for the SPLM.

This chapter suggests that more deeply examining diasporic print forms like the *Update* can advance our knowledge of religion's movement and sociopolitical usage in the African diaspora. Advances in communications and technology have facilitated the flow of cultures, peoples, and ideas to the point where a "global village" has become realized in the blurring of geographic and virtual spaces.[90] The *Update* connected Sudanese to people and developments back home and served as a printed space in which an imagined community of diasporic readers and contributors could be forged and exposed to the same religious ideas.

* * *

On January 9, 2005, the SPLM and Sudanese government signed the Comprehensive Peace Agreement (CPA). With John Garang and Vice President ʿAli Osman Muhammad Taha as the main negotiators, the CPA ended the Second Civil War. The agreement's main features included separate governance for the South, an even split of oil revenues between North and South, and a six-year transitional period to unity or separation. A southern referendum for unity or secession was mandated to take place in 2011. The issue of religion—which was, during the negotiations, the most contentious issue—was addressed, with Sharia law withdrawn from the South and non-Muslims in the North exempted from its enforcement. Though the boundary of the Abyei region was unresolved, the national assembly approved the agreement. Like the process leading up to the Addis Ababa Agreement, the church played an influential role in reaching peace, including ECS archbishop Daniel Deng serving as an architect and the Sudan Council of Churches advocating for peace and reconciliation.[91] The CPA catapulted Garang to further heights of adoration. The feeling in Khartoum when Garang was sworn in as first vice president of Sudan (and president of South Sudan) was triumphant. Millions came to see him. Christian elements imbued his swearing-in ceremony; he placed his left hand on a Bible, and cries of Alleluia accompanied his booming English oath. Field marshal al-Bashir and Muhammad Taha were sworn in in Arabic, with their hands on a Koran and accompanied by shouts of Allahu Akbar. One commentator noted that "the Southern Sudanese in the crowd went wild, perhaps at the substance of the words, more likely at the contrasts John evoked."[92]

The manner in which Garang's life ended cemented the Mosaic narrative. Despite the intimate relationship that Moses enjoyed with God, he was prohibited from entering the promised land after an act of disobedience (Num. 20:6-12). In Deuteronomy 31 Moses spoke before Israel and told them that Joshua would cross the Jordan River with them, and he died three chapters later on Mount Nebo. After Garang's swearing in, he returned from Khartoum and called all the important cabinet members. Salva Kiir, an early follower of Garang who had fought in the first war and stayed with him amid the factionalism of the second, was present.[93] Garang took Kiir by the arm and brought him aside. They talked for roughly two hours, with no one aware of what they were discussing. When they returned, Garang told the people that Kiir was their leader and charged him with the task of taking care of them. "That is why some people now," Bishop Ezekiel Diing expressed to me, "say Salva is Joshua, because of what they heard when Garang" spoke.[94] Garang decided to go to Uganda. He was about to leave for Kampala with his wife, Rebecca, when she refused to accompany him. After meeting with President Museveni, the Ugandan presidential helicopter carrying Garang back to Sudan crashed into a mountain in the Imatong Range. He died.[95] According to Diing, Moses and Garang had given their lives in the same way: "Moses end up his life on the mountain. . . . Garang also end up his life on the mountain. . . . When Moses . . . knew that he was living but that he was not going to continue . . . and he looked beyond at the land that the people had, but he will not cross, go back and talk to Joshua."[96]

Garang's funeral was held at Juba's All Saints Cathedral. Thousands of soldiers patrolled the streets, and President al-Bashir pledged that Khartoum would not back away from the peace agreement. Despite this showing of solidarity, anti-Arab sentiment was violently tangible. Much of Juba's Arab community fled the city after clashes resulted in the deaths of at least fifteen people. Many Muslim-owned shops were burned down. One man in Juba was quoted as saying, "The northerners hate us, we hate them, so we demand our own country."[97]

5

The Troubled Promised Land

In the 60s and 70s, our elders knew and called themselves by names but today we referrer [sic] to each other as Lado the Barri [sic], Chol the Dinka, Duoth the Nuer, etc. We are digressing in thinking instead of progressing. When are we going to stop this Stone Age behaviour so that once again South Sudan becomes a place of milk and honey and not multiple grave yards?

—Jimmy Onge Aremo, *Sudan Tribune*, February 19, 2015

The book of Exodus chronicles the story of the Hebrew leader Moses. As an infant, Moses was placed in a basket and sent down the Nile after all Jewish baby boys in Egypt were ordered to be killed. Seen by Pharaoh's daughter and retrieved by her slave, Moses was subsequently reared in luxury. One day Moses, now a grown man, became incensed at the sight of an Egyptian beating a Hebrew. Moses slayed the abuser and fled to Midian, presumably to spend the rest of his days in obscurity. God, however, had other plans. He appeared to Moses from a burning bush and commissioned the stutterer to lead his people out of bondage. After a series of plagues and the providential killing of every firstborn son in Egypt, Pharaoh—whose own son had been killed in the purge—acceded to Moses's request. After the Hebrew flight from Egypt had already commenced, Pharaoh had a change of heart and pursued the Israelites. In what is perhaps the Old Testament's most iconic scene, God parted the Red Sea before the fleeing host so that they could escape over dry land. When God unbridled the floodgates, Pharaoh's army was annihilated.[1] After forty years in the wilderness, Moses's successor Joshua led the chosen people into their promised land.

Ridley Scott's Hollywood adaptation *Exodus: Gods and Kings* debuted in 2014. Toward the end of the film, Moses—played by Christian Bale—sits down and talks to Joshua. Having just crossed the Red Sea with the rest of the Children of Israel, Moses acknowledged that they were as big as a nation of tribes. This concerned him. When Joshua questioned him about this, Moses looked at his comrade and retorted, "You have to ask?" "But we all have the same goal," responded Joshua. "We do now," said Moses. "What happens when we stop running?"[2] While that particular scene is rooted in creative license and is not found in the biblical account, it nevertheless points to the internal Israelite squabbling that the Bible does record following the Exodus. Despite the romantic Exodus narrative, the Pentateuch frames the Israelites as a grumbling, unfaithful people throughout their journey to Canaan. At the sight of the Egyptian pursuit, the Israelites derisively asked Moses if he had led them out to the desert because there were no graves in Egypt (Ex. 14:11). After entering the promised land, the Israelites experienced the period of the Judges, arguably the darkest era of their history before the Babylonian exile. Throughout the Old Testament are numerous reminders for the Israelites to remember God's liberating acts during the Exodus. These admonitions were not enough to make or keep them obedient.

Ugandan president Yoweri Museveni was the chief guest at the first anniversary of South Sudanese independence celebrations in Juba in July 2012. Recounting the history of the fight for independence and paying tribute to the SPLM, Museveni lamented the tendency among black people to be prone to division. He urged President Salva Kiir to reach a deal with the Sudanese government and used the Israelite example as a cautionary tale for South Sudanese: "Museveni has called on the people of South Sudan not to be like the Biblical children of Israel who were about to back-track to Egypt when faced with challenges. 'You should stand firm and make sure that judgment is attained. Be strong, the modern world doesn't have a place for the weak hearted,' he said."[3] Less than three years into independence—or, to use the Exodus idiom, three years after southerners had "stopped running"—the nation found itself at war again. In December 2013, a conflagration drawn heavily by ethnic lines (primarily Nuer v. Dinka) was kindled. What became of the rhetoric that the "Joshua" Kiir had led the nation into the promised land? What of all the flowery invocations of Cush and claims that Isaiah's ancient prophecy had been realized?

This chapter begins with a description of developments since the 2005 Comprehensive Peace Agreement (CPA). Division and enmity between southern factions persisted during the postwar years, and independence was not sufficient to keep some from recognizing serious challenges facing the country. Matters came to a head in December 2013, when violence broke out between members of the presidential guard, precipitating violence throughout the country between forces led by Salva Kiir and Riek Machar. Between then and 2018, tens of thousands died, more than two million fled to neighboring countries, and nearly two million more became internally displaced.[4]

The war debunked any notion that southerners felt a sense of pan-Christian solidarity strong enough to subsume ethnicity or prevent ethnic tension. And yet, the war produced a dynamic crucible of religious thought. As with earlier periods, Christian political imagination was not limited to ordained clergy but was formulated by lay politicians and civilians alike. The post-CPA period is distinct, however, for the efflorescence of ideas that appeared online. No longer limited to physical print media, online venues like the *Sudan Tribune* were spaces where those throughout the diaspora could make their expressions known. A second observation gleaned from this period is the endurance of an idea expressed during the condominium era—that intergroup fighting was a spiritual "evil" and that uniting under God was the solution to this problem. Unlike Fr. Attiyah's contention that all ethnicities were one in Christ, however, two bishops affirmed God's handiwork in diversity. Finally, the church's evolving but consistent proximity to political happenings mirrored the way in which political theology similarly evolved but remained consistently present. Various intellectuals found it fit to relate particular scriptures and theologies to the situation. Religious thought still functioned as a political technology despite the fundamentally changed scope of who and what constituted us and them, good and evil, heroes and villains.

COMPREHENSIVE PEACE TO CIVIL WAR

The end of the Second Civil War did not mask the realities of internal divisions and simmering problems. Since its founding, the SPLM struggled to maintain legitimate internal democratic practices and was forced to rely on tenuous alliances to maintain stability. The CPA was negotiated between the SPLM/A and Sudan's ruling National Congress Party; other opposition groups were excluded. Many southern groups were absorbed into the SPLM/A in the years that followed, but a joint platform reflecting the interests of an increasingly diverse membership was never adopted. Furthermore, divisions between combatants and communities following the 1991 Nasir split were not reconciled during the CPA period. The massive Nuer South Sudan Defence Forces (SSDF) was, like all other armed groups, required during the interim period to ally with the Sudan Alliance Forces (SAF) or SPLA, and violence between the SPLA and other southern armed groups continued. The 2006 Juba Declaration—which Kiir announced in his attempt to manage divisions—led to the SSDF's incorporation into the SPLA and other security services, as well as the creation of a more unified military front leading up to the referendum.[5]

In 2007 Rebecca Garang—widow of John Garang and minister of roads and transport for the government of South Sudan (GOSS)—called on people to support the CPA, calling it "the Bible of the marginalized communities." Despite accusations against senior government ministers (herself included), she encouraged people to have confidence in the GOSS's capacity to deliver expected services and emphasized the need for construction, public works, and the development of mass media to improve communication.[6] The following year, continued frustration at corruption and lack of development led journalist Roba Gibia to write a scathing editorial in the *Sudan Tribune*. Founded in 2003, the *Tribune* is a Paris-based nonprofit website that is run by independent Sudanese and international journalists and editors. Gibia compared GOSS members to the Jewish scribes during the time of Christ. The GOSS officials and leaders, Gibia contended, were behaving like the scribes and priests who claimed to be pure "but are the very people responsible for the suffering of their people, because they have cut off themselves from their own people and do not know their . . . day-to-day problems."[7] Gibia also noted that some southern ethnicities saw themselves as superior to other groups: "Tribalism and nepotism has infested GOSS which breeds corruption, and has become the definite enemy of South Sudanese."[8]

Gibia was joined a year later by Mawut Guarak, who also used the Bible in his antigovernment critique. Guarak had spent time as a child soldier and several years in a refugee camp before arriving in Syracuse, New York, as a Lost Boy in 2001. After attending Onondaga Community College, he earned a master's degree from SUNY-Binghamton.[9] In February 2009, the *Tribune* published his piece "Conflict of Interest?," in which he cited the fact that top government officials had been taking jobs as executives in oil and other mining companies. Many of these politicians, Guarak claimed, condemned corruption in the media. He noted that Jesus, as a teacher in

Jerusalem and Judea, asked his disciples how Satan could cast out Satan. Just as a house divided against itself cannot stand, a divided Satan cannot stand either (Mark 3:23–26). "Based on interpretation of the above verses," he argued, "it is hard . . . for a government official to serve public purposes in Juba and be [an] executive in major oil companies and expect to not be corrupted. How can regional officials . . . fight corruption when they are lobbying against government (as executive[s] in the oil companies)?"[10]

South Sudan faced manifold issues. While all children were supposed to have access to formal or informal education by 2010 (with a new curriculum), education continued to suffer from untrained teachers, inadequate school buildings, overcrowded classes, and lack of educational materials. Healthcare facilities were unevenly distributed. Economic recovery and progress occurred primarily in urban areas. One study found that in 2009 alone, intra-South violence had resulted in 2,500 deaths and 350,000 displaced people. Another study noted three uprisings by dissident SPLM/A members. Following the conclusion of the electoral process in April 2010, General George Deng—a former independent candidate for the Jonglei state governorship and former SPLA deputy chief of general staff—left Bor with his soldiers and clashed with SPLA troops. Human Rights Watch documented rights violations during the elections and reported growing instability in the central Equatoria, Jonglei, Unity, and western Bahr el-Ghazal states.[11]

Amid frustration at the national leadership and overall state of affairs, a national anthem was drafted that highlighted the continued salience of Christian symbolism. By late summer 2010, the government, along with some individuals, began to brainstorm ideas for the anthem. The task was officially entrusted to the 2011 Machar-chaired taskforce. After conducting an anthem workshop, Col. Malaak Ayuen—who led the information and public relations desk at SPLA's general headquarters—appeared on South Sudan TV to report the outcome of his group's efforts. Ayuen explained that the group preferred to refer to South Sudan as the "Land of Cush."[12] An early draft of the anthem—written by forty-nine poets—followed guidelines set by the government and army and included the following lyrics:

> Oh God! We praise and glorify you / For your grace upon Cush, / The land of great warriors. . . . / Lord bless South Sudan! / Oh black warriors! / Let's stand up in silence and respect, / Saluting millions of martyrs whose / Blood cemented our national foundation. . . . / Oh Eden! / Land of milk and honey and hard-working people, / Uphold us united in peace and harmony.[13]

The seven elements to be considered in the anthem would include History, Land, People, Struggle, Sacrifices, Destination, and Flag. The religious components dealt most specifically with History, People, and Land. According to Ayuen, God was the architect of ancient world civilization and the glory, ethics, and values of South Sudanese history. The land was the Garden of Eden blessed with riches like oil, abundant water, mountains, and the people who loved their land. The South Sudanese, furthermore, "are Biblical Africans as revealed in Isaiah 18; have unity in diversity [and are] people with determination, commitment to hard work and nation building."[14]

The anthem was met with criticism over what was perceived to be a flawed, even dangerous use of religious idioms. Gordon Buay, a signatory of the 2008 Washington Declaration that merged the SPLM and SSDF, wrote an editorial arguing for the removal of military officers from the anthem committee. Buay noted that neither Major General Kuol Deim Kuol nor Colonel Malaak—the two men who came up with the "Land of Cush" idea— were biblical historians who could defend the claim that southern ethnic groups were the only Cushitic people in the Horn of Africa. The question in the minds of educated southerners, Buay continued, was why those officers would title the anthem "Land of Cush" if South Sudanese were not Africa's only Cushitic people. He argued that the idea to use Cush was rooted in John Garang, who used the Good News Bible (which references Cush as "Sudan" in its version of Isaiah 18) as propaganda to support his argument for the creation of a New Sudan. Buay asserted that since "the SPLA officers do not read books on biblical history, they think Dr. John Garang was a religious expert although most educated Southerners know that John Garang was [an] Agro-economist, not biblical historian."[15] Buay's sentiments were echoed by Deng Riak Khoryoam, who argued in the *Tribune* that South Sudan was the best name for the new nation. Khoryoam argued against the use of Cush because of its ambiguities: "Kush" simply meant "black" like *Sudan*, and southerners were not the only black peoples in the Sudan or Africa. He also noted that Cush was not appropriate because people had historically taken up arms to liberate Sudan, not Cush.[16] In the end, Cush was not chosen as the country's official name, and many of the religious idioms in the anthem's early draft form were removed. Only the mention of God remained in the anthem's first and last lines.[17]

The independence referendum took place between January 9 and 15, 2011. Toward the end of the referendum, Benjamin Mkapa, chair of the UN secretary general's Panel on the Referenda in the Sudan, stated that it had gone quite smoothly and even exceeded expectations. His briefing was followed by that of Haile Menkerios, special representative of the secretary general and head of the UN's Mission in the Sudan, who reported that the Southern Sudan Referendum Commission would announce final results on February 7 and any appeals a week later. In the end, 98.3 percent of participants voted for independence. Despite the elimination of Cush from the national anthem, the Isaiah 18 prophecy continued to hold great weight. In February 2012, the *Tribune* reported that southern Christians were planning a pilgrimage to the Holy Land and to present gifts on Mount Zion. Vice President Machar's press secretary conveyed that church leaders had explained to him that the pilgrimage had been promised by God in Isaiah's prophecy three millennia ago.[18]

Interestingly—and perhaps not coincidentally—Kiir chose Israel as one of the sites for his first presidential visits. Israel had been one of the first nations to recognize South Sudan's independence. Though his December 20, 2011, trip lasted less than twenty-four hours, Kiir met with Deputy Foreign Minister Danny Ayalon, President Shimon Peres, Prime Minister Benjamin Netanyahu, Foreign Minister Avigdor Lieberman, and Defense Minister Ehud Barak. In addition to sharing that South Sudan and Israel "shared values" and conquered "similar struggles," Kiir made sure to note his enthusiasm to—representing all South Sudanese—"set foot in the Promised Land."[19]

DESCENT TO WAR

Despite the thrill of independence, dissatisfaction increased. Many blamed the national leadership for failing to deliver on important services.[20] On the first independence anniversary, the *Tribune* published a piece by Jacob K. Lupai that listed corruption, illiteracy, insecurity, and tribalism/nepotism as the country's categories of challenges. Lupai paid most attention to tribalism and nepotism, noting that one ethnic group controlled about 43 percent of ministerial positions, even though more than fifty groups may have participated in the liberation struggle. He concluded, "It is an open question whether it is tribalism/nepotism that influences appointments or [whether] they are made on merit."[21] In a disagreement with Khartoum over how much the new nation should pay to export oil using Sudan's infrastructure and port, South Sudan decided to shut off its oil production six months after independence. Allegations of corruption were legitimated when President Kiir admitted that more than seventy officials had stolen $4 billion. When southern troops entered a contested oil field, clashes began that spurred fear of war. After threats from the United States, troops pulled out and oil was turned back on eighteen months later.[22]

In October 2012, Zechariah Manyok Biar heard a message in his church that "sent chilly air" through his bones, something that made him fearful about the country's future.[23] Biar's life points to the influential role of Christian networks and infrastructure. As a twelve-year-old, Biar signed up to join the army and walked hundreds of miles to an SPLA camp in Ethiopia. United Nations aid brought some gospel-bearing teachers, and Biar was baptized in 1989. He became an army chaplain in 1994 and, five years later, was offered a chance to continue his education by his battalion commander. He enrolled in a two-year Bible college and subsequently earned a theology diploma from a three-year Bible college (Timothy Training Institute). Biar eventually encountered Kansas native Mike Smith, who was doing medical mission work in Sudan. Smith asked Biar to help him learn Dinka and Arabic, and as a result of their connection, Biar earned a bachelor's degree from Kampala International University. Smith used his contacts with Abilene Christian University (ACU) to help Biar acquire a scholarship to cover his graduate school costs there. In the process of earning his master's from ACU's Graduate School of Theology, Biar wrote columns on governance for Sudanese newspapers. He graduated in 2010 and later became executive director in South Sudan's Interior Ministry.[24]

On the last Sunday of October 2012, Biar wrote that many people had called his pastor, asking him to advise other preachers to refrain from criticizing the government from the pulpit. Most recently, he had been called by the president's office, which asked him to do the same. Earlier that month, a journalist from a popular Juba radio program had told Biar that he had been repeatedly called by security officials and told that discussion topics must first be licensed by National Security. This led Biar to state his belief that

> [Kiir] would be the last person to do this. However, I could be wrong if his Office can call pastors to stop them from preaching biblical chapters which criticize leaders. The Bible . . . talks about good and bad leadership . . . why are preachers prevented from talking about good governance today when we know they were encouraged by the same leaders to talk about it during the North-South civil war? Or is it because the leaders then were in Khartoum and not in Juba?[25]

The church, to be sure, did collaborate with the South Sudanese government during the CPA period; pulpits were used to encourage people to participate in the 2008 census, the 2010 elections, and the 2011 referendum. The South Sudan Council of Churches, founded in 1990 by the region's

Christian churches, actually led efforts that proved quite influential in the CPA and was involved in the process that led to the referendum. It was not the first time that the government had had direct contact with the church regarding the nature of disseminated messages. In 2009, a government minister had asked churches to assist the government in preaching a message of peace and in holding reconciliation initiatives to foster unity in the lead-up to the referendum.[26] Yet, this particular attempt to influence pulpit messages appeared to compel Biar to lament that "I am now [more] afraid than before that Juba is going back to Khartoum."[27]

Infringement on church messaging became a serious issue for Juba's Bakhita Radio during the 2005–13 period. Founded in 2006, Bakhita Radio was the Catholic Radio Network's first and central station (the CRN is owned by the Sudan Catholic Bishops' Conference). Sister Sierra, its first director, described the station as "a significant and vital forum for information and entertainment[, allowing] people to express their views as citizens and as Christians . . . our Radio station engaged on civic education, gender, health, and religious programs, prayer vigils, meetings, and training workshops."[28] Martin Agwella, the Archdiocese of Juba's secretary general from 2006 to 2012, noted that the radio project was intended to contribute to the work of peacebuilding and reconciliation following the long civil war: "A community radio that would give ordinary people voice regarding issues"—such as those of a political, sociocultural, or economic nature—"that affect their lives."[29] And yet, Agwella notes that the station found itself in the crosshairs of security operatives who did not want some programs to be aired. "Our radio staff were frequently harassed, arrested. . . . I was involved in meeting and talking with key security officials and concerned offices at the ministry of information regarding those unfortunate incidences." He explained that problems were often settled without reaching the offices of the president, the ministers of information and security, or the Catholic archbishop. While Sr. Sierra similarly noted that "Bakhita Radio was often under siege," she offered that "with a team of Sudanese personnel, most of them women, we stood strong in the face of confrontation, political pressure and harassment from police and other government forces."[30]

CIVIL WAR

In time, Kiir's actions became increasingly sweeping. He reshuffled the army, retired many generals, and stripped Machar of his vice presidential powers in July 2013. Kiir also replaced most of the cabinet, dissolved some key party institutions, and suspended SPLM secretary general Pagan Amum pending a corruption investigation. Contentious reshuffling of state-level party and national leadership even led in one instance to an armed confrontation between SPLM members in the Upper Nile parliament. Sacked officials tried to fight back. On December 6, 2013, Rebecca Garang, Pagan Amum, and many dismissed cabinet members held a press conference in Juba denouncing the SPLM's lack of direction. On December 14, at a meeting of the SPLM's National Liberation Council, Kiir gained approval for Amum's removal and for future votes to be done by show of hands rather than secret balloting. Dismissed officials and their supporters boycotted the following day's session.[31]

On the evening of December 15, 2013, a fight broke out between Dinka and Nuer soldiers of the presidential guard in a military barracks near Juba's city center. Sporadic fighting continued throughout the night before order was restored the following morning. While the government blamed Machar for planning a coup attempt, he responded that the violence had begun when Dinka (Kiir's ethnic group) soldiers tried to disarm Nuer (Machar's ethnic group) soldiers.[32] That the conflict had the presidential guard at its epicenter presented a saddening irony. Known to Jubans as the Tigers, the guard was a multiethnic unit meant to bind members of various ethnic groups.[33]

"Riek W" was not openly known as a Nuer to his colleagues in the presidential guard. In sharing how the fighting between Nuer and Dinka Tigers developed into anti-Nuer civilian violence throughout the city, he stated that "they took people who were not soldiers and tied their hands and shot them. I saw this with my own eyes, I was there wearing the same uniform as them." Afraid for his life and frightened by civilian murders, he abandoned his post in the presidential compound the weekend after the violence broke out. Stating that the curfew was being used as a period to remove bodies, Riek claimed to have seen "large trucks" towing bodies.[34] Machar's house was bombarded and surrounded. Jickson Gatjang, a distant relative of Machar's who was in the compound that night, stated that the buildings had been destroyed and that members of Machar's bodyguard were executed before more general bloodletting commenced.[35] "When they know you are Nuer they don't have any more questions," he said. "It's just a bullet to your head."[36]

The following day, Kiir—dressed in Tiger battalion uniform—announced on national television that Machar had attempted a coup, that the government was in full control of the security situation in Juba, and that forces were pursuing the attackers. He also stated that an overnight curfew would be imposed and remain in effect indefinitely. Eleven senior figures were arrested for their alleged involvement within two weeks' time. While Machar escaped and refuted any involvement, he soon declared himself leader of the armed opposition movement, SPLM/A in Opposition (SPLA-IO). The SPLA-IO quickly seized control of significant parts of Jonglei—where fighting between Dinka and Nuer also broke out in a military barracks—as well as the Upper Nile and Unity states. Fighting also spread to other areas.[37] Concomitant with the spread of violence was the increasingly apparent ethnic tenor of the maelstrom. With reports of ethnically targeted killings filtering out from Juba and reaching areas like the Nuer-dominated Unity state, copycat mayhems occurred.[38] By late December, the *Guardian* reported that the UN base in Juba already housed ten thousand people. A handmade sign hung from rolls of razor wire with words of solace: "The lord is our best defender."[39]

The White Army (WA) emerged as one of the prominent faces of the anti-Dinka violence. Although the WA was not a unified organization, people began referring to Nuer-speaking militias as the WA in 1991. Used when describing groups of armed civilians who were purportedly loyal to Nuer-speaking prophet Wutnyang Gatatek, the *White Army* descriptor has broadened to refer to all Nuer-speaking militias who are not members of a salaried, uniformed army.[40] When in 1991 Machar and Lam Akol broke from the SPLM/A, the WA was involved in the Bor Massacre that year, which claimed the lives of roughly two thousand Dinka civilians. This event led to some of the most ferocious fighting of the Second Civil War, the increasingly ethnic division of southern forces, and the targeting of civilian populations based on ethnicity.[41] In response to the systematic violence levied on Nuer by Dinka elements in the presidential guard and other security forces, the WA targeted Dinka in more than twelve locations. In one instance, a force of two thousand Lou Nuer youths—WA elements—overran a UN base in Jonglei and killed at least twenty people (mainly Dinka government officials and two UN peacekeepers). By late December, an estimated twenty-five thousand members of the WA were reported to be marching toward a contested state capital.[42]

In May 2014 the UN Security Council shifted the mission's mandate from nation building to civilian protection, granting UN troops the right to use force. Two months later, the Security Council declared that South Sudan's food crisis was the worst in the world (violence had prevented farmers from planting or harvesting crops). In February 2017 a famine was declared in

South Sudan, the world's first since 2011. Armed conflict, low harvests, and skyrocketing food prices were blamed for the crisis. While the country was declared to no longer be in a state of famine by June 2017, a UN-backed report noted that the situation was still extreme.[43]

* * *

Peace talks began in January 2014. Responding quickly to the conflict, three envoys (Ambassador Seyoum Mesfin of Ethiopia, General Lazarus Sumbei-ywo of Kenya, and Sudan's General Mohammad Ahmed Mustafa al-Dhabi) shuttled between Juba, opposition-controlled territory, and Addis Ababa, where peace talks were held. Negotiations produced a ceasefire in January 2014 that was violated almost immediately with the partial recapture of Malakal. Mediation efforts were handicapped by the presence of Ugandan troops supporting Salva Kiir's side. Peace deals continued to materialize and evaporate, with Kiir and Machar reaching four agreements by early July 2014 that each fell through in a matter of days. Both parties and other splinter groups violated the ceasefires on multiple occasions. March 5, 2015, was set as a deadline for Kiir and Machar to sign a comprehensive peace agreement, but they could not agree on issues like power sharing and security arrangement. The 2015 national elections were postponed, and in late March 2015, MPs passed Constitutional Amendment Bill 2015, extending President Kiir's term until 2018.[44]

Kiir and Machar signed a peace agreement on August 26, 2015, following several rounds of negotiations supported by the Intergovernmental Authority on Development (IGAD) and under threat of international sanctions. As the first step toward ending the conflict, Machar returned to Juba on April 26, 2016, and was sworn in as vice president. Violence between the government and opposition groups broke out yet again just months later. Scores of people were again displaced, Machar fled the country, and Kiir installed a new vice president, General Taban Deng Gai (one of Machar's deputies, who now claimed to lead the SPLA-IO).[45] While yet another ceasefire was signed on December 21, 2017, US ambassador to the UN Nikki Haley stated that Salva Kiir had violated the agreement days later by preventing millions from receiving aid despite a pledge of unencumbered access and by promoting three generals sanctioned by the Security Council for massacring civilians. In January 2018, Haley stated that the United States was stopping its support for Kiir, calling him "an unfit partner." She urged the

Security Council to support an arms embargo, which the United States established by early February.[46]

In June 2018, Kiir and Machar participated in negotiations that were mediated by bordering states Sudan and Uganda. The following month the two belligerents signed the Khartoum Declaration of Agreement, a settlement that included a ceasefire and promise to negotiate a power-sharing agreement to conclude the conflict. In August and at long last, Kiir and Machar signed one last ceasefire and power-sharing agreement. This agreement was followed by the Revitalized Agreement on the Resolution of the Conflict in South Sudan—an arrangement signed by the government, Machar, and other rebel factions. This Revitalized Agreement reinstated Machar to his former VP role and included a new power-sharing structure. Machar returned to the country in October 2018 for a nationwide celebration to commemorate the end of the war.[47]

The war's statistics tell a sordid tale. Less than two weeks after the initial violence, UN special representative for South Sudan Hilde Johnson stated that more than one thousand people had been killed. By early July 2014, the *Economist* reported that there were at least ten thousand dead. Added to those killed are those who sustained violent wounds. By early January 2014, the World Health Organization had documented 2,566 cases of gunshot wounds across six of the country's ten states, and by early February, the UN Office for the Coordination of Humanitarian Affairs counted 4,895 patients who had been treated for gunshot wounds since December 15. By early January 2014, more than two thousand people were fleeing to Uganda per day, while more than thirty thousand had already fled to neighboring countries like Kenya, Uganda, Ethiopia, and Sudan. This number was dwarfed by the more than two hundred thousand internally displaced, including sixty thousand at UN compounds. By mid-July 2014 one million were said to have fled their homes, with the number housed at UN compounds having risen to one hundred thousand. As of late February 2018—a little over four years after the first shots were fired—the Council on Foreign Relations estimated that more than fifty thousand had been killed and four million displaced.[48]

WARTIME RELIGIOUS POLITICS

In April 2014, people flocked to churches to celebrate Easter. President Kiir, a Catholic, marked Good Friday at Juba's Kator Cathedral. The service was attended by several government ministers and foreign diplomats. In his remarks, Kiir called for forgiveness and the burying of political differences. "As Christians and people of God," he said, "we should pray hard that this country celebrate the next Easter in peace." Paulino Lukudu Loro, the archbishop of Juba Diocese, conducted a prayer service at the cathedral that day.[49] Three years earlier, Loro had co-led the October 2011 symposium "One Church from Every Tribe, Tongue and People" at Juba's Nyakuron Cultural Centre. The title was borrowed from Revelation 7:9, where John describes his apocalyptic vision of an innumerable multitude from every tribe, tongue, and people dressed in white, holding palms, and standing before the throne and the Lamb. Organized by the Catholic Church, Loro led the symposium with Cardinal Gabriel Zubeir Wako.[50] In the symposium's opening address, Loro delivered a powerful argument concerning diversity and unity in the new nation:

> We cannot—and must not—be afraid of our tribes. Unless we recognise and believe in our tribes first of all as gifts of God, we will have a problem, and we may fight because of our tribal background. . . . We must recognise ourselves indeed as a part of our tribe, so that we will be able to be together in honesty. It is useless for us to deny ourselves, "Oh, let us not mention our tribe and background." Wrong! We are then hiding something. We are what we are. . . . If I realise myself, and each one of you in your tribe, that you are what you are and that we can be together, then we can make one nation from every tribe, tongue and people.[51]

At the Easter 2014 service, approximately two-and-a-half years after his comments (and months after violent ethnic conflict had exploded in Juba), Archbishop Loro applied elements of the resurrection story to the contemporary situation. "The message of Easter is a message of man finally returning to the love and care that he used to enjoy with his Father before he sinned," he shared. "If all of us can remember that the Lord has freed us, being reconciled with God and with one another but as long as we are missing out on that fact, we will continue being alienated from each other and from our God." Claiming that politicians seemed to be losing sight of the fact that they had only one country, Loro observed that the conflict showed that politicians lacked tolerance and respect for human rights: "There are some selfish individuals in our midst [who] have got power and money . . . young people, unfortunately, who are not having anything to do, are easily bought and they start to engage in violence . . . if we blow [the country] up . . . we will have no place to run to."[52]

Despite conflicting reports regarding the new nation's religious composition, Christianity is South Sudan's primary faith; a 2012 Pew Research

Center report estimated that approximately 60 percent of the country was Christian, followed by 33 percent who followed African traditional religions, 6 percent Muslim, and the remainder unaffiliated.[53] The remarks made by President Kiir and Archbishop Loro at the Easter service are but one example of efforts made by the government, church officials, and laypeople to inject Christian thought into comments concerning the conflict. Ranging from outright condemnations (of Kiir, Machar, and the government more broadly) to pleas for peace, these episodes illustrate the continued utility that South Sudanese have found in using the Bible and theology to levy political messages. Those who have opined that God is central to any chance of peace in this ethnically driven conflict subliminally hearken back to the days of the Nugent School, when officials there similarly expressed the need for God to achieve transethnic amity. Thus, not only has politicized Christian thought been unrestricted to the two civil wars with Khartoum, it has also continued to dovetail with the pre-1956 issue of intrasouthern relations.

* * *

Church leaders—at least within the conflict's first year—were hitherto unable to seriously influence politicians and generals. The warring groups refused church participation in peace negotiations until June 2014 (six months into the conflict), and the parties repeatedly boycotted subsequent talks to avoid participation from religious groups and other non-armed actors. Anglican bishop Enoch Tombe said, "The political leaders think that their side of the story is always correct. [They ask us], why do you speak as if you are with the rebels?" Jason Patinkin reported that some believed that top politicians' disrespect for the church reflected a deeper problem that hit at the core of South Sudan's traditionally accepted history—one that posited the independence struggle as a fight for religious freedom for the primarily Christian South against Khartoum's Islamist government. This, however, was inaccurate—the SPLA was initially backed by Ethiopian Communists and began as a Marxist-influenced movement. Bishop Tombe opined that the war's atrocities destroyed the myth that the SPLA were Christian liberators. Noting that the politicians could not claim to be Christian, Tombe stated, "Even if they go to church on Sunday they are not guided by Christian values only. They may be Christian by name, but Christian values have not really penetrated."[54]

Patinkin, reporting for the *Christian Science Monitor* in December 2014, noted that churches or clergy were attacked in Juba, Bor, and Malakal—locations that witnessed some of the most vicious fighting. Priests were murdered, and civilians were occasionally slaughtered in the very churches where they had sought safety. Catholic radio stations in government-controlled areas were censored and shut down (along with staff being imprisoned), and government security agents attempted to quell a December 2014 peace march in Juba led by the Catholic Church to mark the war's one-year anniversary. Rebel hardliners reportedly threatened or attacked pastors who preached moderation in their areas.[55] Four years later Vice President James Wani Igga accused priests of promoting violence, while others have accused the church of being inactive during the conflict.[56]

These criticisms notwithstanding, some members of the warring parties (and, postconflict, formerly warring parties) reached out to or worked with the church. In 2016 Nadia Arop, national minister of youth and sport, called on churches to pray for peace in the country. Accompanying Arop's call that year was a report that Kiir, first VP Machar, and second VP Wani Igga were expected to attend a special prayer function for peace and healing that May. Organized by the South Sudan Council of Churches, a source close to the SSCC shared that the event would be held in Juba and presided over by church leaders, including Catholic archbishop Loro and the Anglican Church's Daniel Deng Bul. A source familiar with the program disclosed that prayers would usher in the new cabinet and scriptures would be employed to lessen mistrust between political leaders.[57] The report concerning the aforementioned prayer breakfast was published in the *Christian Times*, a South Sudanese fortnightly newspaper that Anglican priest John Daau launched in 2004. Printed in Nairobi and with offices in Juba, it is also published online.[58]

The following year Rev. General Mabil de Awar Yuot, the head of the National Police Chaplaincy Service, visited the Juba office of Samaritan's Purse (an evangelically minded organization that, as of 2018, operated relief projects from five primary bases in the country). Yuot wanted Samaritan's Purse to train his chaplains. The first training was held months later in Aweil state, and others were later held in Juba and Mundri. In the latter two sessions, Samaritan's team trained more than one hundred government leaders, including officials, members of the military, police chaplains, and others. The Reverend Moses Telar, director general of the Ministry of Religious Affairs, stated, "Let us take the Bible instead of the gun," and "Our country needs to change, even our minds need to change. As chaplains, it is your role. Let us disarm the heart. God is with us."[59] In 2018, the warring parties negotiating in Addis Ababa called on the SSCC to help them overcome their differences (something the IGAD, working as mediator, had failed to accomplish).[60]

The council's work points to other work that the church conducted during the war. From the outset priests, pastors, and nuns protected civilians from extremists on both sides and occasionally stood up to armed men while unarmed themselves. Bishop Emmanuel Murye of the Anglican Diocese of Kajo Keji acknowledged that several partners had supported them in education, trauma-healing workshops, empowerment for girls who had dropped out of school, and other areas. The SSCC—which, according to John Ashworth, "took a breather to rebuild and repair" after the 2005 Comprehensive Peace Agreement—had a renewed impetus that included implementing an Action Plan for Peace, recognizing the need for a long-term peace process to resolve both the current conflict and unresolved effects of previous conflicts. The SSCC shared that this plan could continue for as long as twenty years.[61]

Perhaps the most compelling actions taken by clerical figures occurred in the arena of discourse. Clergy urged civilians not to blindly follow the warlords, lamented politicians' disregard for those who had died, called the nation's leaders "dry bones" that required spiritual renewal, and termed the fighting "evil."[62] The decision to spiritualize the violence in a negative light is particularly significant given a similar strategy employed by Llewellyn Gwynne decades earlier with respect to ethnic conflict. In December 2016, Bishop Isaiah Dau of the Pentecostal Church of Sudan spoke during a Christmas celebration organized by the Presbyterian Evangelical Church in Hai Jalaba, Juba. Warning South Sudanese and politicians to cease all violence, Bishop Dau told a cheering congregation, "Shedding blood is the work of the devil and anybody who is killing people is doing the work of the devil." Peace, he declared, could not be achieved through donors but only if people reconciled with God and one another. "Men and women who do not have peace with God try to make peace[;] that is why there is no peace." He identified love of God as the medicine for the nation's tribalism. The same *Christian Times* piece that reported Dau's fiery sermon noted that Awien Mawien, deputy speaker of the Transitional National Legislative Assembly, said that South Sudan was suffering because of its people's sins.[63]

Dau was joined in his condemnation of violence by a seminarian whose piece, "'No More of This!' Jesus' Condemnation of Violence and the War," appeared in the *Christian Times* in March 2018. The writer referenced the Gospel passage in which political and religious leaders sent armed men to arrest Christ on Holy Thursday (Mark 14:43). After recounting the facts that Jesus was found in the garden, Judas identified him with a kiss, and the soldiers subsequently led him away, the writer opined:

> This is similar to what is happening in South Sudan today. Leaders are seeking to protect their power or gain power by shedding innocent blood. Soldiers are arresting and targeting people in the nighttime. Though they call Jesus "teacher," they honor his name falsely, just as Judas did. They have robbed hungry villagers, raped innocent schoolgirls, forced boys to commit atrocities . . . such brutal violence is not from God. On the contrary, it is from the devil who "was a murderer from the beginning" (John 8:44).

Further on, the seminarian referred to the episode when Peter attempted to protect Christ by cutting off the ear of one of Jesus's arresting soldiers. Noting Jesus's command for Peter to put his sword away, the writer offered that "in this, South Sudan's hour of darkness, we must trust in God, not in weapons. Our example is Jesus, a healer and a peacemaker—not a killer. Though the darkness may last for 'an hour,' Jesus will shatter it and conquer death."[64] Three years later, none other than Salva Kiir would make a public declaration of forgiveness in the postwar state. During the fall of 2018, thousands of people cheered around Juba's John Garang Memorial Park celebrating a new peace deal. Machar, returned from exile, took the stage with Kiir. After the president reiterated that the war had ended, Kiir promised that he had forgiven his rival and that Machar had returned the favor. "To forgive," Kiir told the crowd, "is not an act of cowardice. It is a Christian obligation."[65]

In Daniel Deng's 2015 Christmas message, the Anglican archbishop explained that peace was needed in Sudan and South Sudan and that it simply was not possible without God. "We need to liberate this country spiritually from the moral decay. . . . It is better to be peace builders and makers than being destroyers of God given peace. . . . God will heal our land and us. . . . We are hostile against each other. Time has come to rediscover love of God[,] the source of our healing." By asking for God's forgiveness, Deng stated, they opened themselves for his love, compassion, and grace. He, like Fr. Attiyah during the second war against Khartoum, used Galatians 3:28 to state that Christ broke down the barriers that divided them "racially, tribally and ethnically; no Jew or Gentile, slave or free, male or female[;] all are one in Christ." Later on in the message, however, Deng commented on ethnicity's relationship with the divine in a way that echoed Archbishop Loro's words four years earlier. "Let us celebrate our diversity," he said, "by honoring one another. Our diversity is a God given thing; we did not make ourselves to be who we are in our various ethnic groups."[66] In this way, Deng used Galatians to confirm the overarching unity of faith that transcended ethnicity while affirming that none other than God had created diversity, diversity should be celebrated, and such celebration is done by honoring one another.

PARTISAN READINGS

Kong Tut used scripture to levy his displeasure with the president in "Theological Reflections on Juba Nuer Massacre." Posted shortly after Christmas 2014, Tut's essay cited Herod's killing of infant boys as an occasion to draw a direct parallel to the ethnic killings in Juba that had initiated the conflict. While Herod ordered the infanticides to kill Jesus, Kiir—according to Tut—ordered the killing of innocent Nuer out of hatred and as a means to hunt down "the democratic reformer" Machar. Tut added that the book of Revelation stated that while Christ was in the desert, the beast attempted to destroy Jesus with his messenger but to no avail. Machar, according to Tut's logic, represented the baby Jesus, while Kiir was the beast, and Museveni the messenger. To this end, the Egyptian desert was analogous to Unity, Jonglei, and Upper Nile. While Jesus began his ministry in the Gospels of Matthew and Luke by proclaiming the nearness of God's Kingdom and removing all oppression, "reflections have it that Riek Machar's address of Pagak Conference marks the road forward to the end."[67] There are moments, to be sure, where the accuracy of Tut's biblical references must be called into question; namely, Christ's appearance in the desert in the book of Revelation and the appearance of the beast and messenger in the Nativity story. Nevertheless, it is useful to recognize his attempt to provide spiritual strength behind his benevolent presentation of Machar and villainous portrayal of Kiir.

Prorebel supporters like Akol and Tut were countered by Joseph de Tuombuk and Elhag Paul, who have each been published in online venues, including the *Sudan Tribune, Pachodo.org, Gurtong,* and *South Sudan News Agency.*[68] Tuombuk wrote a piece, "Tribalism in South Sudan: Let's Read from Matthew 7:1-5," published on *Gurtong* in January 2015, in response to an article by Machar spokesperson James Gatdet Dak. Tuombuk stated that tribalism in South Sudan was a fact of life and that everyone hailed from some tribe; indeed, "even the Israelites had twelve tribes." The problem, according to Tuombuk, begins "when highly educated people like Riek Machar . . . try to use our cherished diversity as a way to short-circuit the democratic process and access power through illegal means." He cited the fact that the rebellion's top command was 92 percent Nuer and that Machar had relied heavily on anti-Dinka sentiment to rally a Nuer section "to his unholy cause." On the other hand, Kiir had an administration that was unprecedented for its diversity. As Machar and his supporters had killed Nuer who stood up for their country rather than their ethnic group, Tuombuk returned to the Matthew scripture and charged that "Riek has lost the moral high ground to call Kiir's administration some kind of a tribal entity led by corrupt 'Dinka clan.' Riek has demonstrated that he can use tribal politics as a means to an end: destroying our nascent democracy."[69]

Tuombuk was joined in his anti-Machar criticism by Elhag Paul. Paul accused Machar of wearing layers of disguise, which were gradually being peeled off to reveal his true character. Though Machar offered hope by embracing democracy and federalism, Paul noted that he was now out for his own personal gain, used dictatorial approaches, and had no intention to deliver on promises to some of the country's oppressed people. "The saying that a leopard can not change its spots," Paul contended, "seems to be true in the case of Machar and the SPLM leaders. . . . Machar can not change. . . . He has once again squandered a golden opportunity for him to wash himself clean from his controversial past to emerge as a true leader."[70] Paul informed me that the leopard phrase was a common expression that was suitable for his article and not necessarily used because of any biblical roots.[71] However, the leopard-spot idiom is found in the book of Jeremiah 13:23 (NIV): "Can an Ethiopian change his skin or a leopard its spots? Neither can you do good who are accustomed to doing evil."

* * *

"The blood of the tribe," remarked Bishop Tombe in 2014, "has become thicker than the blood of the Christ."[72] After five decades of racial and religious conflict with North Sudanese, South Sudan's early independence years were wracked by internal violence rent along ethnic lines. Any notion that southerners felt a sense of pan-Christian solidarity strong enough to subsume ethnicity or prevent ethnic tension was violently debunked. And yet, the war—rather than spurring widespread disavowals of Christianity—produced a dynamic crucible of religious thought. From contextual interpretations of specific scriptures to more general theological applications to fit the situation, a diverse array of lay and clerical figures used similarly varied media to make their expressions known. As one sign of the differing opinions that emerged from the war, Tombe's aforementioned comment contrasts with Bishop Murye's message, that "though we are a multi-tribal nation, we are one in Christ," and Bishop Deng's 2015 Christmas plea:

> Christ welcome[s] every tribe and nation because God has purchased us all with His blood. . . . God created and placed us here in South Sudan to live together in peace and harmony. . . . [W]e have been prisoners of our own ethnic violence and wars. . . . Let pride of tribe or clan or class . . . not obscures [sic] our focus on the future for this nation. . . . As we celebrate the birth of Christ, let us celebrate one another, as one family of God. . . . Let us celebrate our diversity by honoring one another. Our diversity is a God given thing; we did not make ourselves to be who we are in our various ethnic groups.[73]

While the independence years have been largely destructive, the period has nevertheless witnessed a vibrant environment for religious discourse.

The religious thought examined in this chapter contains elements that illustrate not only the post-CPA period's unique nature but also its constituent position within the region's longer train of political theology. As with earlier periods, Christian political imagination was not limited to ordained clergy but was formulated by lay politicians and civilians alike. What makes the post-CPA period different in this respect, however, was the efflorescence of ideas that could be found online. No longer limited to physical print spaces like personal correspondences or newspapers, venues like the *Sudan Tribune* and *Christian Times* continued online in the tradition of the *SPLA Update* as spaces where those throughout the Sudanese diaspora could make their expressions known (though to a potentially wider audience than the *Update* ever could).

A second observation gleaned from this period is the endurance of an idea expressed by Gwynne and Nugent School staff during the condominium era: that intergroup fighting was a spiritual "evil" and that uniting under God was the solution to this problem. Yet, unlike the move that Thomas Attiyah previously made in the *Update* (that, borrowing from 1 Corinthians, there was no more Dinka or Nuer but simply those in Christ), Bishops Deng and Loro affirmed the value of ethnicity as a God-given identity even as tribalism was tearing the young nation apart. Rather than approaching Christian identity as one meant to completely subsume ethnic identity, they instead presented it as a pan-ethnic framework that not only can but must accommodate ethnic diversity. South Sudanese Christians, in this paradigm, were a chosen people religiously and chosen peoples ethnically, a venerable "mixed multitude" like their figurative predecessors.[74]

Finally, the church's evolving but consistent proximity to political happenings mirrored the way in which political theology similarly evolved but remained consistent. As South Sudan's internal conflict was not racialized or religionized in the oppositional manner that the wars against Khartoum were (Arab v. Black, Christian v. Muslim), various intellectuals related particular scriptures and theologies to the situation. While Arabs, Muslims, and the Sudanese government were no longer the targets of religiously infused language, Kiir, Machar, and the South Sudanese government filled this void in some respects. The Exodus narrative so previously lionized was replaced by far more references to the New Testament. Despite a framework that differed from the twentieth-century civil wars, religious thought still operated as a political technology.

Conclusion

We must rise to defend our liberation credentials and bring hope to our people who pinned their future on the historical legacy of this party. We must rise so that the words of Prophet Isaiah ring true. SPLM must lead, the SPLM must inspire, SPLM must unleash its liberation zeal and captivate the imagination of our people yet again.
—Salva Kiir, 2018

This book has examined theology's role in the ideological construction of the South Sudanese nation-state. The condominium period was critical for the institutionalization of mission work in the South, administrative attempts to insulate the South from Arab-Islamic influences, and the cultivation of an English-speaking, biblically literate elite. That period was followed by the First Civil War, which witnessed the emergence of a black liberation theology that buttressed arguments for southern liberation. Foundational to this theology was the sense that southerners were God's people and that he was concerned with liberating them from their northern, Arab, and Islamic "oppressors." This stream of thought was revived during the Second Civil War in the *SPLM/A Update* to contribute a sense of spiritual destiny to the war effort and serve as a unifying mechanism in the face of internal division. Thus, the religious nationalism displayed at independence in 2011 did not emerge spontaneously but was merely another chapter in a genealogy of thought.

This religious thought is noteworthy for its endurance and racialized nature, with a black/African "chosen" and "oppressed" and Arab "oppressors." While John Mbiti identified southern Africa as a context in which black theology could exist, this study suggests that South Sudan was also a space where religious ideology was heavily informed by racialized political realities. Unlike South Africa (and a host of other African contexts), the population framed as "oppressive" was not white and Christian but Arab and Muslim. Far from being isolated from or insensitive to the sociopolitical realities of the times, religious thought in South Sudan has historically served as an arena for thinkers to define and respond to their circumstances. Rather than the historical North-South conflict being whittled down to race or religion, religious thought was an important space in which racial differences and behaviors were defined.

Race's centrality in the theological paradigm, however, must not overshadow the religious approaches taken to interethnic relations—relations that, since December 2013, have been openly and violently broadcasted for the world to see. This study has shown that from a Christian perspective, approaches to ethnicity have been ambivalent. During the condominium the state was bent on preserving, rather than eliminating, indigenous cultures. The CMS Nugent School encouraged ethnically driven competition, and moments of division were lamented. Oliver Allison, John Parry, and others contended that Christianity was needed for interethnic amity to exist, while the Catholic *Messenger* newspaper published one editorial that told its readers that "Christianity is now your tribe," a sentiment that could only be read as an argument for the supremacy of one's Christian identity over ethnic heritage. While Fr. Thomas Attiyah would later use scripture to inform his *SPLA Update* readers that there were no longer ethnic differences but only those in Christ, Archbishop Paolino Loro offered in 2011 that ethnicities were gifts of God and not to be feared. There has never been an overwhelming sense that ethnicity should be repudiated in favor of Christianity or, conversely, that ethnic identity should reign supreme.

While there has been ambivalence on that point, one element has been particularly consistent—that South Sudanese, in blending their Christian and political imaginations, rarely offered wholesale demonization of Islam. While Muslim individuals and Islamizing governments and policies may have been the targets of rebuke, Islam as a world religion was not altogether vilified in the print mediums—at least, most notably, not by the Sudanese writers quoted in this study. The same cannot be said of the Europeans and Americans who, in the first half of the twentieth century, discussed Islam in antagonistic, martial terms. Thus, despite the reality that religion certainly was a pivotal factor in the twentieth-century civil wars, the South Sudanese intellectuals under study did not generally frame the conflict as a war against Islam itself. This reality is not only imperative for those who would wish to clothe the civil wars as "Christianity v. Islam" struggles but also illustrates the capacity for adherents of one religion to marshal that faith for their own political (and perhaps revolutionary) purposes without castigating the faith(s) of their political enemies.

IMPLICATIONS FOR SUDAN AND BEYOND

I believe that the narrative presented in this study holds several implications for the study of religion and politics in Africa and beyond. To begin, I believe that one of this book's most critical interventions is the fact that South Sudanese did not stop using the Bible and Christian theology for political purposes after the end of the war in 2005 or the attainment of independence in 2011; on the contrary, such thinking has continued during the post-CPA era. The primary danger of limiting one's focus on southern religious politics to the civil war years with the North is the inaccurate presumption that southerners only appropriated Christianity in opposition to Islam (and, consequently, that Christianity was no longer politically expedient or useful with the removal of the northern threat). Such a reading would connote that those southerners under study had a narrow objective when invoking God and scripture. The fact that political theology has continued in South Sudan testifies to the more compelling reality that southerners have not forsaken the idea that the spiritual is intimately connected with the material, or that scripture is a useful political resource with a pertinent word for every situation. Given this state of affairs, it would be useful to compare the nature of religion in other national contexts that have emerged after lengthy periods of conflict. In what ways does the manner of religious ideation change when states transition from wartime to postwar status? Charting such changes—or consistencies—across time and space can expand our knowledge about religion's use as an instrument of war, mouthpiece, resource, and building block for nationalism.

The SPLA Update's use of scripture and theology to interpret enemies and justify violence can lead us to consider other communities that similarly invoked biblical narratives. In Uganda, the Lord's Resistance Army (LRA) wants to establish a theocratic state based on Old Testament and Acholi tradition. With Joseph Kony believing himself to be God's spokesperson and a medium of the Holy Spirit, the LRA began from the remnants of the Holy Spirit movement, which fought against the Ugandan state in the late 1980s.[1] Hutu preachers in Rwanda used the memory of King Saul and his divinely sanctioned actions against the Amalekites (killing every man, woman, and child) to justify Tutsi destruction.[2] It will be imperative to note if and how biblical passages are or have been invoked to stoke violence in conflict between Christians and Muslims in places like the Central African Republic.[3]

Beyond the use of scripture in a bellicose environment, there is also the broader matter of state appropriations of the Bible or Christianity for partisan purposes. How have African and non-African states used religious rhetoric to encourage peace or policy agendas? Amid the war on terror, President Donald Trump's Muslim ban, and the terrorist attacks that have hit France, this question is particularly relevant and revealing for the contemporary geopolitical climate. While one could argue that we are living in an era similar to the late nineteenth century (when some envisioned a global "Christianity v. Islam" struggle), a sign I encountered on the lawn of a Minneapolis church reading "Jesus was a Refugee" in the wake of Trump's ban reinforces the need to look for dissenting undercurrents of religious thought. Just as political theology in Sudan has contained a diversity of appropriations, one must look for the multiplicity of ways that state, nonstate, church, and secular actors use scripture to address issues like the US immigration crisis, global warming, abortion, and all forms of state violence against marginalized communities. How, for example, are Catholic immigrants from South and Central America using theology to bolster their claims for access to US citizenship? How are Black Lives Matter activists using religion to buttress arguments for social, economic, and political enfranchisement? How are Muslim citizens in France, the United States, and South Sudan using the Koran as a basis from which to petition those respective governments for equal status in those countries?[4] The South Sudanese case proves that religion can function as a productive and dynamic technology with which to empower, encourage, and enlighten those in the midst of a violent, revolutionary struggle. Similarly, work must be done on the ways in which clerical and lay theologians the world over are marshaling religion to advance sociopolitical projects in spaces that are defined not by military warfare but instead by more seemingly pacific conflicts.

The international nature of Sudan's civil wars can help students and scholars to think in different ways about religion's mobility in the diaspora. Religion is a space where individuals can stake claims in communities that are much larger than their own. Conversion to Christianity and Islam in

Africa has been described as an entryway into a "global system" that revitalizes Yoruba religion's "vital core," and in sub-Saharan Africa independent churches rejuvenated African identity by making "inter-ethnic and transcultural associative networks" that are linked by "overarching symbols and doctrines."[5] While Matthew Kustenbauder once noted that mobile phones, airplanes, and news media linked seemingly isolated refugee camps and villages to the wider world system, I believe that one of the more fascinating dimensions of my study is the way in which political theology is shown advancing from diasporic print mediums like the *Voice of Southern Sudan* and *SPLA Update* to online venues like the *Sudan Tribune*. How, then, are refugees, immigrants, and all others who are geographically distant from their homes using the internet as figurative pulpits to moralize domestic issues? The internet has made it easier than ever for politically attentive laypeople to broadcast their views to a global audience, making the authorship of those disseminating religiously infused civic messaging more egalitarian. Building off work that Timeka Tounsel and D. S. Williams have done on black women, I believe that by inserting biblical language into online articles and blogs, political discourse can become the stuff of everyday hermeneutics, revealing both the capacity for clerical and lay citizens to express their interpretations through public discourse and their willingness to do so.[6] The study of African religious politics stands to be strengthened by seriously considering the internet as a venue for religious expression.

Perhaps one of the more curious implications of this study concerns the use of religion in arguments for diversity and inclusion. One may walk away from this book believing that South Sudanese Christians used their faith as a weapon against the North Sudanese racial and religious Other. Such a reading would frame the theology that infused the liberation effort as not only partisan but essentially divisive and exclusive, an ideology that encouraged separatism rather than reconciliation across racial, religious, and political lines. Such a conclusion, however, would be problematic for several reasons. First, it flies in the face of the reality that this theology never demonized Islam or Muslims wholesale. Second, it would fail to account for the ways in which theology was used to encourage peace during South Sudan's internal conflict. Third, it would fail to account for the severe pressures that southerners faced in their struggles against Khartoum. The religious ideations presented in this book were created by people living with crushing circumstances, and that such theology could emerge from such extraordinary circumstances sheds light on Joseph Taban's assertion that "If there's a book the South Sudanese cannot remove from their lives, it's the Bible." Rather than viewing their theology as one that was essentially antagonistic, it would be more accurate to take note instead of their ability to make positive meaning of themselves and their futures despite their perilous circumstances.

Finally, the competing contentions that "Christianity is now your tribe" and that tribes are "gifts from God" are fascinating to think about when considering other contexts in which intergroup relations—whether racial, ethnic, or national—are controversial. Should religions that propose themselves to be predicated on love (whether Christianity or otherwise) justify the inherent value of distinct identities in a world where identity politics are so fraught? Should the priority, conversely, be to accentuate sameness, shared values, and communal identities? While these questions are bound to conjure polarizing answers depending on one's experiences and perspectives, I think that there is something right, compelling, and even urgent about Loro's claim that ethnicities are gifts from God. While religious identities may be essentially transcendent by their connection with the divine, it is dangerous to consider identity politics in a zero-sum manner. Celebrating one must not mean relegating another. On the contrary, seeing that there is intimate connection between one's faith, race, ethnicity, and gender can open the door for honest dialogue and mutual understanding. I pose the same questions for South Sudan that Kristin Anderson did for race in the United States. Is colorblindness good for people of color? In a multicultural and multiethnic South Sudan, what does it mean for people to ignore ethnicity in their interactions? If ethnicity matters in society and in everyday life, what are the implications of not seeing it?[7] The decision not to see one's race or ethnicity comes with the consequences of ignoring the beauty, pain, culture, and history that accompanies those identities.

CLOSING THOUGHTS

It has been a singular time in which to produce a book on South Sudanese history. Since work for this study began in 2010, South Sudan has transitioned from being a part of the Republic of the Sudan to independence to a nation that has emerged from its own civil war. While the history of southern nationalism—and indeed, the history of the nation—is still evolving, some conclusions can be drawn at this particular moment.

Despite the temptation to marvel at the fact that an internal war erupted less than three years into independence, the recent conflict did not occur spontaneously. Nor does the violence signify a total failure of the national project, a turning away from the long-standing racial and cultural identifications with blackness and Africanness. This study shows how race, in response to conflicts with North Sudanese, came to dominate identifications of self and community. Changing times call for changing responses, however, and race in the current environment has become less salient than ethnicity. Still, the appalling ferocity of ethnic violence since 2013 raises some legitimate questions. How effective was Christianity's contribution in encouraging a sense of cross-ethnic nationalism? How should one assess the true impact of the Biblical idioms that infused political rhetoric before and after the CPA? In a religious thought that placed such importance on race in defining oppressor and oppressed, how does the current state of ethnic division complicate ideological understandings of the South Sudanese nation-state?

South Sudan is not a singular case. Almost every nation has had to contend with existential disputes, problems, and civil wars that threatened their principles and existences. One needs to look no further than the Sudan, which had to deal with the consequences of the Torit Mutiny mere months before its 1956 independence. Others might argue that South Sudan's current trauma proves that Frantz Fanon wrote with prophetic accuracy in the following excerpt from *The Wretched of the Earth*:

> Nationalism, that magnificent hymn which roused the masses against the oppressor, disintegrates in the aftermath of independence. Nationalism is not a political doctrine. . . . If we really want to safeguard our countries from regression, paralysis, or collapse, we must rapidly switch from a national consciousness to a social and political consciousness. The nation can only come into being in a program elaborated by a revolutionary leadership and enthusiastically and lucidly appropriated by the masses.[8]

It is tempting to conclude that South Sudan proves Fanon correct that, upon independence, the aims and utility of religious nationalism were achieved but never actually possessed the power to construct and preserve national peace and unity. Gordon Buay's critique of government attempts to push the Cush moniker on the new nation illustrates the tenuousness of biblical insertions in the construction of national identity. He raises legitimate questions about South Sudan's exclusive claims to being the Land of Cush and the educational and theological backgrounds of the military officers who tried to insert Cush into the national anthem. What value, then, does the infusion of religious idioms into national identity have if those connections are thin or inaccurate? Is it mere propaganda—as Buay termed Garang's actions—or is it constructive? The veracity of the claim that religious (and other) nationalisms are not fit to sustain the nation-state may also be proved by the civil war's dead, refugees, and shattered dreams.

And yet, the utility of religious thought in the nation's political sphere historically or moving forward cannot and should not be wholly rejected. On the contrary, recent years have shown that the Bible's continued appropriation in political claims making is an outgrowth of longer-term behaviors. Biblical borrowings since the CPA have been used to celebrate, discuss, and critique South Sudanese authority and nationhood. One of my interview participants, Bishop Anthony Poggo, authored *Come Let Us Rebuild: Lessons from Nehemiah* (2013). He looks to the book of Nehemiah to provide lessons for the construction of South Sudan. While he was still in the writing process, Poggo shared his reasoning behind the project with me:

> I'm looking at . . . the lessons that we learn from Nehemiah on building the nation, and so a number of things that are in my view are relevant to [the] South Sudan context. . . . We need to be Nehemiahs to be able to build this nation. . . . Nehemiah was patriotic . . . a pray-er . . . a planner . . . patient in the face of the challenges that he faced. . . . We are talking of lessons and principles that we can learn from the word of God that can be useful and important.[9]

A couple of months before the war's first shots were fired, I met with two students from the Juba Diocesan Model Secondary School and was taken aback by their use of the Old Testament to express their hopes and wishes for the government. One of the students, Grace, called on government ministers to come to church, pray, and ask God to give them wisdom so that they could rule wisely. She noted that the fear of the Lord is the beginning of wisdom (Prov. 9:10), and that if leaders go to church and fear the Lord, "they'll do good." The other student, Diana, mentioned that when God asked Solomon what he desired, the king responded with wisdom. She also quoted from Proverbs 21:1, stating that the king's heart is in the Lord's hands. With these thoughts in mind, she expressed her wish for the authorities to come to the Lord. "If they did not call on the Lord to come and guide our country," Diana opined, "it will be in vain. . . . They should call on the Lord and then they can be in control. God will be the one guiding them . . . just following his footsteps."[10] Even anthem-critic Gordon Buay illustrated the continued potency of biblical borrowings when he responded to claims about his loyalty to the Kiir regime. Appointed by Kiir as an ambassador in 2014, Buay was alleged to be involved in a coup plot. He dismissed the charge and was quoted in early January 2015 as likening his relationship with the president to that between "Jesus Christ and Jehovah."[11]

South Sudanese have repeatedly found the Bible to be a critical source for sociopolitical power, dissent, defense, and meaning making. Whether biblical Cush was or was not limited to South Sudan's modern boundaries means little in comparison to the power of being able to claim that one's tribulations and liberation were prophetically foretold. It does not matter that elements of the Moses-Joshua narrative are inconsistent with John Garang and Salva Kiir; it is the script that allows southerners to envision themselves as moving toward and reaching the promised land, whatever that place might be. The Bible, in South Sudan as elsewhere, has provided a script for action, a lexicon for resistance, a vehicle for defining "us" and "them," and ways to understand and respond to various circumstances. Its mutability in South Sudanese history is rivaled only by its endurance as a politically relevant text.

Continued appropriations of biblical symbolisms and themes in southern political discourse warrant continued study on the meanings of such invocations. Rather than symbolizing the failure of religious thought in the national project, this period of conflict could prove to be yet another in a list of chapters in which Christian thought is appropriated to fit contemporary circumstances. Rather than the traditional Arab enemy and black African oppressed, new heroes and villains are bound to emerge to fit a new type of theology. Regardless of what the future may hold, the Bible—with its characters, narratives, themes, and symbols—will continue to be a source of political inspiration, argument, and vocabulary to address and define issues facing the nation.

Sources and Methodology

The nature of my inquiry and the agents in my narrative largely dictated the primary source base for this study. I envisioned this history of nationalism as a history of discourse, ideology, and thought. As my chronological scope stretched from the condominium to Sudanese independence to South Sudanese nationhood, the ideologies that form the basis of my investigation were espoused by agents that varied in nationality, profession, religion, period, race, and a host of other socioeconomic indexes. Furthermore, the means by which their views were expressed were fashioned in various media, including newspapers, magazines, speeches, government and ecclesiastical correspondences, private letters, song, poetry, and sermons. Given the international scope of government and mission work in the Sudan, research necessitated visits to government, religious, and university archives in South Sudan, Egypt, England, Italy, and various American locations (the complete list of archives can be found in the bibliography). While each research site contributed to the formulation and construction of my project, the most significant archives proved to be the South Sudan National Archives (SSNA), Durham University's Sudan Archive (SAD), and Rome's Comboni Mission Archive (CMA).

The SSNA is a government archive flush with official documents from the Anglo-Egyptian administration and early Sudanese governments. Holdings include government and missionary correspondences, mission school inspection reports, official government newspapers, and a host of other memoranda. Mission school reports were particularly useful for gaining insight into condominium educational curriculums, student body makeups, and socio-pedagogical priorities. Authored primarily by British administrators like resident inspector A. G. Hickson, these documents also offer private insights and clues regarding British positions on the social objectives and ramifications of their work. The archive's holdings concerning the aftermath of the Torit Mutiny allowed me to chart and analyze accounts from individuals who participated in the violence. Many of the early independence documents pertain to the controversial process of Arabization and Islamization, and of chief importance are those materials produced by Ali Baldo, the governor of Equatoria during the late 1950s and early 1960s. Indeed, the SSNA is a critical resource with which to chronicle official dimensions of the Sudanese government's cultural and religious objectives in South Sudan during the early years of Sudanese independence.

For any work that seriously interrogates Sudanese Catholic history, Rome's Comboni Mission Archive is a collection of the first magnitude. With primarily English-language materials (along with those in Latin and Italian), the CMA proved to be the most important repository I visited with respect to primary sources produced by Sudanese Catholic priests and refugees. Letters written by priests and other refugees afforded me the opportunity to trace the ideological and spiritual contours of refugee experiences. What biblical narratives, for example, did refugees reference in their letters? How did they recognize God in the midst of their suffering? Other CMA documents of great use included those concerning the Anyanya movement and foreign press coverage of developments in the country. In many respects, perhaps the most pleasant surprise from the CMA was the *Sudanese Catholic Clergy* volume that is kept downstairs in the Comboni Library. The *SCC* contains not only mini-biographies of Sudanese clerics but also contact information with which I was able to track down and connect with several priests through questionnaires and during my 2013 trip to Juba.

Durham University's Sudan Archive combines the best elements of the SSNA and CMA by offering a prodigious amount of religious and government materials. Like the SSNA it contains documents authored by colonial officials concerning various spheres of administration (including a comprehensive roll of annual reports and Sudan government gazettes), as well editions of periodicals, including the *Grass Curtain*, *SPLM/A Update*, and *Sudan Diocesan Review*. Unlike the CMA, whose church/mission holdings are overwhelmingly Catholic, the SAD houses an abundance of materials pertaining to Protestant church work. This includes, for example, the Oliver Allison papers and materials concerning the Church Missionary Society. I was fortunate enough to visit Durham shortly after the library had received the translated collection of Kuku-Balokole songs I mention in Chapter 3.

Following in the vein of Daniel Magaziner, my focus was not limited to people and organizations; I also studied circulating texts and ideas that allow me to chronicle change over time. This entailed looking at poems, songs, letters, sermons, prayers, speeches, and newspapers crafted by southern and Euro-American individuals and organizations. My heavy use of newspapers published in South Sudan and throughout sites in the Sudanese diaspora enabled me to note the evolution of thought concerning various Khartoum governments, treatment of church and missionary institutions, and southern self-determination. Examining poetry in newspapers and magazines allowed me to examine political views, laments, and thoughts from contributors around the world as well as to put their ideas in conversation with those of others of varying professional, personal, and geographic backgrounds. By incorporating voices throughout the diaspora, I show the ways in which South Sudanese religious and political thought was not just developed within the political borders of South Sudan but evolved and proliferated throughout the Sudanese diaspora.

In addition to archival work, I gathered interviews with clerical and non-clerical figures during my trips to Juba. As I was very much interested in the southern church's political actions and thought both historically and present, many of my participants were southern clergy. This notwithstanding, I prioritized the inclusion of laypeople and non-Sudanese clerical figures who have spent time in the country. Participants included a member of parliament; various church brothers, sisters, priests, and bishops; the former general secretary of the Sudan Council of Churches; a man who has since been appointed as an ambassador; employees at Juba's Catholic Radio Bakhita; an Anyanya veteran; an SPLA chaplain related to John Garang; the president of the Mothers' Union; and several Lost Boys. Life histories and stories passed down from elders resulted in my receiving intimate perspectives on some of the most formative elements in my study, including the Juba Conference, the Torit Mutiny, refugee experiences, education, Anyanya, and SPLA-church relations. What I heard was beautiful, macabre, and transformative. While my questions varied depending on factors like age, background, and experience, I invariably sought to capture the ways in which they related or could relate the history of South Sudan to the providence of God. While I did not include every interview or questionnaire in this study, those used allowed me to complement archival research—that dealt, for all intents and purposes, with southern history pre-2006—with thoughts and memories on more recent developments.

While I contend that the diversity of my print and oral sources equipped me to craft a rigorous history of religious nationalism, there must naturally be room for source critique. To begin, there is the matter of who produced the sources and for whom they were intended. Print media like the *Sudan Diocesan Review* were intended for a generally Christian audience and may have had an implicit (or explicit) bias in their description of the government, Muslims, Christian churches, and/or their adherents. Yet and still, they provided a look into the daily life of the Nugent School and the perspectives of figures like Ian Watts and Llewellyn Gwynne. The *Sudan Diocesan Review*'s information on interethnic conflict allowed me—in conjunction with reports from the SSNA—to paint a more comprehensive portrait of interethnic relations at the school. The *SPLA Update* was a decidedly propagandist medium, and though I did not use it as an authoritative information source on the Second Civil War, it is still an enlightening and relevant lens into the SPLA's public use of Christianity. Its nature as propaganda, furthermore, actually enhances its importance as a partisan repository of religious rhetoric during that conflict.

My decision to rely heavily on Christian clerics as interview participants was the fruit of the access I had to them as a result of my stays at the Episcopal Church of Sudan's guest house in Juba. Standing in the shadows of All Saints Cathedral, Anglican bishops from throughout the country regularly frequented the guest house (note, however, that I also interviewed Catholics during my research). Rather than representing a privileged minority class of South Sudanese Christians, my interviews and questionnaires with clerics allowed me to better understand their lives as laypeople during the history under study, their subsequent experiences as Christian leaders, and their insight on providence in South Sudanese history. Not simply clerics, they brought a diversity of perspectives to their interactions with me—they were former refugees, witnesses, students, and sons (and grandsons) with family history to share. Given the attention that I give to clerics throughout the book (their public and private writings provide a healthy share of the political theology I highlight), engaging with contemporary clerics allowed me to offer a more comprehensive examination of the words and actions of ordained southerners for the better part of the last half-century.

Last but not least, there is my decision to rely on English sources. I do not work in Arabic, and given the fact that many southern activists are primarily Arabic speakers and that the North was a major theater of southern activism (particularly during the second civil war), I acknowledge that certain slices are missing from this study. How, for example, did Arabic-speaking southern Christians inject Christian thought into their political dialogue in Arabic print media? Aside from primarily Arabic-speaking South Sudanese, the class and gender dynamic is impossible to ignore; English was taught in schools that a relatively low percentage of the population attended, and of that population, most were boys. In this way, my focus on English print media necessarily means that the primary subjects of study are those who had privileged access to published and proliferating English print media— educated southern men.

While demographically limited in one sense, the global archival network of twentieth-century Sudanese history is fraught with English-language materials written by and about South Sudanese Christians. As a language that representatives of the Anglican, Presbyterian, and Catholic denominations each conversed in (and one encouraged at the expense of Arabic for religious reasons), English has a focal role in the history of Sudanese Christianity. Many refugee letters, mission/church and secular publications, and materials that circulated internationally were written in English and were written by southerners. My approach to English secular sources is an attempt to expand the scope of the sources we can examine to interrogate the injection of religious thought into the public political sphere. As such, this study can be placed in conversation with other works that are principally concerned with Sudanese Christianity from a local, ethnic, or anthropological lens to paint a fuller picture of political Christianity in South Sudan.

Notes

ABBREVIATIONS

CMA   Comboni Mission Archive
CMSA   Church Missionary Society Archive, University of Birmingham
PHS   Presbyterian Historical Society
SAD   Sudan Archive, Durham University Libraries
SSNA   South Sudan National Archives

INTRODUCTION

1 "The Wind of Change—Harold Macmillan's African Tour of 1960," National Archives (UK), accessed August 20, 2012, http://www.nationalarchives.gov.uk /news/421.htm.

2 Boddy-Evans, "Chronological List of African Independence."

3 *East Africa and Rhodesia* 37, no. 1187 (September 9, 1960), folder EP.46.B.2, box EP 373, SSNA.

4 Øystein H. Rolandsen notes that though the First Civil War is popularly dated 1955–72, full-scale violence did not begin until 1963. See Rolandsen, "False Start," 105. Others had previously made this point: for example, Johnson and Prunier, "Foundation and Expansion," 117–41; Johnson, "Sudan People's Liberation Army," 53–72; Johnson, *Root Causes* (2003); and Johnson, "Twentieth-Century Civil Wars," 122–32.

5 United Nations Security Council, "Southern Sudan Referendum Was Timely"; and United Nations Mission in the Sudan, "Independence of South Sudan."

6 "Sudan Referendum."

7 Natsios, *Sudan*, 18; and Jok, *War and Slavery*, 100.

8 "South Sudanese Christians Plan."

9   Acting Governor, Episcopal Church of the Sudan (ECS) Independence Service,
    July 8, 2012 (Juba, South Sudan).

10 Natsios, *Sudan,* xvii.

11 Prayer given during same service.

12 Salomon, *For Love of the Prophet.* For a sense of the prodigious scholarship,
    the fourth edition of the *Historical Dictionary of the Sudan* lists in its "Law and
    Islamization" bibliography twenty-nine books and articles published in that
    area between 1971 and 2012. See Kramer, Lobban, and Fluehr-Lobban, *Historical
    Dictionary of the Sudan,* 512–13 (as taken from Tounsel, "Khartoum Goliath," 145n3).

13 Jok, *War and Slavery,* 40.

14 Sanneh, "Religion, Politics, and National Integration," 151.

15 Moyn, *Christian Human Rights,* 24, 145.

16 Mahmood Mamdani's *Saviors and Survivors* is of particular interest (especially
    6–7, 279–80, 300).

17 Glassman, *War of Words,* 6–7; and Magaziner, *Law and the Prophets.*

18 See Feierman, *Peasant Intellectuals.* According to Feierman, the purpose of
    studying intellectuals' social position was to comprehend those within peasant
    society best capable of shaping discourse, their location within an oppressive
    framework, and the relationship between their status and political language
    (4–5; see also 39, 263).

19 "South Sudan's Kiir Reiterates Call"; Natsios, *Sudan,* xii, xv; and Harris, "U.S.
    Imposes Arms Ban." For dating of conflict, see "Global Conflict Tracker [South
    Sudan]."

20 Barnaba Marial Benjamin and Desmond Tutu, ECS Independence Service
    (July 8, 2012). For Deng's ministerial position, see "Barnaba Marial Benjamin";
    and Ngor, "S. Sudan Says China to Help."

21 F. M. Deng, *War of Visions,* 15; see also Tesfai, *Holy Warriors,* where the same
    quotation is cited on p. 18.

22 Minter, "Pro Veritate"; and Walshe, "Evolution of Liberation Theology," 19.

23 Magaziner, *Law and the Prophets,* 3.

24 "Challenge to the Church."

25 Akanji, "Black Theology," 177; Pinn, "Cone, James Hal"; and Cone and Wilmore,
    "Black Theology and African Theology," 463n.

26 Cone and Wilmore, "Black Theology," 467. Information on the essay's publica-
    tion history can be found on 463n.

27 Cone and Wilmore, "Black Theology," 467.

28 Mbiti, "African Views," 477, 478.

29 Mbiti, "African Views," 481.

30 F. M. Deng, *War of Visions,* 222–23.

31 F. M. Deng, *War of Visions,* 210, citing Bona Malwal, *People and Power in Sudan: The
    Struggle for National Stability* (London: Ithaca Press, 1981), 16–17.

32 Johnson, "Future of Southern Sudan's Past," 39–40; Leonardi, "South Sudanese
    Arabic," 351, 371; Woodward, "Religion and Politics," 170; and Gray, "Epilogue,"
    188–89, 198–99.

33 Fadlalla, "Neoliberalization of Compassion," 212–13.

34 Launay, "An Invisible Religion?," 189–90; and Ware, *Walking Qur'an*, 19.

35 Launay, "An Invisible Religion?," 190.

36 Ware, *Walking Qur'an*, 19–20.

37 Steve Paterno, email to Christopher Tounsel (questionnaire response), October 4, 2013.

38 Jok, *War and Slavery*, 77–78.

39 Leonardi, *Dealing with Government*, 182; Ryle, "Peoples and Cultures," 33; and Hutchinson, *Nuer Dilemmas*, 354.

40 Mutua, "Racism at Root."

41 Johnson, "Sudanese Military Slavery," 148–49.

42 Sikainga, *Slaves into Workers*, xii–xiii; and Idris, *Conflict and Politics*, 4, 6, 20.

43 Lee, *Unreasonable Histories*, 5.

44 *Africanism* emerged from the colonial native question, broadly construed, being deeply racialized in the first instance and firmly entrenched in the ethnic politics of the customary in the second; see Lee, *Unreasonable Histories*, 8.

45 D. Chang, *Citizens of a Christian Nation*, 9; Longman, "Church Politics," 168–69; and Keto, "Race Relations," 600–601, 612, 626. In the Sudanese context, incoming British brought their own conception of labor along ethnic lines and certain perceptions about the working capacity of each ethnic group. See Sikainga, *Slaves into Workers*, xiii.

46 See, for example, Hall, *History of Race*, 2; Brennan, *Taifa*, 1–2; Glassman, *War of Words*, 6–7; and Magaziner, *Law and the Prophets*.

47 Mamdani, *Citizen and Subject*, 7–8.

48 Breidlid, Said, and Breidlid, *Concise History of South Sudan*, 148–49; and Johnson, *Root Causes* (2011), 15.

49 See Leonardi and Jalil, "Traditional Authority," 115.

50 Gordon, *Invisible Agents*, 3.

51 See Collins, *Land beyond the Rivers*; Collins, *Shadows in the Grass*; and Sanderson, *Education, Religion and Politics*.

52 See Coleman, "Race as Technology," 177.

53 Gray, *Black Christians and White Missionaries*, 2–4.

54 See Chidester, *Savage Systems*, 118; and Elbourne, *Blood Ground*, 18–20.

55 Stanley, "Introduction," 6–7 (for Derek Peterson's chapter, "The Rhetoric of the Word: Bible Translation and Mau Mau in Colonial Central Kenya," see 164–82).

56 Rolandsen, *Guerilla Government*, 17. For work done by Nikkel on Dinka Christianity, see his *Dinka Christianity* and "Christian Conversion," 162–68.

57 See Loro, "Opening Address," 14; and Bul, "Christmas Message 2015."

58 Sanneh, "Preface," 9.

59 Gray, "Epilogue," 195, 196; and Hasan, "Role of Religion," 24, citing a quotation from Francis Deng in *Management of the Crisis in the Sudan*, ed. Abdel Ghaffar M. Ahmed and Gunnar M. Sorbo (Khartoum: Khartoum University Press, 1989), 47.

60 Van der Veer and Lehmann, introduction, 6. In n17, they cite *Many Are Chosen: Divine Election and Western Nationalism*, ed. William R. Hutchison and Hartmut Lehmann (Minneapolis, MN: Fortress Press, 1994). "It is essential," van der Veer and Lehmann write, "to follow the transformation of religious notions when they are transferred from a purely religious context to the sphere of national politics" (7).

61 See Salomon, "Religion after the State," 447–69.

62 Marshall, *Political Spiritualities*, 17–18.

63 Marshall, *Political Spiritualities*, 19. Marshall took her second question from a billboard she saw in Lagos that read, "Jesus is the Answer." See Marshall, *Political Spiritualities*, 268.

64 Oliver O'Donovan clarifies what is meant by political theology with this explanation: "Let us be clear that political theology (except in some ideal-type of civil religion) . . . does not suppose a literal synonymity between the political vocabulary of salvation and the secular use of the same political terms. It postulates an analogy—not a rhetorical metaphor only, or a poetic image, but an analogy grounded in reality—between the acts of God and human acts, both of them taking place within the one public history which is the theatre of God's saving purposes and mankind's social undertakings." See O'Donovan, *Desire of the Nations*, 2.

65 Asad, *Formations of the Secular*, 186.

66 Casanova, *Public Religions*, 3.

67 An-Na'im, "Islam and National Integration," 31.

68 See Attiyah, "Challenge of Peace in Sudan," 8 (Attiyah borrows from and cites Colossians 3:10–11); and Loro, "Opening Address," 12, 14 (paraphrased "gifts of God" from 14).

69 See chapter 1 for such connections between ethnic conflict and spirituality. Bush's post-9/11 characterization of the "axis of evil" is one such example.

70 Anthias and Yuval-Davis, introduction, 2.

71 Ali, *Gender, Race, and Sudan's Exile Politics*, 1, 3, 18, 41–42.

72 Decker, *In Idi Amin's Shadow*, 6. In footnote 18 Decker cites a quotation from Judith Butler, "Performative Acts and Gender Constitution: An Essay in Phenomenology and Feminist Theory," *Theater Journal* 40, no. 4 (December 1988): 519.

73 Decker, *In Idi Amin's Shadow*, 2, 7.

74 I borrow the idea of imagined community from Benedict Anderson, who argues that toward the end of the eighteenth century, certain European cultural artifacts became transplantable to a variety of social spaces. Printed vernaculars are a foundational part of his thesis: as a tool of administrative centralization, a shared print culture could contribute to the formation of "imagined communities." Even though their members may never encounter one another, these communities set the stage for the creation of modern nations. See Anderson, *Imagined Communities*, 4, 6, 40, 46.

75 Tounsel, "Khartoum Goliath."

CHAPTER 1. THE NUGENT SCHOOL AND THE ETHNO-RELIGIOUS POLITICS OF MISSION EDUCATION

1 "Llewellyn H. Gwynne," 9; "The Builder of the Foundations," in *The Anglican Diocese of the Sudan: A Handbook* (1951), 1, 3, ACC300 Z5, CMSA; "Thanksgiving," 14–15 (this includes G. H. Martin's speech from December 16, 1957); and Llewellyn H. Gwynne obituary, *Times* (London), December 4, 1957, as taken from *Sudan Diocesan Review*. For full obituary and information, see "Bishop Gwynne" and Llewellyn H. Gwynne obituary, *Times* (London), December 4, 1957.

2 Churchill, *River War*, 269.

3 W. H. T. Gairdner, *The C.M.S. in the Anglo-Egyptian Sudan* (London: Clowes, 1919), reprinted from the *Church Missionary Review*, June 1919, 4, ACC6 F15/1, CMSA.

4 Gairdner, *C.M.S.*, 4.

5 Gairdner, *C.M.S.*, 5; and "Thanksgiving," 15.

6 Stevenson, "Protestant Missionary Work," 197.

7 See Sharkey, "Christians among Muslims," 55, where she quotes from General Committee Resolution, December 13, 1899, G3/E/P1/1900, CMSA.

8 Snape, *Redcoat and Religion*, 225; Ahmed, *Sudan*, 62; Kramer, Lobban, and Fluehr-Lobban, "Baring, Evelyn, Earl of Cromer (1841–1917)," in *Historical Dictionary of the Sudan*, 87; Sharkey, "Christians among Muslims," 56; and W. W. Cash, "Gordon Memorial Mission to Southern Sudan," 1928, 1, G/Y/S2 (1–122), CMSA.

9 "Copy of Journal of the Rev. Archibald Shaw, Southern Soudan, 1905–9," entry for October 17, 1905, 1, ACCIII F2, CMSA.

10 "Thanksgiving," 15.

11 F. M. Deng, *War of Visions*, 210, citing Malwal, *People and Power in Sudan*, 16–17.

12 Sidahmed, *Politics and Islam*, 5.

13 Sanderson, *Education, Religion and Politics*, 8.

14 Rolandsen, "Colonial Backwater," 17; and Barsella and Guixot, *Struggling to Be Heard*, 11–12.

15 See Watson, *Sorrow and Hope*, 131; and Sanderson, *Education, Religion and Politics*, 18–19.

16 See Watson, *Sorrow and Hope*, 131; and Voll, "Imperialism, Nationalism and Missionaries," 40.

17 Collins, *Southern Sudan*, 22–23, 44–45; and Johnson, "Prophecy and Mahdism," 45n11 (citing J. M. Schuver, letter dated August 16, 1883, *Afrique Explorée et Civilisée* 5 [1884]: 7).

18 Johnson, "Prophecy and Mahdism," 43, 51–53 (quotation on 53). For the hymn Johnson cites in footnote 35, see Lienhardt, *Divinity and Experience*, 164–65.

19 Baum, "Sudan," 1795; Kramer, Lobban, and Fluehr-Lobban, *Historical Dictionary of the Sudan*, 14–15; and Sharkey, "Christians among Muslims," 57. Though Baum uses "spirits of the sky" (1795) when referring to those entities that inspired the prophets (a term that Edward Evans-Pritchard also employed with respect to Nuer vocabulary), it is an outdated term. Douglas Johnson found Lienhardt's

terminology better suited than Evans-Pritchard's for dealing with the common elements of Nilotic religious life. See Johnson, *Nuer Prophets*, 59–60.

20 Sharkey, "Christians among Muslims," 57; Watson, *Sorrow and Hope*, 131–32; Ahmed, *Sudan*, 59–60; and Pitya, "History of Western Christian Evangelism," 159–60, 167–68.

21 House of Commons, *Egypt No. 1 (1920)*, 132.

22 [Archibald Shaw], "Sudan Notes," no. 14, January 1918, 3–4, ACIII F4, CMSA.

23 C. A. Lea-Wilson speech at the New Alliance Club, December 8, 1922, 15, ACCIII FI/12, CMSA; A. M. Gelsthorpe, "The Bishop Bullen Memorial Chapel" (from the Nugent School, January 1, 1944), 1, ACC300 Z5, CMSA; C. A. Lea-Wilson, "Tidings of the School at Juba, the School-house Being the Gift of Friends in Beloved Memory of Sophia M. Nugent," August 20, 1920, 1, ACCIII FI/9, CMSA; and C. A. Lea-Wilson, "Tidings of the Juba School 1920–1921," 1, ACCIII FI/10, CMSA.

24 "TREK No. 1. (Lado Enclave 3rd Jan.–30th. Jan.)," ACCIII FI/2, CMSA, p. 2; Grace B. M. Riley, *No Drums at Dawn*, 45, ACC284 Z1, CMSA; Cash, "Gordon Memorial Mission," 4; Gelsthorpe, "Bishop Bullen Memorial Chapel," 1; H. G. Selwyn to Miss Nugent, October 13, 1928, p. 1, ACCIII FI/22, CMSA; Watts, "From Mr. I. H. Watts," 5–6; Beare, "From Miss J. M. Beare," 18; and Sharland, "From the Rev. C. T. Sharland," 20–21.

25 Lea-Wilson, "Tidings of the School at Juba," 1.

26 Gelsthorpe, "Bishop Bullen Memorial Chapel," 1.

27 Lea-Wilson speech, 15–16.

28 Lea Wilson, "Tidings of the Juba School," July 31, 1921.

29 Effie K. Kitching to Miss Nugent, March 16 [year unknown], 1, ACCIII FI/19, CMSA; and Lea-Wilson, "Tidings of the Juba School," 2.

30 Castillo, *Maltese Cross*, 75, 79–80; and Keating, "Who Are the Knights of Malta?"

31 Sharkey, "Jihads and Crusades," 271–72n53, citing Janice Boddy, *Civilizing Women: British Crusades in Colonial Sudan* (Princeton, NJ: Princeton University Press, 2007), 2, 5, 24, 54, 106.

32 Lea-Wilson speech, 17.

33 Wöndu, *From Bush to Bush*, 32.

34 H. Parry, "From Mrs. Helena Parry," 16; and "History," Urban Saints, accessed July 29, 2019, https://www.urbansaints.org/history.

35 H. Parry, "From Mrs. Helena Parry," 15–16.

36 J. I. Parry, "From Mr. J. I. Parry, the Nugent School," 14; and de Sarum, "Church in the Sudan," 32.

37 J. I. Parry, "From Mr. J. I. Parry, the Nugent School," 14.

38 Parsons, *Race, Resistance*, 5–6, 18, 23, 26 (quotation on 18).

39 Tounsel, "Render to Caesar," 347; see also 344–51 for examples of this discourse.

40 Watts, "Mr. Ian Watts," 14.

41 Collins, *Land beyond the Rivers*, 319.

42 Collins, *Shadows in the Grass*, 199, 239.

43 Peterson, *Ethnic Patriotism*, 6–7, citing Lamin Sanneh, *Translating the Message: The Missionary Impact on Culture* (Maryknoll, NY: Orbis, 1989); and Andrew Walls, *The Missionary Movement in Christian History* (Maryknoll, NY: Orbis, 1996).

44 Lienhardt, "Dinka and Catholicism," 83.

45 Nikkel, *Dinka Christianity*, 31; and F. M. Deng, "Dinka Response to Christianity," 158.

46 F. M. Deng, "Dinka Response to Christianity," 158, 161.

47 Lea-Wilson, "Tidings of the Juba School," 1; Lea-Wilson, "Tidings of the School at Juba," 1; "Circular [letter] from the Rev. C. Lea Wilson," November 18, 1920, 1, ACCIII F1/8, CMSA; and "Tidings from the Rev. C. Lea-Wilson, in Charge of the School for the Cons of Chiefs," October 20, 1920, 1, ACCIII F1/8, CMSA.

48 Lea-Wilson speech, 16; Lea-Wilson, "Tidings of the Juba School," 2; and "Circular," 1.

49 Blakemore, "From Mr. Blakemore Harrop," 5. For another description of the school's diversity, see Beare, "From Miss J. M. Beare," 19.

50 J. I. Parry, "From Mr. J. I. Parry," 18–19.

51 J. G. Matthew, "Rejaf Language Conference 1928," No. E.H.Etc.17.J.9 (October 30, 1927), 1, 5, folder SCR.17.J.1 (August 2013 designation), box TD 42, SSNA; Anderson, Werner, and Wheeler, *Day of Devastation*, 272; and Hatoss, *Displacement, Language Maintenance and Identity*, 65.

52 Memorandum, January 25, 1930, 1, CS.1-C-1, Civil Secretary's Office.

53 *Southern Sudan Disturbances August 1955: Report of the Commission of Enquiry, 1956*, Report of the Sudan, 14, A/87/2, CMA; and Wheeler, "Gateway to the Heart of Africa," 17. For more on Britain's pre-1930 policy toward the South, see Wawa, "Background," 8.

54 A. G. Hickson, "Christian Names—English Form or Italian," June 22, 1933, 1, folder EP.46.A.1 (summer 2012 designation), box 372, SSNA. For Hickson's position, see "Torit Trades School, Visited May 22nd, 1933," 2, folder 46.C.3.2.A, EP 380, SSNA.

55 J. B. de Sarum [Saram], "The Nugent School, C.M.S. Loka (Report for the Year 1945)," December 16, 1945, 4, 7, folder EP.46.C.1.12 (summer 2012 designation), box 379, SSNA.

56 "Extracts from a Report on the Nugent School, Loka, the Intermediate School of the Church Missionary Society in the Southern Sudan (Given at Prize Day, December 6th 1944, by the Acting Headmaster)," 2, G/Y/S2 (1–114/4), CMSA; H. Parry, "From Mrs. Helena Parry," 16; G. F. Earl to [C. W. M.] Cox, September 7, 1937, 670/6/38–39, SAD; and Watts, "Mr. Ian Watts," 10.

57 Mangan, "Ethics and Ethnocentricity," 368; Mangan cites in footnote 32 G. F. Earl, "A School's Opportunity in the Southern Sudan," *Church Missionary Outlook* (July 1937): 154.

58 A. G. Hickson, "Review of Education Progress" [1933], 29, folder ZD.17.E (summer 2012 designation), box ZD 29, SSNA.

59 "Appendix C: Documents from the (So Called) Missionary Press which Deal with the Religious Situation in the Sudan," in *The Black Book of the Sudan: On the*

Expulsion of the Missionaries from Southern Sudan, An Answer (Milan: Artigianelli, 1964), 174; and "Editor of Catholic Paper Expelled from Sudan," January 1963, 1, A/93/9/6, CMA. The Ayok, Kwajok, and Jambite articles are cited in Pitya, "History of Western Christian Evangelism," 445n337, 586n228, 773.

60 Mason, "Controversy," 28.

61 Mason, "Controversy," 28; and de Cruz, "New Era of Peace," 47.

62 See, for example, Nebel, *Dinka-Dictionary*; Huffman, *Nuer-English Dictionary*; and Kiggen, *Nuer-English Dictionary*.

63 Kiggen, *Nuer-English Dictionary*, 171, 207, 252–53, 278.

64 Kiggen, *Nuer-English Dictionary*, 124, 186, 206, 252.

65 J. I. Parry, "From Mr. J. I. Parry," 19.

66 G. F. Earl, "The Nugent School, C.M.S. Loka. Report for the Year 1946," January 31, 1946, 1, folder EP.46.C.1.12 (summer 2012 designation), box EP 379, SSNA.

67 Watts, "From Mr. I. H. Watts," 6.

68 J. I. Parry, "C.M.S. Nugent School, Loka," 32.

69 W. B. Adair to Dr. Grice, June 30, 1954, folder 3, box 12, United Presbyterian Church in the U.S.A. Commission on Ecumenical Mission and Relations Records, PHS.

70 Unnamed author to W. B. Adair, July 21, 1954, folder 3, box 12, United Presbyterian Church in the U.S.A. Commission on Ecumenical Mission and Relations Records, PHS.

71 De Sarum [Saram], "From Mr. J. B. de Saram," 8; and Simeon, "Allison, Oliver C."

72 Allison, "From Bishop O. C. [Oliver] Allison," 22–23.

73 De Sarum [Saram], "From Mr. J. B. de Saram," 8–9.

74 J. I. Parry, "From Mr. J. I. Parry," 19–20.

75 B. M. de Sarum (9.5.45), "The Nugent School, C.M.S. Loka (Report for the Year 1944)," 3–4, folder EP.46.C.1.12 (summer 2012 designation), box 379, SSNA.

76 Migido, "To Charm," 16.

77 Kuyok, "Benjamin Lowki (1918–1974)," in *South Sudan*, 124–25, and "Paulo Logali (1909–1965)," in *South Sudan*, 202; Rev. H. Gordon to Miss Nugent, November 11, 1926, ACCIII F1/19, CMSA; and Johnson, *South Sudan*, 122. It should be noted that the Nugent School eventually became known as the Loka Intermediate School, explaining Lwoki's connection with the Nugent School, though Kuyok doesn't mention Nugent by name. See Wöndu, *From Bush to Bush*, 32n29.

78 "Faith" questionnaire.

79 Kuyok, *South Sudan*: "Bullen Alier (c. 1918–1968)," 127; "Dak Dei (1919–1976)," 147; "Jon Majak (1913–1965)," 175; "Aggrey Jaden (1928–1986)," 229 and 232. More examples can be found in Pitya, "History of Western Christian Evangelism," 409, 411–14 (part of his "Education for Leadership in Southern Sudan" section; see x).

CHAPTER 2. THE EQUATORIAL CORPS AND THE TORIT MUTINY

1 "*Quo Vadis* (1951)," IMDb, accessed October 10, 2017, http://www.imdb.com/title/tt0043949/?ref_=nv_sr_1; see also John Oswalt, "Storyline," IMDb, accessed October 10, 2017, http://www.imdb.com/title/tt0043949/?ref_=nv_sr_1. For

a summary of the *Quo Vadis* episode, see the Acts of Peter, 35, in "Acts of Peter," 152.

2   *Morning View* (Sudan), April 13, 1954, 803/9/5, SAD.

3   As stated in the introduction, several have countered the 1955 start date.

4   Allison, "Church History in the Making," 7.

5   Daly, *Empire on the Nile*, 254–55; Kramer, Lobban, and Fluehr-Lobban, "Lado Enclave," *Historical Dictionary of the Sudan*, 257; Pitya, "History of Western Christian Evangelism," 48–49; House of Commons, *Egypt No. 1 (1911)*, 76; and Breidlid, Said, and Breidlid, *Concise History of South Sudan*, 134.

6   Daly, "Wingate, Sir (Francis) Reginald"; Kramer, Lobban, and Fluehr-Lobban, "Wingate, Francis Reginald (1861–1953)," *Historical Dictionary of the Sudan*, 460; and Anderson, Werner, and Wheeler, *Day of Devastation*, 217–19, 223.

7   Daly, *Empire on the Nile*, 116; Watson, *Sorrow and Hope*, 188; and Artin, "S. S. 'Omdurman,' 16th December, 1908," in *England in the Sudan*, 164.

8   Kumm, *From Hausaland to Egypt*, 4–5, 268.

9   Archibald Shaw, copy of personal journal, August 14, 1910, 8, ACCIII F3, CMSA.

10 Reginald Wingate to Eldon Gorst, March 1, 1911, 300/3/2, 9, 10, SAD. See also Daly, *Empire on the Nile*, 116.

11 Daly, *Empire on the Nile*, 117; and S. S. Poggo, *First Sudanese Civil War*, 30.

12 Daly, *Empire on the Nile*, 117; and Robert O. Collins, "Africa Begins at Malakal," paper presented at the Religion and Politics in Sudan conference, Centre de Recherches Africaines Paris, June 22–24, 1988, 9, E/675/6/2, CMA.

13 Ruay, *Politics of Two Sudans*, 38.

14 S. S. Poggo, *First Sudanese Civil War*, 30, 62; and Johnson, *Root Causes* (2011), 18.

15 Decker, *In Idi Amin's Shadow*, 29, quoting from Timothy Parsons, *The African Rank-and-File: Social Implications of Colonial Military Service in the King's African Rifles, 1902–1964* (Portsmouth, NH: Heinemann, 1999), 5. Decker also cites 1908 KAR regulations taken from Parsons, *Rank-and-File*, 54, which was used to craft this section.

16 Johnson, "Sudanese Military Slavery," 148–49.

17 Streets, *Martial Races*, 1.

18 Johnson, "Sudanese Military Slavery," 149; for longer direct quotation, Johnson, n111, cites Enloe, pp. 27, 30–31, presumably Cynthia H. Enloe, *Ethnic Soldiers: State Security in Divided Societies* (Athens: University of Georgia Press, 1980), as taken from Lamothe, *Slaves of Fortune*, 211.

19 Johnson, *Root Causes* (2011), 18; Cisternino, *Passion for Africa*, 502, 506; Haddon, "Mr. J. H. Driberg," 257; Johnson, *South Sudan*, 107–8; Mohammed, "Militarism in the Sudan," 21.

20 Cisternino, *Passion for Africa*, 515, 520; and "Ye also Helping Together by Prayer," ACCIII FI/9, CMSA.

21 "Notes of the Address Given By Archdeacon Shaw at the New Alliance Club on December 8, 1922," ACCIII FI/12, CMSA.

22 Civil Secretary's Office, memorandum, January 25, 1930, 1, CS.1-C-1, folder SCR.17.J.1 (August 2013 designation), box TD 42, SSNA.

23 Civil Secretary's Office, memorandum, 3–4.

24 Tape 7A, vol. 1, Missions-General, piece 51 46.A.1, box 10, 913/1/1, SAD.

25 John G. Buyse, October 3, 1949, folder 8, box 16, collection 081, Billy Graham Center Archives.

26 C. M. Lamb, August 28, 1954, folder 6, box 35, collection 081, Billy Graham Center Archives.

27 Johnson, *South Sudan*, 118; Baum, "Sudan," 1796; and Kramer, Lobban, and Fluehr-Lobban, *Historical Dictionary of the Sudan*, 16.

28 Johnson, *South Sudan*, 118–19; Baum, "Sudan," 1796; and Kramer, Lobban, and Fluehr-Lobban, *Historical Dictionary of the Sudan*, 16–17.

29 Gino Barsella and Miguel Ángel Ayuso Guixot, "A List of Major Dates in the Modern History of the Sudan," Nairobi, 2, 624 266.009 AAV Brack II, Comboni Mission Library.

30 Johnson, *South Sudan*, 123; Kramer, Lobban, and Fluehr-Lobban, *Historical Dictionary of the Sudan*, xxxix, 17; and Baum, "Sudan," 1796.

31 Johnson, *South Sudan*, 124–26; and Kramer, Lobban, and Fluehr-Lobban, *Historical Dictionary of the Sudan*, 17.

32 Leonardi, *Dealing with Government*, 129; Leonardi cites Hilary Paul Logali, "Autobiography," 890/1/1–80, SAD; and J. F. Tiernay, Deputy Governor, to all DCs and heads of department, July 11, 1946, and Civil Secretary to Governor Equatoria, July 24, 1946, National Records Office, Khartoum, EP 1/4/17.

33 Kramer, Lobban, and Fluehr-Lobban, "Southern Party," *Historical Dictionary of the Sudan*, 393.

34 Ruay, *Politics of Two Sudans*, 67; Collins, *History of Modern Sudan*, 62; Wawa, "Background," 12–13; and Lobban, Kramer, and Fluehr-Lobban, "Liberal Party [Southern]," "Southern Liberal Party," and "Southern Party," in *Historical Dictionary of the Sudan*, 166, 264.

35 S. S. Poggo, *First Sudanese Civil War*, 38, 41–42; and Kuyok, "Daniel Jumi (1923–2013)" and "Marko Rume (c. 1925–1991)," in *South Sudan*, 268, 370–71.

36 For both quotations and the information on Brown, see W. B. E. Brown, "Some Reminiscences and Personal Views Concerning *Sudanisation* of the Equatorial Corps, Sudan Defence Force in 1954," paper presented to the Durham Sudan Historical Records Conference, 1982, 533/9/3–4, SAD.

37 Kuyok, "Marko Rume (c. 1925–1991)," in *South Sudan*, 371.

38 Woodward, "South in Sudanese Politics," 187–88; Sanderson, *Education, Religion and Politics*, 343–44; S. S. Poggo, *First Sudanese Civil War*, 40 (regarding what would happen to southern troops in Khartoum, Poggo includes a quotation that is presumably from the *Report of the Commission of Enquiry*, 106); and Kuyok, "Saturlino Oboyo (?–1955)," *South Sudan*, 419–20.

39 Interview with Elizabeth Noel, September 2, 2013 (Juba, South Sudan).

40 Johnson, "Sudanese Military Slavery," 153.

41 Anderson, Werner, and Wheeler, *Day of Devastation*, 367–68; and "The Southern Troops Mutiny," 721/3/193–94, SAD. This is a section of Alberto Marino's larger memoir, *Sudan*.

42 Alberto Marino, *Sudan*, 721/3/193–94, SAD.

43 S. S. Poggo, *First Sudanese Civil War*, 42; Yangu, *Nile Turns Red*, 40; Riley, "No Drums at Dawn," 148–49; and Marian I. Farquhar, "What Do You Fear," 1956, 2, RG 424, PHS.

44 See Osman El Tayeb, October 19, 1955, 1 (353), folder EP.41.C.1 (August 2013 designation), EP 507, SSNA; and M. A. Abu Rannet "Note on Confirmation of Findings and Sentences by the Chief Justice," October 30, 1955, 1, 4, folder EP.41.C.1 (August 2013 designation), EP 507, SSNA.

45 Osman El Tayeb, October 12, 1955, 1 (323), folder EP.41.C.1 (August 2013 designation), EP 507, SSNA. A "Mr. Williams of the C.M.S." contributed this quotation to the report.

46 Glassman, *War of Words*, 256.

47 "Trial of Airo Ogwana," October 18, 1955, 1; attached "Note," 1, and "Notes on Confirmation of Findings and Sentence by the C. J. M. A. Abu Rannat Chief Justice of the Sudan," October 29, 1955, all in folder EP.41.C.1 (August 2013 designation), EP 507, SSNA.

48 "Notes on Confirmation of Findings and Sentence," 1.

49 Yangu, *Nile Turns Red*, 45.

50 Yangu, *Nile Turns Red*, 45; and Kuyok, "Alexis Mbale (1924–1985)," in *South Sudan*, 243–44.

51 Yangu, *Nile Turns Red*, 45; Shea, "Second Glances"; and "Gabriel Dwatuka," in *Sudanese Catholic Clergy*, 28, both in A/96/2/11, CMA.

52 Shea, "Second Glances."

53 "Profile: Marian I. Farquhar," November 1966, RG 360-46-17, PHS.

54 Farquhar, "What Do You Fear," 2–3.

55 Anderson, Werner, and Wheeler, *Day of Devastation*, 368; and Yangu, *Nile Turns Red*, 43.

56 Yangu, *Nile Turns Red*, 43.

57 S. S. Poggo, *First Sudanese Civil War*, 46–47.

58 Dorothy Rankin, November 23, 1955, folder 23, box 1, Dorothy L. Rankin Papers, PHS.

59 S. S. Poggo, *First Sudanese Civil War*, 49–50, citing in footnote 5 interview no. 84 by John Ukech Lueth and Paul Urbac (January 28, 1980); Yangu, *Nile Turns Red*, 40, 46; Johnson, "Twentieth-Century Civil Wars," 123; and Johnson, *Root Causes* (2011), 28.

60 Collins, *Southern Sudan*, 14; Hill, *Egypt in the Sudan*, 7; Fahmy, *All the Pasha's Men*, 80; Wawa, "Background," 3; and Khalid, *War and Peace in the Sudan*, 8.

61 Collins, *Southern Sudan*, 14.

62 Pitya, "History of Western Christian Evangelism," 46; Collins, *Southern Sudan*, 14; Ibrahim and Ogot, "Sudan in the Nineteenth Century," 368; Johnson, "Sudanese Military Slavery," 143; Beswick, *Sudan's Blood Memory*, 201; and Dunn, *Khedive Ismail's Army*, 33.

63 Pitya, "History of Western Christian Evangelism," 47; Dunn, *Khedive Ismail's Army*, 33; Searcy, "Sudanese Mahdi's Attitudes," 63, 71.

64 Warburg, "Ideological and Practical Considerations," 257–58, citing Memorandum to Mudirs, Enclosure No. 1, in Cromer to Salisbury, March 17, 1899, FO 78/5022. For continued discussion, see 258–59.

65 Andrew Wieu, as quoted in Deng and Daly, *Bonds of Silk*, 191. For Wieu's biographical information, see 237.

66 Southern Staff, Aweil, Bahr el Ghazal Area, Equatoria Province, on the future of the Southern Sudan, April 20, 1947, 519/2/16, SAD, as taken from Wawa, *Southern Sudanese Pursuits*, 28, 29.

67 Anonymous, "SUDAN Late 50s/Early 60s," 1, 2, Historical Documents by Country (1950) 1960–1994 1908 + 1909, folder 6, box 102, collection 081, Billy Graham Center Archives.

68 S. S. Poggo, *First Sudanese Civil War*, 49–50.

69 Lyrics and story from "Naborju's Song," 393/2/46, SAD. The Martin and Margo Russell Papers, SAD, 393/2/1–65, contain manuscript lyrics to southern Sudanese songs with translations from the 1950s through the 1970s that were gathered in 1979. Enoch Lobiya likely translated and transcribed this song (Francis Gotto, e-mail to author, August 20, 2020).

70 Quotations taken from Yangu, *Nile Turns Red*, 43–44.

71 Hansen, "Sudan," 1–4; and Allison, *Travelling Light*, 38.

72 Paterno, *Rev. Fr. Saturnino Lohure*, 41, 208–9; Akol, *Southern Sudan*, 58–59, citing in footnote 29 Severino Fuli Boki Ga'le, *Shaping a Free Southern Sudan* (Nairobi: Paulines Africa, 2002), 190; Kramer, Lobban, and Fluehr-Lobban, with Scopas S. Poggo, "Taffeng [*sic*] Lodongi, Amadeo (Emilio)," in *Historical Dictionary of the Sudan*, 417; Collins, *History of Modern Sudan*, 79; Jean-François Chauvel, "The Sudan: Africa Bleeds," *Le Figaro*, March 30, 1966, 28, A/87/7/1, CMA; Kuyok, "Emilio Tafeng (1917–1980s)," in *South Sudan*, 303; and Allison, *Travelling Light*, 38.

73 Allison, *Travelling Light*, 38.

74 Kramer, Lobban, and Fluehr-Lobban, "Port Sudan," in *Historical Dictionary of the Sudan*, 355; Hansen, "Suakin," 3; and Perkins, *Port Sudan*, 165–66; for the "servants" quotation found on p. 165, Perkins cites Gov., RSP, to the Special Commissioner on Slavery, December 19, 1925, 2/38/240, Slavery, Central Record Office, Khartoum.

75 393/2/14, SAD. That Jacob Sebit likely transcribed and translated these lyrics is inferred from the phrase "TRND JS. LATUKA. JUBA June 15, 1979" attached to this song (Francis Gotto, e-mails to author, August 20, 21, 2020).

76 Lane and Johnson, "Archaeology and History of Slavery," 518, 520–21; and Kuyok, "Alexis Mbale (1924–1985)," *South Sudan*, 243.

77 Yangu, *Nile Turns Red*, 47–48.

78 Barsella and Guixot, "List of Major Dates," 3; and Sanderson, *Education, Religion and Politics*, 352.

79 See Woodward, *Condominium*, 155; Yoh, "Historical Origins," 8; Daly, *Imperial Sudan*, 387; and Leonardi, *Dealing with Government*, 77, 131.

80 Yoh, "Historical Origins," 8.

81 Lako Logono to Governor of Equatoria, February 18, 1954, MI SCR 1/C/15, as taken from Woodward, *Condominium*, 148; see also 205n24 and 207n49.

82 "[Report on the Southern Mutiny]: despatch no 128 from Sir E Chapman-Andrews to Mr Selwyn Lloyd commenting on the Cotran Report. *Minute* JSR Duncan," October 30, 1956, no. 87, 371/119604, Foreign Office (FO), as taken from Johnson, *Sudan*, 504.

83 *Report of the Commission of Enquiry*, 81, A/87/2, CMA.

84 *Report of the Commission of Enquiry*, 5–6.

85 "[Report on the Southern Mutiny]," as taken from Johnson, *Sudan*, 506. For biographical information on Chapman-Andrews, see 518.

86 Daniel Jumi Tongun interview with Nathan Wojia Pitia in Yei, *Southern Sudan* (2004), as taken from S. S. Poggo, *First Sudanese Civil War*, 51.

87 "SUDAN Late 50s/Early 60s," 3–4.

88 "Street Manners Tells Lot about a Country," 1, folder 13 ("Sudan"), box 3, Toward Freedom Newsletter Records, Melville J. Herskovits Library of African Studies, Northwestern University.

89 Jean-Marie Garraud, "The Sudan: An Unknown War Has Been Ravaging the Upper Valley of the Nile for Three Years," *Le Figaro*, March 24, 1966, 5–6, A/87/7/1, CMA.

CHAPTER 3. LIBERATION WAR

1 "Lamentations," 1292–93, 1305.

2 Mazrui, "Shifting African Identities," 163.

3 Mabuong's version combines the English Standard Version and Authorized King James Version of the *Holy Bible*.

4 Conor O'Brien notes that "nationalism as a collective emotional force makes its first appearance in the Hebrew Bible. Nationalism at this stage is indistinguishable from religion, one and the same thing. God chose a particular people and promised them a particular land." See O'Brien, *God Land*, 2–3.

5 McCauley, *Logic of Ethnic and Religious Conflict*, 147–48.

6 Ministry of Foreign Affairs, 1956, Foreign Policy of the Sudan, No. 2, p. 23, in "Sudan's External Relations," 13.

7 Lobban, Kramer, and Fluehr-Lobban, "Arab-Israeli Conflict," in *Historical Dictionary of the Sudan*, 27; Kramer, Lobban, and Fluehr-Lobban, "Islamization," in *Historical Dictionary of the Sudan*, 223; Barsella and Guixot, "List of Major Dates," 3. See G. Vantini, "Church to Be Annihilated in Africa" (March 8, 1966), 1, A/93/15/5, CMA; and K. Cherono and T. K. Rubale, "A Petition by the East African Students in the United Kingdom and Ireland to President Ibrahim Abboud of the Republic of the Sudan during His State Visit to the United Kingdom" (May 21, 1964), 2, A/90/3/1, CMA; Wawa, "Background," 14; "The Question of Mission Schools in the Sudan," 2, E/693/6/1, CMA; and "Candidates for Election to the Executive Board: Curriculum Vitae, Mr. Ziada Arbab (Sudan)," October 27, 1960,

1–2, II/C/NOM/18, UNESCO Archives, http://unesdoc.unesco.org/images/0016
/001631/163147eb.pdf.

8 Barsella and Guixot, "List of Major Dates," 3; Breidlid, Said, and Breidlid,
Concise History of South Sudan, 183, 185, 187; Wawa, "Background," 14; and Pitya,
"Role of the Local Church," 120.

9 Corne, "Thorns from Khartoum," 32; and Barsella and Guixot, "List of Major
Dates," 3–4.

10 "Educational Planning Committee to . . . On New Educational System," *Bahr
El Ghazal Daily*, no. 12 (December 27, 1958): 4, folder EP 36.F.21 (summer 2012
designation), box 314, SSNA.

11 Anderson, Werner, and Wheeler, *Day of Devastation*, 375.

12 Barsella and Guixot, *Struggling to Be Heard*, 109.

13 Anderson, Werner, and Wheeler, *Day of Devastation*, 375; Breidlid, Said, and
Breidlid, *Concise History of South Sudan*, 211; Holt and Daly, *History of the Sudan*,
122; Deng, *War of Visions*, 138.

14 S. S. Poggo, *First Sudanese Civil War*, 57, 63, 115; Lobban, Kramer, and Fluehr-
Lobban, "Oduho, Joseph H. (ca. 1930–1993)," in *Historical Dictionary of the Sudan*,
218; Gray, "Some Reflections," 120–21; Paterno, *Rev. Fr. Saturnino Lohure*, 150–51;
and Heraclides, *Self-Determination*, 114.

15 S. S. Poggo, *First Sudanese Civil War*, 63–64; Paterno, *Rev. Fr. Saturnino Lohure*, 152;
Anthony Carthew, "Inside Southern Sudan: A Story to Shock the World," type-
script of *Daily Mail*, February 1, 1966, 6, A/96/9/4, CMA; Kramer, Lobban, and
Fluehr-Lobban, with S. S. Poggo, "Lagu, Joseph Yakobo," in *Historical Dictionary
of the Sudan*, 257; Lagu, *Sudan*, 105–6; and Akol, *Southern Sudan*, 81.

16 S. S. Poggo, *First Sudanese Civil War*, 64–65.

17 Ben Machar, correspondence with Christopher Tounsel, May 13, 2019; and
Malith Kur, email to Jesse Zink, May 8, 2019. Many thanks to Machar, Kur, and
Zink for their translation assistance.

18 Collins, *History of Modern Sudan*, 80; Barsella and Guixot, "List of Major Dates,"
4; Suleiman, "52nd Anniversary"; Kramer, Lobban, and Fluehr-Lobban, "Al-
Turabi, Hasan (1932–)," in *Historical Dictionary of the Sudan*, 430–31.

19 Kyle, "Southern Problem," 515–16; S. S. Poggo, *First Sudanese Civil War*, 118; Kuyok,
"Aggrey Jaden (1928–1986)," in *South Sudan*, 229–31; Collins, *History of Modern
Sudan*, 80.

20 Collins, *History of Modern Sudan*, 79; Kramer, Lobban, and Fluehr-Lobban,
"Round Table Conference of 1965," and "Sudan African National Union
(SANU)," in *Historical Dictionary of the Sudan*, 370–71 and 399; and Johnson, *Root
Causes* (2011), 32.

21 Voll, "Imperialism, Nationalism and Missionaries," 42.

22 Zink, *Christianity and Catastrophe*, 41–42; Johnson, *Nuer Prophets*, 315; Davies,
"Population Change," 249; Pitya, "History of Western Christian Evangelism,"
647–49, tables 4-2, 4-3, and 4-4, 699.

23 Pitya, "History of Western Christian Evangelism," 698; Johnson, *Nuer Prophets*,
315–16; Zink, *Christianity and Catastrophe*, 41; "Daniel Ferim Deng Sorur," "Guido

Akou," and "Ireneo Wien Dud," in *Sudanese Catholic Clergy*, 23–24 and 29–37; Anderson, Werner, and Wheeler, *Day of Devastation*, 360–61, 363, 395; Wheeler, "Richard Jones," 174.

24 Pitya, "History of Western Christian Evangelism," 704; Rolandsen, "Colonial Backwater," 22; Johnson, *Root Causes* (2011), 30–31, and footnote 12, citing Karl-Johan Lundström, "The Lotuho and the Verona Fathers: A Case Study of Communication in Development" (PhD diss., Uppsala, 1990), 191.

25 "Sudan to Deport."

26 Johnson, *Root Causes* (2011), 31n12, citing James, *Listening Ebony*, 241–52; James, *Listening Ebony*, 207; Sanderson, "Sudan Interior Mission," 38–39.

27 Hutchinson, *Nuer Dilemmas*, 133, 318; and Johnson, *Nuer Prophets*, 316.

28 Johnson, *Nuer Prophets*, 315–16; and Zink, *Christianity and Catastrophe*, 164–65; "prophets" quotation on 64, citing E. E. Evans-Pritchard, *Nuer Religion* (Oxford: Oxford University Press, 1956), 287–310.

29 Zink, *Christianity and Catastrophe*, 46.

30 Nikkel, "Christian Conversion," 163.

31 Nikkel, "Christian Conversion," 163; and Zink, *Christianity and Catastrophe*, 35, 44, 46.

32 Zink, *Christianity and Catastrophe*, 46.

33 "The Sudan Question and the Refugees," July 16, 1970, 1–2, A/108/3/11, CMA; and Wheeler, "Christianity in Sudan."

34 Wheeler, "Christianity in Sudan."

35 Zacharia Duot de Atem to D. T. Casson, 1963, 1, 804/8/65–66, SAD.

36 Ga'le, *Shaping a Free Southern Sudan*, 233, 242; Paterno, *Rev. Fr. Saturnino Lohure*, 148, 149, 186; and S. S. Poggo, *First Sudanese Civil War*, 113. I believe that the Southern Sudan Christian Association and the Sudanese Christian Association in East Africa—each based in Kampala—are one and the same.

37 Ibrahim Nyigilo, Southern Sudan Christian Association (Kampala) to Heads of Christian Churches, Heads of African States, and Secretary-General of the UN, 1962–1963, 804/8/53, SAD.

38 SACNU to Milton Obote, February 20, 1963, 817/10/57–59, SAD; and Manoeli, *Sudan's "Southern Problem,"* 47n26.

39 Ireneo Dud to Minister of Interior, August 1, 1965, A/95/8/1, CMA.

40 Letter dated November 29, 1965, A/107/5/63, CMA.

41 Kramer, Lobban, and Fluehr-Lobban, "Southern Sudan Association," in *Historical Dictionary of the Sudan*, 395; Rolandsen, *Guerrilla Government*, 24n32; Alexander C. Wilson (2) to Claude de Mestral and George Carpenter, January 18, 1956, 1, folder "K. Sudan 1954–1959," box 33 (536), CBMS.ICCLA, School of Oriental and African Studies, Special Collections Library; Ga'le, *Shaping a Free Southern Sudan*, 247; "Announcement," 8; and Lagu, *Sudan*, 239.

42 Deng, "Who Is behind Abbass?," 34; and Tutu, "A Reply," 16–17.

43 Lagu, "Dynamics of Co-operation," 4, 6.

44 "Father Herman Gerard Te Riele," Catholic Hierarchy, accessed August 27, 2014, http://www.catholic-hierarchy.org/bishop/bte.html; "Bishop Edoardo Mason,"

Catholic Hierarchy, accessed August 27, 2014, http://www.catholic-hierarchy
.org/bishop/bmasone.html; "Bishop Domenico Ferrara," Catholic Hierarchy,
accessed August 27, 2014, http://www.catholic-hierarchy.org/bishop/bferrarad
.html; and "Bishop Sisto Mazzoldi," Catholic Hierarchy, accessed August 27,
2014, http://www.catholic-hierarchy.org/bishop/bmazzoldi.html.

45 "To Our Brother in Christ, Bishop Ireneo Dud, to all of the Clergy and
Laity in the Church of Southern Sudan," October 31, 1965, 1, 2, A/95/9/8,
CMA.

46 "Arkangelo Ali Konogo" and "Barnada Deng, MCCJ," in *Sudanese Catholic Clergy*,
25, 33.

47 See "Avellino Wani Longa," in *Sudanese Catholic Clergy*, 26; and P. Avellino Wani
to Ireneo [Dud], November 25, 1965 (1), A/95/9/22, CMA.

48 Levi, *Bible or the Axe*, 23.

49 Levi, *Bible or the Axe*, 89–91, 91–92.

50 Michael Maror Liec to Angelo Confalonieri [1964; inferred from previous two
correspondences of the same designation], 1, A/95/3/14, CMA.

51 Elia Seng Majok to A. Matordes, April 28, 1964, 1, A/95/3/29, CMA.

52 See Juliano Kita to Bro. Mariotti, April 29, 1964, 1, A/95/3/35, CMA.

53 "Summons to an Accused Person," April 24, 1961, folder 7, box 1, Dorothy L.
Rankin Papers, PHS.

54 Gordon Tower to Andrew Das and John Smith, August 28, 1961; and A. Karrar
to Dorothy Rankin, August 20, 1961, both in folder 7, box 1, Dorothy L. Rankin
Papers, PHS.

55 "More Word from Dorothy Rankin," 2; and Dorothy Rankin, "Excerpts from
Letters," 2, September 14, 1961, Dorothy L. Rankin Papers, PHS.

56 For information on the Biblical Ishmaelites, see Porter, "Ishmaelites."

57 "Jerome Bidai," in *Sudanese Catholic Clergy*, 26.

58 Fr. Jerome Bidai Siri to Mons. Ferrara, February 11, 1966, 1, A/95/10/36,
CMA.

59 Kuyok, "Severino Fuli (1922–)," in *South Sudan*, 435.

60 Ga'le, *Shaping a Free Southern Sudan*, 222–23.

61 Ga'le, *Shaping a Free Southern Sudan*, 331–32; see 325–27 for more on the act, trophies, and uses for the liberation movement.

62 S. S. Poggo, "Kuku Religious Experiences," 129–30.

63 S. S. Poggo, "Kuku Religious Experiences," 130–31, quotation on 133. *Balokole* is a
Luganda word meaning "the saved people" and the name by which revivalists in
Uganda's Anglican Church were known. See Peterson, *Ethnic Patriotism*, 288–89;
and Ward, "Tukutendereza Yesu." Peterson cites in his explanation Amos
Kasibante, "Revival and Pentacostalism in My Life," in *The East African Revival:
History and Legacies*, ed. Kevin Ward and Emma Wild-Wood (Kampala: Foun-
tain, 2010). See Peterson, *Ethnic Patriotism*, 289n37.

64 Byaruhanga, "Dronyi." The claim that Dronyi brought thousands to Christ
comes from Lusania Kasamba, a team leader in Uganda's revival movement,
who was interviewed by Byaruhanga and is cited in his article on Dronyi.

65 393/2/17, SAD. These songs, though crafted in the mid-1960s, were translated in the late 1970s. SAD 393/2/1–65 contain manuscript lyrics to southern Sudanese songs with translations from the 1950s–1970s that were gathered in 1979. Enoch Lobiya translated 393/2/17, 393/2/26, and 393/2/27, which have no titles (Francis Gotto, e-mail to author, August 20, 2020).

66 393/2/26, SAD.

67 393/2/27, SAD.

68 See Adelino Fuli to "Fr. Bresciani," June 14, 1965, A/95/7/12, CMA.

69 Athian Joseph to Rev. Fr. Nebel, August 18, 1965, 1, A/95/8/11, CMA.

70 Felix Doka Kule to Alexis Gangi, February 11, 1966, 1, A/95/10/37, CMA.

71 "D. Paul," "Clergy: Activities, After the Expulsion of the Missionaries from the S. Sudan in February, 1964," 3, A/98/1/5, CMA.

72 Alfredo Akot Bak to Fr. Ciccacci, April 22, 1964, A/95/3/25, CMA.

73 Gabriel Ngor to Giuseppe Gusmini, July 30, 1965, A/98/45/22, CMA. For Gusmini's title, see "April 2004," Comboni Missionaries, accessed May 29, 2015, http://www.comboni.org/en/contenuti/100204-april-2004.

74 "Report on the Activities of the Arab Security Forces against the Church in Rumbek Vicariate" [1965], 19, A/93/14/14, CMA.

75 See Richard Gray, "Christianity in Post-Colonial Africa, Paper for Discussion on November 15th: The Churches' Role in the Sudan," Centre for African Studies, 3, A/108/1/23, CMA. Here Gray cites *Nouvel Observateur*, March 1967. See also Hastings, *History of African Christianity*, 134.

76 "52," 393/2/35, SAD.

77 393/2/50, SAD.

78 Rodolfo Deng to Rev. Fr. Nebel, October 20, 1965, 1, A/95/9/3, CMA.

79 Emidio Tapeng [Tafeng] Lodongi, "We Aclaim [*sic*] His Holiness' Arrival in Africa," July 31, 1969, 2, A/90/14/11, CMA. For biographical information on Tafeng, see Lobban, Kramer, and Fluehr-Lobban, "Tafeng, Emidio," in *Historical Dictionary of the Sudan*, 287.

80 Lobban, Kramer, and Fluehr-Lobban, "May Revolution of 1969" and "Nimeiri, Ja'afar (Numayri) (1930–)," in *Historical Dictionary of the Sudan*, 184–85 and 210.

81 See Collins, *History of Modern Sudan*, 109; [Allison], "Bishop's Letter," n.p.; Stephen Whittle, "A Peaceful Prospect for the Sudan," *Ecumenical Feature Service* no. 2, 45–46, in Ramsey Papers, 242:45-48, Lambeth Palace Library; and Scott, "Sudan Peoples' Liberation Movement," 69.

82 Levi, *Bible or the Axe*, 69.

83 See Allison, *Through Fire and Water*, 81–82; and *Sudan Diocesan Review* 24, no. 69 (1973): 46, which contains a picture of this scene. (It is also included in Anderson, Werner, and Wheeler, *Day of Devastation*, 450, which credits the SAD for the photo.)

84 Johnson, *Nuer Prophets*, 316–17.

85 For quotation and postwar church history, see Wheeler, "Christianity in Sudan."

86 Here I am thinking of Glassman's *War of Words* and Magaziner's *Law and the Prophets*.

1 1 Samuel 17, New International Version.

2 Kim, *Identity and Loyalty*, 189–91.

3 Jobling, *1 Samuel*, 197, 208, 215. Jobling takes the Arnold quotation, found on 208, from *The Complete Prose Works of Matthew Arnold*, 11 vols., ed. R. H. Super (Ann Arbor: University of Michigan Press, 1960–77), 3:112.

4 "Great Expectations: The Civil Roles of the Churches in Southern Sudan," *African Rights*, Discussion Paper No. 6 (April 1995): 14–15, E/678/3/1, CMA.

5 Sidahmed, "Unholy War," 83, 91, 92, 94; Hutchinson, "Curse from God?," 307–31; Mark Nikkel, "The Cross as a Symbol of Regeneration in Muonyjang bor Society," unpublished paper, M 624 266.009 AAV Brack IV, Comboni Mission Library; Nikkel, *Dinka Christianity*; and Haumann, *Travelling with Soldiers and Bishops*. For the theme of suffering, see LeMarquand, "Bibles, Crosses," 554, 561, 574, 577–78; Kustenbauder, "Politicization of Religious Identity," 400–401; Anderson, Werner, and Wheeler, *Day of Devastation*, 529–30, 533; and Sharkey, "Jihads and Crusades," 276.

6 Guarak, *Integration and Fragmentation*, 285; Okiech, "Organisational Report," 16; and Kramer, Lobban, and Fluehr-Lobban, "National Islamic Front (NIF)," in *Historical Dictionary of the Sudan*, 315–16.

7 See Frahm, "Defining the Nation," 37–39; and James, "Multiple Voices," 201 and 198, where she comments on radio's influence in shaping warfare and moral rhetoric.

8 Ashworth and Ryan, "One Nation from Every Tribe," 49; and Hanzich, "Struggles in South Sudan," 40.

9 Idris, *Conflict and Politics*, 67; Hutchinson, *Nuer Dilemmas*, 312, 314; and F. M. Deng, *War of Visions*, 219.

10 Tanenbaum Center for Interreligious Understanding, *Peacemakers in Action*, 188, 198.

11 Lobban, Kramer, and Fluehr-Lobban, "Bashir, Umar Hasan al- (1944–)" and "National Islamic Front (NIF)," in *Historical Dictionary of the Sudan*, 49–50 and 205–6; and Kramer, Lobban, and Fluehr-Lobban, "National Islamic Front (NIF)," in *Historical Dictionary of the Sudan*, 315–16.

12 "72—SPLM/SPLA Radio Broadcast to the Sudanese People on the Continuation of the War after the Overthrow of Sadiq El Mahdi by Omar el Bashir (9 August 1989)," from Wawa, *Southern Sudanese Pursuits*, 379. See also 377 for reference to the manifesto.

13 Kustenbauder, "Politicization of Religious Identity," 401.

14 Hutchinson, "Spiritual Fragments," 145; Guarak, *Integration and Fragmentation*, 284; and Madut-Arop, *Sudan's Painful Road to Peace*, 103.

15 Guarak, *Integration and Fragmentation*, 285. Lawrence Soley states that Radio SPLA returned to the air from South Sudan in October 1991, though it's unclear for how long. See Soley, "Heating up Clandestine Radio," 139.

16 Nikkel, "Cross," 23; "Great Expectations," 10–11; *Sudan: A Cry for Peace. Report of a Pax Christi International Mission January 1994*, prepared by Jan Gruiters and

Efrem Tresoldi (Brussels: Pax Christi International, 1994), 43, E/677/7/5, CMA; and Zink, *Christianity and Catastrophe*, 90. See also Hamberg, "Transnational Advocacy Networks," 161–62.

17 "Interview with Bishop Seme," 15; and Hutchinson, "Curse from God?," 308.

18 Anderson, Werner, and Wheeler, *Day of Devastation*, 650–51, 660–61.

19 Tanenbaum Center for Interreligious Understanding, *Peacemakers in Action*, 187, 196, 198–99.

20 Hamberg, "Transnational Advocacy Networks," 161–62.

21 McAlister, *Kingdom of God*, 176, 177, 179; and Fadlalla, *Branding Humanity*, 17, 30.

22 McAlister, *Kingdom of God*, 175–76, 182.

23 McAlister, *Kingdom of God*, 177; and Moyn, *Christian Human Rights*, 145.

24 "Great Expectations," 38–39.

25 F. M. Deng, *War of Visions*, 222–23.

26 "Great Expectations," 38–39; and Hutchinson, "Spiritual Fragments," 148.

27 "Great Expectations," 39.

28 Guarak, *Integration and Fragmentation*, 285; Okiech, "Organisational Report," 18; Elhag Paul questionnaire 1; and Johnson, *Root Causes* (2011), 190.

29 Atem, "Juba Diary 4."

30 Elhag Paul questionnaire 2.

31 "Transitional Executive Council," 4; "Archbishop Visits," 1, 5; Malek, "Condolences," 10; Kalulu (Nairobi), "Wake Up," 11; Luri (Lesotho), "Truth Shall Tell," 3; Michael (Germany), "Weapons," 5–6; Alley (Paterson, NJ), "Dear Editor," 6; Lomuro (Dar es Salaam), "Dear Editor," 6; Thiik (London), "Soldiers of the SPLA," 11; and Arik (Harare), "I Hate You," 11.

32 Ayiei, "Return of the Lost Boys," 1–2.

33 Interview with Abraham Nihal, August 5, 2013 (Juba, South Sudan); Ayiei, "Return of the Lost Boys," 1–2; and Lesch, *Sudan*, 90. Douglas Johnson states that the unofficial estimate of Sudanese refugees around the Itang, Fungyido, and Dimma camps in February 1991 was around 222,000–262,000. See Johnson, *Root Causes* (2011), 88–89.

34 Ayiei, "Diaspora Commission"; Collins, *History of Modern Sudan*, 240–41; Nhial interview; "Abraham Nhial," Lost Boy No More: The True Story of Abraham Nhial—One of the Lost Boys of South Sudan, accessed July 25, 2016, http://lostboysnomore.org/lost-boy-abraham.

35 Elhag Paul questionnaire 1; and "Faith" questionnaire.

36 Elhag Paul questionnaire 1.

37 Ayiei, "Diaspora Commission."

38 Chang, "Time for Southern Sudanese Youth to Stand Up," 3.

39 Lesch, "Abuja Conferences," 46–47.

40 "Commentary: Reliable Enemy," 11.

41 Malith, "SPLA Keeps Goliath at Bay," 11.

42 Lobban, Kramer, and Fluehr-Lobban, "Sudanese Peoples' Liberation Movement (SPLM), Sudanese Peoples' Liberation Army (SPLA)," in *Historical Dictionary of the Sudan*, 280–81; Africa Watch Committee, *Denying "the Honor of Living,"*

153; and G. N. Anderson, *Sudan in Crisis*, 71. For information on the Sudan Alliance Forces and their efforts against the government, see Lobban, Kramer, and Fluehr-Lobban, "Sudan Alliance Forces (SAF)," in *Historical Dictionary of the Sudan*, 270–71; Kramer, Lobban, and Fluehr-Lobban, "Sudan Alliance Forces (SAF)," in *Historical Dictionary of the Sudan*, 400; and G. N. Anderson, *Sudan in Crisis*, 71.

43 Attiyah, "Cost of Freedom," 5. For biographical information on Attiyah, see Omolo, "Father Thomas Oliha."

44 Attiyah, "Christ the 'Good Shepherd,'" 7.

45 Izale, "Joint Front," 8.

46 Attiyah, "Challenge of Peace," 8. Attiyah borrows from and cites Colossians 3:10–11.

47 James, *War and Survival*, 173, 249–50, quotation on 250; and Rule, "Refugees from Sudan."

48 "Brief Life History."

49 Jaden, "Khartoum by Night," 11.

50 Watkins, *With Kitchener's Army*, 207.

51 Wheeler, "Gateway to the Heart of Africa," 11.

52 Kuyok, *South Sudan*, 731–32.

53 Malek, "Condolences," 10. Malek's letter was addressed to George W. Bush with condolences following the 9/11 attacks.

54 Kramer, Lobban, and Fluehr-Lobban, "Bin Laden, Usama (1957–2011)," in *Historical Dictionary of the Sudan*, 94–95; and Hiro, *War without End*, 174.

55 Nhial interview.

56 Pinaud, "'We Are Trained to Be Married!,'" 376; and Beswick, "Women, War, and Leadership," 102–4.

57 Michael, "Weapons," 5.

58 Attiyah, "Cost of Freedom," 5.

59 Riak, "Land of Sudan," 11.

60 Wöndu, "Knights of Lucifer," 2.

61 Jaden, "Politics of Self Destruction," 11.

62 "Christian Leaders," 5 (contextual information on p. 4).

63 Interview with John Daau, August 24, 2013 (Juba, South Sudan); John Daau, email to Christopher Tounsel, May 18, 2016. For information on Daau, see "Meet Rev. John Chol Daau of Sudan," Episcopal Diocese of Central Florida, April 15, 2016, http://www.cfdiocese.org/cfe/meet-rev-john-chol-daau-of-sudan/.

64 The Rt. Rev. Bismark Avokaya questionnaire and "Welcome to the Diocese of Mundri," Diocese of Mundri in the Episcopal Church of Sudan, accessed August 19, 2020, http://www.mundri.anglican.org/index.php?PageID=bishop2.

65 Interview with Angelo Lokoyome, September 4, 2013 (Juba, South Sudan).

66 Mahmoud E. Yousif questionnaire.

67 Michael, "Weapons," 5.

68 Hays, "From the Land of the Bow," 30–31.

69 Description of prophecy taken from Isaiah 18, New International Version.

70 Johnson, *Nuer Prophets*, 342; and Falge, "Countering Rupture," 175.

71 Hutchinson, *Nuer Dilemmas*, 316. Here Hutchinson quotes and cites Deborah Scroggins, *Sunday Journal of the Atlanta Constitution*, March 10, 1991.

72 "New Sudan Brigade (NSB)," 11.

73 Zion, "Military Boots," 3.

74 Abuk, "Sudan Laugh," 11.

75 Johnson, *Root Causes* (2011), 119.

76 Kwaje, "Vision, Perspective, and Position," 19.

77 Hutchinson, "Spiritual Fragments," 148–49.

78 Ajuok, "Response of Southern Sudanese Intellectuals," 133–34, where he discusses John Garang's paper to the AASC.

79 "Faith" questionnaire.

80 Elhag Paul questionnaire 1.

81 Parfitt, *Black Jews*, 102–3, 106, 109.

82 Chidester, *Empire of Religion*, 234. For direct quotation, he cites Magema M. Fuze, *The Black People and Whence They Came: A Zulu View*, ed. A. T. Cope, trans. H. C. Lugg (Pietermaritzburg: University of Natal Press, 1979), iv, 9.

83 Parfitt, *Black Jews*, 133.

84 See Wilson, *I Was a Slave*. An examination of Wilson's life can be found in Johnson, "Salim Wilson," 27–39.

85 Ninan, *Comparative Study*, unpaged abstract.

86 James, *War and Survival*, 274.

87 Nsiku, "Isaiah," 848–49.

88 Weanzana, "1 and 2 Chronicles," 475.

89 Weanzana et al., "Psalms," 616.

90 Olupona and Rey, introduction, 5.

91 Kramer, Lobban, and Fluehr-Lobban, "Comprehensive Peace Agreement," in *Historical Dictionary of the Sudan*, 115–16; Steve Paterno questionnaire; Sudanese Anglican Bishop questionnaire; and interview with Rugaya Richard, August 6, 2013 (Juba, South Sudan).

92 Jabiro, "Ode to GARANG," 10.

93 Kramer, Lobban, and Fluehr-Lobban, "Kiir Mayardiit, Salva (1951–)," in *Historical Dictionary of the Sudan*, 252–53; and interview with Ezekiel Diing, July 11, 2012 (Juba, South Sudan).

94 Diing interview.

95 "Q&A." To be sure, the events leading up to his death have been hotly debated. See, for example, "Death of John Garang."

96 Diing interview.

97 AFP, "Sudan's Garang."

CHAPTER 5. THE TROUBLED PROMISED LAND

1 See Exodus 1–14 for the complete story.

2 "Exodus: Gods and Kings (2014)—Full Transcript," Subslikescript, accessed August 12, 2020, https://subslikescript.com/movie/Exodus_Gods_and_Kings-1528100.

3   "President Museveni Calls for Unity Deal."

4   Harris, "U.S. Imposes Arms Ban on South Sudan."

5   International Crisis Group, *South Sudan*, 3–4.

6   "Sudan's CPA."

7   Gibia, "Who Is Really Virtuous?"; and "About Sudan Tribune," *Sudan Tribune*, accessed June 30, 2020, http://www.sudantribune.com/spip.php?page=about.

8   Gibia, "Who Is Really Virtuous?"

9   Moses, "Former Lost Boy."

10   Guarak, "Conflict of Interest?"

11   Breidlid, Said, and Breidlid, *Concise History of South Sudan*, 333–34, 337.

12   "South Sudan Institutions."

13   Lyrics to "South Sudan Oyee!" from Martell, "A Song for South Sudan." Information on its composition was also taken from this article.

14   "South Sudan Institutions."

15   Buay, "Kiir Should Remove Army Officers."

16   Khoryoam, "New Nation."

17   Rice, "South Sudan's New National Anthem."

18   United Nations Security Council, "Southern Sudan Referendum"; United Nations Mission in the Sudan, "Independence of South Sudan"; and "South Sudanese Christians Plan."

19   McDonnell, "South Sudan President." See also Keinon, "Diplomacy" (which McDonnell cites).

20   International Crisis Group, *South Sudan*, 3.

21   Lupai, "First Anniversary."

22   McNeish, "South Sudan Teeters."

23   Biar, "Juba."

24   Anthony, "You Will See," 42, 45–47; and Tryggestad, "So You Want to Attend."

25   Biar, "Juba."

26   A. Poggo, *Come Let Us Rebuild*, 207; and Jeffrey, "How Christian Churches Are Trying." The South Sudan Council of Churches is an ecumenical body comprising seven member churches and associated churches in the country. See "South Sudan Has Suffered Crucifixion."

27   Biar, "Juba."

28   Sr. Sierra questionnaire; and Martin Ochaya Lino Agwella questionnaire.

29   Agwella questionnaire.

30   Agwella questionnaire; and Sierra questionnaire.

31   McNeish, "South Sudan Teeters"; and International Crisis Group, *South Sudan*, 4–5.

32   Howden, "South Sudan"; Muhumuza, "South Sudan"; Kulish and Sengupta, "New Estimate"; and AFP, "Attempted Coup."

33   McNeish, "South Sudan Teeters"; and Howden, "South Sudan."

34   Howden, "South Sudan."

35   McNeish, "South Sudan Teeters"; and D. H., "Descent."

36   D. H., "Descent."

37 International Crisis Group, *South Sudan*, 1; AFP, "Attempted Coup"; McNeish, "South Sudan Teeters"; "Full Statement by President Salva Kiir"; and "South Sudan's Warring Sides."

38 D. H., "Descent"; and "South Sudan's Army Advances."

39 Howden, "South Sudan."

40 Muhumuza, "South Sudan"; and Stringham and Forney, "It Takes a Village," 185–86.

41 International Crisis Group, *South Sudan*, 5.

42 International Crisis Group, *South Sudan*, i; D. H., "Descent"; and Muhumuza, "South Sudan."

43 "Global Conflict Tracker [South Sudan]"; and "South Sudan No Longer in Famine."

44 "Global Conflict Tracker [South Sudan]"; "Back with a Vengeance," 42; International Crisis Group, *South Sudan*, i and 2; John Chol Daau, email message to Christopher Tounsel, March 13, 2015, re: "South Sudan peace talks update"; "Can Ethnic Differences Be Overcome?," 41; and "S. Sudanese MPs Extend President Kiir's Term."

45 "Global Conflict Tracker [South Sudan]."

46 "South Sudan's Warring Parties"; "Global Conflict Tracker [South Sudan]," which cites "U.S. Cuts Support to South Sudan's President," *Associated Press*, January 25, 2018; Lederer, "US after Supporting South Sudan's Leader Calls Him 'Unfit'"; and "U.S. Bans Weapons Export."

47 "Global Conflict Tracker [South Sudan]."

48 Kulish and Sengupta, "New Estimate"; "Can Ethnic Differences Be Overcome?," 41; Office for the Coordination of Humanitarian Affairs South Sudan, "South Sudan Crisis"; "South Sudan's Army Advances"; and "Global Conflict Tracker [South Sudan]."

49 "South Sudan President Celebrates."

50 "Symposium: One Church from Every Tribe," 6.

51 Loro, "Opening Address," 13–14.

52 "South Sudan President Celebrates."

53 Jeffrey, "How Christian Churches Are Trying."

54 Patinkin, "In S. Sudan, Churches Struggle."

55 Patinkin, "In S. Sudan, Churches Struggle."

56 Jeffrey, "How Christian Churches Are Trying."

57 Radio Tamazuj, "If You Kill People"; and Oduha, "South Sudan Church Leaders."

58 "About Us," *Christian Times*, June 3, 2015, http://www.thechristiantimes.net/index.php/73-about-us/528-about-us; and Lokoyome interview.

59 "Samaritan's Purse Provides Biblical Training to Government Leaders in South Sudan," Samaritan's Purse, accessed March 28, 2018, https://www.samaritanspurse.org/article/samaritans-purse-provides-biblical-training-to-government-leaders-in-south-sudan/.

60 Jeffrey, "How Christian Churches Are Trying."

61 Patinkin, "In S. Sudan, Churches Struggle"; Anglican Communion News Service, "Exiled South Sudanese Anglicans"; and Jeffrey, "How Christian Churches Are Trying" (for Ashworth quotation). For original ACNS article, see Anglican Communion News Service, September 24, 2018, https://www.anglicannews.org/news/2018/09/exiled-south-sudanese-anglicans-pray-peace-will-enable-them-to-go-and-rebuild-our-nation.aspx.

62 Patinkin, "In S. Sudan, Churches Struggle."

63 Radio Tamazuj, "If You Kill People."

64 TCT Correspondent, "No More of This!"

65 Peralta, "Will South Sudan's New Peace Agreement Hold?"

66 Bul, "Christmas Message 2015."

67 Tut, "Theological Reflections."

68 For examples from Joseph de Tuombuk, see his "Is South Sudan Peace Process Doomed to Fail?," "Tribalism in South Sudan," and "Potential Politicization." For Elhag Paul pieces, see "SPLM and Mass Media," "To Achieve Peace in South Sudan" (Paul cites this article in his first completed questionnaire), and "Like a Leopard."

69 All quotations and information from Tuombuk, "Tribalism in South Sudan."

70 Paul, "Like a Leopard."

71 Elhag Paul, email message to Christopher Tounsel, April 27, 2015.

72 Jeffrey, "How Christian Churches Are Trying."

73 Patinkin, "Exiled South Sudanese" (citing *Voice of Hope*, the Kajo Keji's diocesan newsletter); and Bul, "Christmas Message 2015."

74 Exodus 12:38, King James Version, reads, "And a mixed multitude went up also with them; and flocks, and herds, and very much cattle."

CONCLUSION

1 Flock, "Joseph Kony," quoting William Branigin.

2 Stewart, "How Christian Fundamentalists Plan." Stewart quotes and cites Philip Jenkins, *Laying Down the Sword: Why We Can't Ignore the Bible's Violent Verses* (New York: HarperCollins, 1994)

3 "UN: Muslims Ethnically Cleansed"; and "Global Conflict Tracker."

4 For work on Muslims in South Sudan and the issue of religious freedom, see Salomon, "Religion after the State."

5 Olupona and Rey, introduction, 6, quoting Bennetta Jules-Rosette, "The Sacred in African New Religions," in *The Changing Face of Religion*, ed. James A. Beckford and Thomas Luckmann (London: Sage, 1989), 157.

6 See Kustenbauder, "Politicization of Religious Identity," 413. I build off Timeka Tounsel's claim concerning black women's use of the Boaz-Ruth narrative to create edifying views of dating, romance, and marriage. See T. Tounsel, "#WaitingForBoaz," 96. There, Tounsel cites and builds on Williams, "Womanist Theology," 117–25.

7 K. J. Anderson, *Benign Bigotry*, 239–40.

8 Fanon, *Wretched of the Earth*, 142–43.

9 Interview with Anthony Poggo, August 2, 2013 (Juba, South Sudan).

10 Interview with Grace Ropani and Diana Juan Joseph, August 7, 2013 (Juba, South Sudan); for the full name of the school, see "Let There Be Light," Juba Diocesan Model Secondary School, accessed August 11, 2020, http://www.jdmss .co.uk/.

11 "Juba Dismisses Ambassador's Role."

Bibliography

ARCHIVES

Billy Graham Center Archives, Wheaton College, Wheaton, IL
Church Missionary Society Archive, Birmingham University, Birmingham, UK
Comboni Mission Archive, Rome
Comboni Mission Library, Rome
Lambeth Palace Library, London
Melville J. Herskovits Library of African Studies, Northwestern University, Evanston, IL
Presbyterian Historical Society, Philadelphia
School of Oriental and African Studies, Special Collections Library, London
South Sudan National Archives, Juba
Sudan Archive, Durham University Libraries, Durham, UK

INTERVIEWS (JUBA, SOUTH SUDAN)

John Daau, founder of Good Shepherd College and Seminary and founder/editor of
    Christian Times, August 24, 2013
Ezekiel Diing, Anglican bishop of Twic East Diocese, July 11, 2012
Angelo Lokoyome, Justice of Peace coordinator, Catholic Archdiocese of Juba,
    September 4, 2013
Abraham Nhial, Anglican bishop of Aweil, August 5, 2013
Elizabeth Noel, president of the Episcopal Church of Sudan Mothers' Union,
    September 2, 2013
Anthony Poggo, Anglican bishop of Kajo Keji, August 2, 2013
Rugaya Richard, media work for Episcopal Church of Sudan, August 6, 2013
Grace Ropani and Diana Juan Joseph, secondary school students, August 7, 2013
Joseph Taban, principal of Bishop Gwynne College, July 12, 2012

QUESTIONNAIRES

Martin Ochaya Lino Agwella, former secretary general of the Catholic Archdiocese of Juba
Rt. Reverend Bismark Avokaya
"Faith" (pseudonym)
Steve Paterno
Elhag Paul (2)
Sr. Sierra, first director of Radio Bakhita
Sudanese Anglican bishop
Mahmoud E. Yousif, former chairman of New Sudan Islamic Council and South Sudan Islamic Council

OTHER SOURCES

Abuk, Ater Deng. "The Sudan Laugh." *SPLM/SPLA Update*, October 3, 1994.
"The Acts of Peter." In *Lost Scriptures: Books that Did Not Make It into the New Testament*, edited by Bart D. Ehrman, 135–54. New York: Oxford University Press, 2003.
AFP. "Attempted Coup in South Sudan." *Sydney Morning Herald*, December 16, 2013.
AFP. "Sudan's Garang Laid to Rest as Grieving Crowds Mourn Him." *Sudan Tribune*, August 6, 2005.
Africa Watch Committee. *Denying "the Honor of Living": Sudan, a Human Rights Disaster*. Africa Watch Report. New York: Africa Watch Committee, 1990.
Ahmed, Hassan Makki Mohamed. *Sudan: The Christian Design*. Leicester, UK: Islamic Foundation, 1974.
Ajuok, Albino Deng. "Response of Southern Sudanese Intellectuals to African Nationalism." *Journal of Pan African Studies* 2, no. 5 (July 2008): 130–41.
Akanji, Israel. "Black Theology." In *The Oxford Encyclopedia of African Thought*, vol. 1, edited by F. Abiola Irele and Biodun Jeyifo, 177–78. New York: Oxford University Press, 2010.
Akol, Lam. *Southern Sudan: Colonialism, Resistance and Autonomy*. Trenton, NJ: Red Sea Press, 2007.
Ali, Nada Mustafa. *Gender, Race, and Sudan's Exile Politics: Do We All Belong to This Country?* Lanham, MD: Lexington Books, 2015.
Alley, Sabit. "Dear Editor." *SPLM/SPLA Update*, October 31, 1993.
[Allison, Oliver]. "The Bishop's Letter." *Sudan Diocesan Review* 23, no. 66 (Spring 1972).
Allison, Oliver. "Church History in the Making." *Sudan Diocesan Review* 1, no. 3 (July 1949): 7–9.
Allison, Oliver. "From Bishop O. C. [Oliver] Allison, Meridi, via Juba, Southern Sudan, December, 1948." *Southern Sudan Mail Bag*, no. 11 (July 1949): 22–25.
Allison, Oliver. *Through Fire and Water*. London: Church Missionary Society, 1976.
Allison, Oliver. *Travelling Light: Bishop Oliver Allison of the Sudan Remembers*. Bexhill-on-Sea: privately printed, 1983.
Anderson, Benedict. *Imagined Communities: Reflections on the Origin and Spread of Nationalism*. Rev. ed. London: Verso, 2006.

Anderson, G. Norman. *Sudan in Crisis: The Failure of Democracy*. Gainesville: University Press of Florida, 1999.

Anderson, Kristin J. *Benign Bigotry: The Psychology of Subtle Prejudice*. Cambridge: Cambridge University Press, 2010.

Anderson, William, Roland Werner, and Andrew Wheeler. *Day of Devastation, Day of Contentment: The History of the Sudanese Church across 2000 Years*. Nairobi: Paulines, 2001.

Anglican Communion News Service. "Exiled South Sudanese Anglicans Pray Peace Will Enable Them to 'Go and Rebuild Our Nation.'" *Christian Times* (South Sudan), September 24, 2018.

An-Na'im, Abdullahi A. "Islam and National Integration in the Sudan." In *Religion and National Integration in Africa: Islam, Christianity, and Politics in the Sudan and Nigeria*, edited by John O. Hunwick, 11–38. Evanston, IL: Northwestern University Press, 1992.

"Announcement: Formation of the 'Southern Sudan Association.'" *Grass Curtain* 1, no. 1 (May 1970): 8.

Anthias, Floya, and Nira Yuval-Davis. Introduction to *Woman-Nation-State*, edited by Nira Yuval-Davis and Floya Anthias, 1–15. New York: St. Martin's, 1989.

Anthony, Paul A. "'You Will See': Biar Helps Build South Sudan." *ACU Today* (Winter 2012): 41–47.

"Archbishop Visits Refugee Camps." *SPLM/SPLA Update*, August 15, 1994.

Aremo, Jimmy Onge. "Lamentation." *Sudan Tribune*, February 19, 2015.

Arik, Mawien Dhor. "I Hate You." *SPLM/SPLA Update*, June 26, 1995.

Artin, Yacoub. *England in the Sudan*. Translated by George Robb. London: Macmillan, 1911.

Asad, Talal. *Formations of the Secular: Christianity, Islam, Modernity*. Stanford: Stanford University Press, 2003.

Ashworth, John, and Maura Ryan. "'One Nation from Every Tribe, Tongue, and People': The Church and Strategic Peacebuilding in South Sudan." *Journal of Catholic Social Thought* 10, no. 1 (2013): 47–67.

Atem, Atem Yaak. "Juba Diary 4: Please Don't Call Me 'Far Away from War.'" *Gurtong*, February 4, 2010. http://www.gurtong.net/ECM/Editorial/tabid/124 /ctl/ArticleView/mid/519/articleId/3132/Juba-Diary-4-Please-Dont-Call-Me-Far -Away-from-War.aspx.

Attiyah, Thomas. "The Challenge of Peace in Sudan." *SPLM/SPLA Update*, December 2000.

Attiyah, Thomas. "Christ the 'Good Shepherd.'" *SPLM/SPLA Update*, June 6, 1995.

Attiyah, Thomas. "The Cost of Freedom." *SPLM/SPLA Update*, October 11, 1994.

Ayiei, Thon Agany. "Return of the Lost Boys to South Sudan: A Strategy to Building a Stronger South Sudan." Master's thesis, Naval Postgraduate School, 2011.

Ayiei, Thon Agany. "South Sudan Needs Diaspora Commission." *New Sudan Vision*, May 24, 2011. http://newsudanvision.com/columns/2363-south-sudan-needs-a -diaspora-commission.

"Back with a Vengeance: Conflict in South Sudan." *Economist*, March 1, 2014, 42.

"Barnaba Marial Benjamin." *Sudan Tribune*. Accessed July 23, 2019. http://www
.sudantribune.com/spip.php?mot744.

Barsella, Gino, and Miguel Á. Ayuso Guixot. *Struggling to Be Heard: The Christian
Voice in Independent Sudan, 1956–1996*. Nairobi: Paulines, 1998.

Baum, Robert. "Sudan." In *Africana: The Encyclopedia of the African and African American Experience*, edited by Kwame Anthony Appiah and Henry Louis Gates Jr.,
1793–98. New York: Basic Civitas, 1999.

Beare, Joyce M. "From Miss J. M. Beare, of Loka, the Nugent School, Loka,
S. Sudan, 10/11/46." *Southern Sudan Mail Bag*, no. 3 (March 1947): 18–20.

Beswick, Stephanie. *Sudan's Blood Memory: The Legacy of War, Ethnicity, and Slavery in
South Sudan*. Rochester, NY: University of Rochester Press, 2004.

Beswick, Stephanie. "Women, War and Leadership in South Sudan." In *White Nile,
Black Blood: War, Leadership, and Ethnicity from Khartoum to Kampala*, edited by Jay
Spaulding and Stephanie Beswick, 93–113. Lawrenceville, NJ: Red Sea Press, 2000.

Biar, Zechariah Manyok. "Is Juba Going Back to Khartoum?" *Sudan Tribune*, October 28, 2012.

"Bishop Gwynne." *Times* (London), December 4, 1957.

*The Black Book of the Sudan: On the Expulsion of the Missionaries from Southern Sudan, An
Answer*. Milan: SAGA, 1964.

Boddy-Evans, Alistair. "Chronological List of African Independence." Thoughtco.
Accessed November 16, 2020. https://www.thoughtco.com/chronological-list
-of-african-independence-4070467.

Breidlid, Anders, Avelino Androga Said, and Astrid Kristine Breidlid, eds. *A Concise
History of South Sudan*. Rev. ed. Kampala: Fountain, 2014.

Brennan, James R. *Taifa: Making Nation and Race in Urban Tanzania*. Athens: Ohio
University Press, 2012.

"Brief Life History of the Late Richard Latio Lo'Jaden." *Lamentations from the Heart*
(blog), February 28, 2009. http://richardlatios.blogspot.com/2009/.

Buay, Gordon. "Kiir Should Remove Army Officers from National Anthem Committee." *Sudan Tribune*, August 15, 2010.

Bul, Daniel Deng. "Christmas Message 2015—from Archbishop Daniel Deng Bul,
Episcopal Church of South Sudan and Sudan." *Christian Times* (South Sudan),
December 26, 2015.

Byaruhanga, Christopher. "Dronyi, Sosthenes Yangu Ayume." *Dictionary of African
Christian Biography*. Accessed September 9, 2020. https://dacb.org/stories
/uganda/dronyi-sosthenes/.

"Can Ethnic Differences Be Overcome? South Sudan." *Economist*, July 5, 2014, 41.

Casanova, José. *Public Religions in the Modern World*. Chicago: University of Chicago
Press, 1994.

Castillo, Dennis Angelo. *The Maltese Cross: A Strategic History of Malta*. London:
Praeger Security, 2006.

"Challenge to the Church: A Theological Comment on the Political Crisis in South
Africa. The Kairos Document, 1985." South African History Online, June 1, 2012.
http://www.sahistory.org.za/article/kairos-document-1985-0.

Chang, Derek. *Citizens of a Christian Nation: Evangelical Missions and the Problem of Race in the Nineteenth Century.* Philadelphia: University of Pennsylvania Press, 2010.

Chang, Kong P. "Time for Southern Sudanese Youth to Stand Up." *SPLM/SPLA Update,* September 25, 1995.

Chidester, David. *Empire of Religion: Imperialism and Comparative Religion.* Chicago: University of Chicago Press, 2014.

Chidester, David. *Savage Systems: Colonialism and Comparative Religion in Southern Africa.* Charlottesville: University Press of Virginia, 1996.

"Christian Leaders Present Our Tragedy to the Pope." *SPLM/SPLA Update,* February 14, 1993.

Churchill, Winston. *The River War: The Reconquest of the Sudan.* Edited by F. Rhodes. Rev. ed. New York: Longmans, Green, 1902.

Cisternino, Mario. *Passion for Africa: Missionary and Imperial Papers on the Evangelisation of Uganda and Sudan, 1848-1923.* Kampala: Fountain, 2004.

Coleman, Beth. "Race as Technology." *Camera Obscura: Feminism, Culture, and Media Studies* 24, no. 1 (May 2009): 177-207.

Collins, Robert O. *A History of Modern Sudan.* Cambridge: Cambridge University Press, 2008.

Collins, Robert O. *Land beyond the Rivers: The Southern Sudan, 1898-1918.* New Haven, CT: Yale University Press, 1971.

Collins, Robert O. *Shadows in the Grass: Britain in the Southern Sudan, 1918-1956.* New Haven, CT: Yale University Press, 1983.

Collins, Robert O. *The Southern Sudan, 1883-1898: A Struggle for Control.* New Haven, CT: Yale University Press, 1964.

"Commentary: Reliable Enemy." *SPLM/SPLA Update,* June 29, 1992.

Cone, James H. *Black Theology and Black Power.* New York: Seabury, 1969.

Cone, James H., and Gayraud S. Wilmore. "Black Theology and African Theology: Considerations for Dialogue, Critique, and Integration." In *Black Theology: A Documentary History,* vol. 1, *1966-1979,* edited by James H. Cone and Gayraud S. Wilmore, 463-76. Maryknoll, NY: Orbis Books, 1979.

"Contributors." In *Africa Bible Commentary: A One-Volume Commentary Written by 70 African Scholars,* edited by Tokunboh Adeyemo, xiii-xviii. Grand Rapids, MI: Zondervan, 2010.

Corne, Barthelemy. "Thorns from Khartoum." *Worldmission* 19, no. 4 (Winter 1968-1969): 29-36.

Daly, Martin W. *Empire on the Nile: The Anglo-Egyptian Sudan, 1898-1934.* Cambridge: Cambridge University Press, 1986.

Daly, Martin W. *Imperial Sudan: The Anglo-Egyptian Condominium, 1934-1956.* Cambridge: Cambridge University Press, 2002.

Daly, Martin W. "Wingate, Sir (Francis) Reginald, First Baronet (1861-1953)." In *Oxford Dictionary of National Biography.* New York: Oxford University Press, 2011.

Davies, H. R. J. "Population Change in the Sudan since Independence." *Geography* 73, no. 3 (June 1988): 249-55.

"The Death of John Garang." *Economist,* August 4, 2005.

Decker, Alicia C. *In Idi Amin's Shadow: Women, Gender, and Militarism in Uganda.* Athens: Ohio University Press, 2014.

de Cruz, Joaquim Jose Valente. "'A New Era of Peace': St Comboni's Dream of a Developed and Free South Sudan and the Commitment of His Followers to Fulfil It." In *One Church from Every Tribe, Tongue and People: Symposium on the Role of the Church in the Independence of South Sudan*, edited by John Ashworth, 28–52. Nairobi: Paulines, 2012.

Deng, Francis M. "Dinka Response to Christianity: The Pursuit of Well-Being in a Developing Society." In *Vernacular Christianity: Essays in the Social Anthropology of Religion Presented to Godfrey Lienhardt*, edited by Wendy James and Douglas H. Johnson, 157–69. New York: Barber, 1988.

Deng, Francis M. *War of Visions: Conflict of Identities in the Sudan.* Washington, DC: Brookings Institution, 1995.

Deng, Francis M., and Martin W. Daly. *"Bonds of Silk": The Human Factor in the British Administration of the Sudan.* East Lansing: Michigan State University Press, 1989.

Deng, J. M. "Who Is behind Abbass?" *Grass Curtain* 1, no. 4 (April 1971): 34–35.

de Sarum [Saram], J. B. "The Church in the Sudan." *Southern Sudan Mail Bag*, no. 13 (May 1950): 28–33.

de Sarum [Saram], J. B. "From Mr. J. B. de Saram, C.M.S. Akot, via Juba, Southern Sudan, 15th February, 1950." *Southern Sudan Mail Bag*, no. 13 (May 1950): 7.

D. H. "The Descent into Civil War." *Economist*, December 27, 2013.

Dunn, John P. *Khedive Ismail's Army.* London: Routledge, 2005.

Elbourne, Elizabeth. *Blood Ground: Colonialism, Missions, and the Contest for Christianity in the Cape Colony and Britain, 1799–1853.* Montreal: McGill-Queen's University Press, 2002.

Elrayah, Tagelsir H. "Arabic and English in Sudan, 1821–1985." *Islamic Studies* 38, no. 4 (Winter 1999): 603–20.

Fadlalla, Amal Hassan. *Branding Humanity: Competing Narratives of Rights, Violence, and Global Citizenship.* Stanford, CA: Stanford University Press, 2018.

Fadlalla, Amal Hassan. "The Neoliberalization of Compassion: Darfur and the Mediation of American Faith, Fear, and Terror." In *New Landscapes of Inequality: Neoliberalism and the Erosion of Democracy in America*, edited by Jane L. Collins, Micaela di Leonardo, and Brett Williams, 209–28. Sante Fe, NM: School for Advanced Research Press, 2008.

Fahmy, Khaled. *All the Pasha's Men: Mehmed Ali, His Army and the Making of Modern Egypt.* Cambridge: Cambridge University Press, 1997.

Falge, Christiane. "Countering Rupture: Young Nuer in New Religious Movements." *Sociologus: Journal of Empirical Social Anthropology* 58, no. 2 (2008): 169–95.

Fanon, Frantz. *The Wretched of the Earth.* Translated by Richard Philcox. 1963; New York: Grove Press, 2004.

Feierman, Steven. *Peasant Intellectuals: Anthropology and History in Tanzania.* Madison: University of Wisconsin Press, 1990.

Flock, Elizabeth. "Joseph Kony and the Lord's Resistance Army: A Primer." *Washington Post*, October 14, 2011.

Frahm, Ole. "Defining the Nation: National Identity in South Sudanese Media Discourse." *Africa Spectrum* 47, no. 1 (2012): 21–49.

"Full Statement by President Salva Kiir on Attempted Coup." *Gurtong*, December 16, 2013. http://www.gurtong.net/ECM/Editorial/tabid/124/ctl/ArticleView/mid/519/articleId/14151/Full-Statement-by-President-Salva-Kiir-on-Attempted-Coup.aspx.

Ga'le, Severino Fuli Boki Tombe. *Shaping a Free Southern Sudan: Memoirs of Our Struggle 1934–1985*. Limuru: Loa Catholic Mission Council, 2002.

Gibia, Roba. "Who Is Really Virtuous in the Government of Southern Sudan?" *Sudan Tribune*, October 24, 2008.

Glassman, Jonathon. *War of Words, War of Stones: Racial Thought and Violence in Colonial Zanzibar*. Bloomington: Indiana University Press, 2011.

"Global Conflict Tracker." Council on Foreign Relations, last updated July 9, 2020. https://www.cfr.org/interactive/global-conflict-tracker/conflict/violence-central-african-republic.

"Global Conflict Tracker [South Sudan]." Council on Foreign Relations, last updated July 8, 2020. https://www.cfr.org/interactives/global-conflict-tracker#!/conflict/civil-war-in-south-sudan.

Gordon, David M. *Invisible Agents: Spirits in a Central African History*. Athens: Ohio University Press, 2012.

Gray, Richard. *Black Christians and White Missionaries*. New Haven, CT: Yale University Press, 1990.

Gray, Richard. "Epilogue." In *Religion and Conflict in Sudan: Papers from an International Conference at Yale, May 1999*, edited by Yusuf Fadl Hasan and Richard Gray, 195–200. Nairobi: Paulines, 2002.

Gray, Richard. "Some Reflections on Christian Involvement, 1955–1972." In *Religion and Conflict in Sudan: Papers from an International Conference at Yale, May 1999*, edited by Yusuf Fadl Hasan and Richard Gray, 114–25. Nairobi: Paulines, 2002.

Guarak, Mawut. "Conflict of Interest? The Most Dangerous Form of Corruption." *Sudan Tribune*, February 11, 2009.

Guarak, Mawut Achiecque Mach. *Integration and Fragmentation of the Sudan: An African Renaissance*. Bloomington, IN: AuthorHouse, 2011.

Haddon, E. B. "Mr. J. H. Driberg." *Nature: International Journal of Science* 157 (March 2, 1946): 257–58.

Hall, Bruce. *A History of Race in Muslim West Africa, 1600–1960*. New York: Cambridge University Press, 2011.

Hamberg, Stephan. "Transnational Advocacy Networks, Rebel Groups, and Demobilization of Child Soldiers in Sudan." In *Transnational Dynamics of Civil War*, edited by Jeffrey T. Checkel, 149–72. New York: Cambridge University Press, 2013.

Hansen, Erik. *Preservation of Suakin: Sudan—(Mission) October–November 1972*. Paris: UNESCO, 1973.

Hanzich, Ricky. "Struggles in South Sudan: Five Months to Resolve 55 Years of Structural Violence." *Harvard International Review* 33, no. 1 (Spring 2011): 38–41.

Harris, Gardiner. "U.S. Imposes Arms Ban on South Sudan as Civil War Grinds On." *New York Times*, February 2, 2018.

Harrop, Blakemore. "From Mr. B. [Blakemore] Harrop, C.M.S. Nugent School, Loka, via Juba, S. Sudan, October 18th, 1950." *Southern Sudan Mail Bag*, no. 15 (December 1950): 26–28.

Harrop, Blakemore. "From Mr. Blakemore Harrop, C.M.S. Nugent School, Loka, via Juba, Southern Sudan, 27th July, 1949." *Southern Sudan Mail Bag*, no. 12 (December 1949): 5–6.

Hasan, Yusuf Fadl. "The Role of Religion in the North-South Conflict with Special Reference to Islam." In *Religion and Conflict in Sudan: Papers from an International Conference at Yale, May 1999*, edited by Yusuf Fadl Hasan and Richard Gray, 23–47. Nairobi: Paulines, 2002.

Hastings, Adrian. *A History of African Christianity: 1950–1975*. Cambridge: Cambridge University Press, 1979.

Hatoss, Anikó. *Displacement, Language Maintenance and Identity: Sudanese Refugees in Australia*. Amsterdam: Benjamins, 2013.

Haumann, Matthew. *Travelling with Soldiers and Bishops: Stories of Struggling People in Sudan*. Nairobi: Paulines, 2004.

Hays, J. Daniel. "From the Land of the Bow: Black Soldiers in the Ancient Near East." *Bible Review* 14, no. 4 (August 1998): 28–33, 50–51.

Heraclides, Alexis. *The Self-Determination of Minorities in International Politics*. New York: Routledge, 2010.

Hill, Richard. *Egypt in the Sudan: 1820–1881*. New York: Oxford University Press, 1959.

Hiro, Dilip. *War without End: The Rise of Islamist Terrorism and Global Response*. Rev. ed. New York: Routledge, 2002.

Holt, P. M., and M. W. Daly. *A History of the Sudan: From the Coming of Islam to the Present Day*. New York: Routledge, 2014.

House of Commons. *Egypt No. 1 (1911): Reports by His Majesty's Agent and Consul-General on the Finances, Administration, and Condition of Egypt and the Soudan in 1910*. London: His Majesty's Stationery Office, [1911].

House of Commons. *Egypt No. 1 (1920): Reports by His Majesty's High Commissioner on the Finances, Administration, and Condition of Egypt and the Soudan for the Period 1914–1919*. London: His Majesty's Stationery Office, 1920.

Howden, Daniel. "South Sudan: The State that Fell Apart in a Week." *Guardian*, December 23, 2013.

Huffman, Ray. *Nuer-English Dictionary*. Berlin: Augustin, 1929.

Hutchinson, Sharon E. "A Curse from God? Religious and Political Dimensions of the Post-1991 Rise of Ethnic Violence in South Sudan." *Journal of Modern African Studies* 39, no. 2 (June 2001): 307–31.

Hutchinson, Sharon E. *Nuer Dilemmas: Coping with Money, War, and the State*. Berkeley: University of California Press, 1996.

Hutchinson, Sharon E. "Spiritual Fragments of an Unfinished War." In *Religion and Conflict in Sudan: Papers from an International Conference at Yale, May 1999*, edited by Yusuf Fadl Hasan and Richard Gray, 136–61. Nairobi: Paulines, 2002.

Ibrahim, H. A., and B. A. Ogot. "The Sudan in the Nineteenth Century." In *UNESCO General History of Africa*, vol. 6, *Africa in the 19th Century until the 1880s*, edited by J. F. A de Ajayi, 356–75. Berkeley: University of California Press, 1989.

Idris, Amir. *Conflict and Politics of Identity in Sudan*. New York: Palgrave Macmillan, 2005.

International Crisis Group. *South Sudan: A Civil War by Any Other Name*. Africa Report No. 217. Brussels: International Crisis Group, April 10, 2014. https://www .crisisgroup.org/africa/horn-africa/south-sudan/south-sudan-civil-war-any -other-name.

"Interview with Bishop Seme: The Churches Are United against Human Rights Violation." *NSCC Magazine* 1 (December 1996): 14–15.

Izale, Benjamin. "Joint Front." *SPLM/SPLA Update*, October 2001.

Jabiro, Job. "Ode to GARANG." *Sudan Church Review*, Autumn 2005, 10.

Jaden, Latio Lo. "Khartoum by Night." *SPLM/SPLA Update*, February 27, 1994.

Jaden, Latio Lo. "Politics of Self Destruction." *SPLM/SPLA Update*, June 27, 1994.

James, Wendy. *The Listening Ebony: Moral Knowledge, Religion, and Power among the Uduk of Sudan*. Oxford: Clarendon; New York: Oxford University Press, 1988.

James, Wendy. "The Multiple Voices of Sudanese Airspace." In *African Broadcast Cultures: Radio in Transition*, edited by Richard Fardon and Graham Furniss, 198–215. Westport, CT: Praeger, 2000.

James, Wendy. *War and Survival in Sudan's Frontierlands: Voices from the Blue Nile*. New York: Oxford University Press, 2007.

Jeffrey, James. "How Christian Churches Are Trying to Save South Sudan." *American Conservative*, August 20, 2018.

Jobling, David. *1 Samuel*. Edited by D. W. Cotter, J. Walsh, and C. Franke. Collegeville, MN: Liturgical Press, 1998.

Johnson, Douglas. "Future of Southern Sudan's Past." *Africa Today* 28, no. 2 (1981): 33–41.

Johnson, Douglas. *Nuer Prophets: A History of Prophecy from the Upper Nile in the Nineteenth and Twentieth Centuries*. Oxford: Clarendon; New York: Oxford University Press, 1994.

Johnson, Douglas. "Prophecy and Mahdism in the Upper Nile: An Examination of Local Experiences of the Mahdiyya in the Southern Sudan." *British Journal of Middle Eastern Studies* 20, no. 1 (1993): 42–56.

Johnson, Douglas. *The Root Causes of Sudan's Civil Wars*. Bloomington: Indiana University Press, 2003.

Johnson, Douglas. *The Root Causes of Sudan's Civil Wars: Peace or Truce*. Rev. ed. Kampala: Fountain, 2011.

Johnson, Douglas. "Salim Wilson: The Black Evangelist of the North." *Journal of Religion in Africa* 21, no. 1 (February 1991): 26–41.

Johnson, Douglas. *South Sudan: A New History for a New Nation*. Athens: Ohio University Press, 2016.

Johnson, Douglas, ed. *Sudan*. London: Institute of Commonwealth Studies in the University of London, Stationery Office, 1998.

Johnson, Douglas. "Sudanese Military Slavery from the Eighteenth to the Twentieth Century." In *Slavery and Other Forms of Unfree Labour*, edited by Leonie Archer, 142–56. London: Routledge, 1988.

Johnson, Douglas. "The Sudan People's Liberation Army and the Problem of Factionalism." In *African Guerrillas*, edited by Christopher Clapham, 53–72. Bloomington: Indiana University Press, 1998.

Johnson, Douglas. "Twentieth-Century Civil Wars." In *The Sudan Handbook*, edited by John Ryle, Justin Willis, Suliman Baldo, and Jok Madut Jok, 122–32. Suffolk: Currey, 2011.

Johnson, Douglas, and Gerard Prunier. "The Foundation and Expansion of the Sudan People's Liberation Army." In *Civil War in the Sudan*, edited by M. W. Daly and Ahmad Alawad Sikainga, 117–41. London: British Academic Press, 1993.

Jok, Jok Madut. *War and Slavery in Sudan*. Philadelphia: University of Pennsylvania Press, 2001.

"Juba Dismisses Ambassador's Role in Alleged Coup Plot." *Sudan Tribune*, January 5, 2015.

Kalulu, Francis Oliha A. "Wake Up the South Calls." *SPLM/SPLA Update*, February 9, 1995.

Keating, Joshua E. "Who Are the Knights of Malta—and What Do They Want?" *Foreign Policy*, January 19, 2011. http://foreignpolicy.com/2011/01/19/who-are-the-knights-of-malta-and-what-do-they-want/.

Keinon, Herb. "Diplomacy: An Appreciative Partner in Africa." *Jerusalem Post*, December 23, 2011.

Keto, Clement T. "Race Relations, Land and the Changing Missionary Role in South Africa: A Case Study of the American Zulu Mission, 1850–1910." *International Journal of African Historical Studies* 10, no. 4 (1977): 600–627.

Khalid, Mansour. *War and Peace in the Sudan*. London: Kegan Paul, 2003.

Khoryoam, Deng Riak. "The New Nation Should Retain the Name 'South Sudan'!" *Sudan Tribune*, January 30, 2011.

Kiggen, J. *Nuer-English Dictionary*. London: Foreign Missions, 1948.

Kim, Uriah Y. *Identity and Loyalty in the David Story: A Postcolonial Reading*. Sheffield: Sheffield Phoenix Press, 2008.

Kramer, Robert S., Richard A. Lobban Jr., and Carolyn Fluehr-Lobban. *Historical Dictionary of the Sudan*. 4th ed. Lanham, MD: Scarecrow Press, 2013.

Kulish, Nicholas, and Somini Sengupta. "New Estimate Sharply Raises Death Toll in South Sudan." *New York Times*, January 9, 2014.

Kumm, H. Karl W. *From Hausaland to Egypt, through the Sudan*. London: Constable, 1910.

Kustenbauder, Matthew. "The Politicization of Religious Identity in Sudan, with Special Reference to Oral Histories of the Sudanese Diaspora in America." In *Religion on the Move! New Dynamics of Religious Expansion in a Globalizing World*, edited by Afe Adogame and Shobana Shankar, 397–424. Leiden: Brill, 2013.

Kuyok, Kuyok Abol. *South Sudan: The Notable Firsts*. Bloomington, IN: AuthorHouse, 2015.

Kwaje, Samson L. "Vision, Perspective, and Position of the SPLM." In *The Sudan at War: In Search of Peace*, 18–27. Report of a Consultation Convened by Church and Christian Councils of the Great Lakes-Horn of Africa Region, April 7–8, 1998, Karen, Nairobi.

Kyle, Keith. "The Southern Problem in the Sudan." *World Today* 22, no. 12 (December 1966): 512–20.

Lagu, Joseph. "The Dynamics of Co-operation Between the Anya-Nya and the People." *Grass Curtain* 1, no. 4 (April 1971): 4–9.

Lagu, Joseph. *Sudan: Odyssey through a State: From Ruin to Hope*. Omdurman: MOB Center for Sudanese Studies, Omdurman Ahlia University, 2006.

"Lamentations." In *Life Application Study Bible* (New Living Translation), 2nd ed. Carol Stream, IL: Tyndale House, 2007.

Lamothe, Ronald M. *Slaves of Fortune: Sudanese Soldiers & the River War 1896–1898*. Woodbridge, Suffolk: Currey, 2011.

Lane, Paul, and Douglas Johnson. "The Archaeology and History of Slavery in South Sudan in the Nineteenth Century." In *The Frontiers of the Ottoman World*, edited by A. C. S. Peacock, 509–37. Oxford: Oxford University Press, 2009.

Launay, Robert. "An Invisible Religion? Anthropology's Avoidance of Islam in Africa." In *African Anthropologies: History, Critique and Practice*, edited by Mwenda Ntarangwi, David Mills, and Mustafa Babiker, 188–203. New York: Zed, 2006.

Lederer, Edith M. "US after Supporting South Sudan's Leader Calls Him 'Unfit.'" *Associated Press*, January 24, 2018.

Lee, Christopher J. *Unreasonable Histories: Nativism, Multiracial Lives, and the Genealogical Imagination in British Africa*. Durham, NC: Duke University Press, 2014.

LeMarquand, Grant. "Bibles, Crosses, Songs, Guns and Oil: Sudanese 'Readings' of the Bible in the Midst of Civil War." *Anglican and Episcopal History* 75, no. 4 (2006): 553–79.

Leonardi, Cherry. *Dealing with Government in South Sudan: Histories of Chiefship, Community and State*. Oxford: Currey, 2013.

Leonardi, Cherry. "South Sudanese Arabic and the Negotiation of the Local State, c. 1840–2011." *Journal of African History* 54, no. 3 (2013): 351–72.

Leonardi, Cherry, and Musa Abdul Jalil. "Traditional Authority, Local Government and Justice." In *The Sudan Handbook*, edited by John Ryle, Justin Willis, Suliman Baldo, and Jok Madut Jok, 108–21. Suffolk, UK: Currey, 2011.

Lesch, Ann. "Abuja Conferences." In *Historical Dictionary of the Sudan*, 4th ed., edited by Robert S. Kramer, Richard A. Lobban Jr., and Carolyn Fluehr-Lobban, 46–47. Lanham, MD: Scarecrow Press, 2013.

Lesch, Ann. *The Sudan: Contested National Identities*. Bloomington: Indiana University Press, 1998.

Levi, William. *The Bible or the Axe: One Man's Dramatic Escape from Persecution in the Sudan*. Chicago: Moody, 2005.

Lienhardt, R. G. "The Dinka and Catholicism." In *Religious Organization and Religious Experience*, edited by John Davis, 81–95. New York: Academic Press, 1982.

Lienhardt, R. G. *Divinity and Experience: The Religion of the Dinka.* Oxford: Clarendon, 1961.

"Llewellyn H. Gwynne, 1863–1957." *Sudan Diocesan Review* 11, no. 30 (Spring 1958): 9.

Lobban, Richard A., Jr., Kramer, Robert S., and Carolyn Fluehr-Lobban. *Historical Dictionary of the Sudan.* 3rd ed. Lanham, MD: Scarecrow Press, 2002.

Lomuro, L. "Dear Editor." *SPLM/SPLA Update*, October 31, 1993.

Longman, Timothy. "Church Politics and the Genocide in Rwanda." *Journal of Religion in Africa* 31, no. 2 (May 2001): 163–86.

Loro, Paulino Lukudu. "Opening Address." In *One Church from Every Tribe, Tongue and People: Symposium on the Role of the Church in the Independence of South Sudan,* edited by John Ashworth, 12–14. Nairobi: Paulines, 2012.

Lupai, Jacob K. "First Anniversary of Independence of South Sudan." *Sudan Tribune,* July 9, 2012.

Luri, Kichere Joseph. "The Truth Shall Tell." *SPLM/SPLA Update*, March 13, 1995.

Mabuong, P. K. "Southern Leaders Remember the South." *SANU Youth Organ Monthly Bulletin,* no. 2 (November 1967): 16–17.

Madut-Arop, Arop. *Sudan's Painful Road to Peace: A Full Story of the Founding and Development of SPLM/SPLA.* Charleston, SC: BookSurge, 2006.

Magaziner, Daniel. *The Law and the Prophets: Faith, Hope, and Politics in South Africa, 1968–1977.* Athens: Ohio University Press, 2010.

Malek, Nyandeng. "Condolences to the American People." *SPLM/SPLA Update,* September 2001.

Malith, Isaac Dongrin. "SPLA Keeps Goliath at Bay." *SPLM/SPLA Update,* March 3, 1995.

Manoeli, Sebabatso C. *Sudan's "Southern Problem": Race, Rhetoric and International Relations, 1961–1991.* Cham, Switzerland: Palgrave Macmillan, 2019.

Mamdani, Mahmood. *Citizen and Subject: Contemporary Africa and the Legacy of Late Colonialism.* Princeton, NJ: Princeton University Press, 1996.

Mamdani, Mahmood. *Saviors and Survivors: Darfur, Politics, and the War on Terror.* New York: Doubleday, 2009.

Mangan, J. A. "Ethics and Ethnocentricity in British Tropical Africa." *International Journal of the History of Sport* 27, nos. 1–2 (January–February 2010): 362–88.

Marshall, Ruth. *Political Spiritualities: The Pentecostal Revolution in Nigeria.* Chicago: University of Chicago Press, 2009.

Martell, Peter. "A Song for South Sudan: Writing a New National Anthem." *BBC News,* January 12, 2011.

Mason, E. "The Controversy over the Belanda." *Messenger,* May 1946, 28.

Mazrui, Ali A. "Shifting African Identities: The Boundaries of Ethnicity and Religion in Africa's Experience." In *Shifting African Identities,* edited by Simon Bekker, Martine Dodds, and Meshack M. Khosa, 153–75. Pretoria, SA: Human Sciences Research Council, 2001.

Mbiti, John. "An African Views American Black Theology." In *Black Theology: A Documentary History,* vol. 1, *1966–1979,* edited by James H. Cone and Gayraud S. Wilmore, 477–82. Maryknoll, NY: Orbis Books, 1979.

McAlister, Melani. *The Kingdom of God Has No Borders: A Global History of American Evangelicals*. New York: Oxford University Press, 2018.

McCauley, John F. *The Logic of Ethnic and Religious Conflict in Africa*. Cambridge: Cambridge University Press, 2017.

McDonnell, Faith. "South Sudan President Salva Kiir Makes First Official Visit to Israel." *Weekly Standard*, January 7, 2012.

McNeish, Hannah. "South Sudan Teeters on the Brink." *Al Jazeera*, December 17, 2013.

Michael, Amosa Johnson. "Weapons to Defeat the NIF in the Bible." *SPLM/SPLA Update*, July 24, 1995.

Migido, Tarcisio. "To Charm." *Messenger*, February–March 1937, 16.

Minter, William. "Pro Veritate." *Aluka*, January 2007. https://www.jstor.org /stable/10.2307/al.sff.document.ae000040.

Mohammed, Ahmed El Awad. "Militarism in the Sudan: The Colonial Experience." *Sudan Notes and Records* 61 (1980): 15–26.

"More Word from Dorothy Rankin." *Twin Tower Light* 16, no. 9 (October 1961): 2, 4.

Moses, Sarah. "Former Lost Boy Gives Back to His Native Community in Sudan through Education." *Syracuse.com*, June 1, 2011. http://www.syracuse.com/news /index.ssf/2011/06/former_lost_boy_gives_back_to.html.

Moyn, Samuel. *Christian Human Rights*. Philadelphia: University of Pennsylvania Press, 2015.

Muhumuza, Rodney. "South Sudan: 'White Army' Militia Marches to Fight." *USA Today*, December 28, 2013.

Mutua, Makau. "Racism at Root of Sudan's Darfur Crisis." *Christian Science Monitor*, July 14, 2004.

Natsios, Andrew S. *Sudan, South Sudan, and Darfur: What Everyone Needs to Know*. New York: Oxford University Press, 2012.

Nebel, Arthur. *Dinka-Dictionary with Abridged Grammar*. Verona: Missioni Africane, 1936.

"The New Sudan Brigade (NSB): Notes on the NSB, SPLM and New Sudan." Special edition, *SPLM/SPLA Update*, March 20, 1995.

Ngor, Mading. "S. Sudan Says China to Help Build New Airport in Juba." *Reuters*, August 17, 2012. https://in.reuters.com/article/southsudan-airport/s-sudan-says -china-to-help-build-new-airport-in-juba-idINDEE87G0DP20120817.

Nikkel, Mark R. "Christian Conversion among the Jieng Bor." In *Religion and Conflict in Sudan: Papers from an International Conference at Yale, May 1999*, edited by Yusuf Fadl Hasan and Richard Gray, 162–68. Nairobi: Paulines, 2002.

Nikkel, Mark R. *Dinka Christianity: The Origins and Development of Christianity among the Dinka of Sudan with Special Reference to the Songs of Dinka Christians*. Faith in Sudan No. 11. Nairobi: Paulines, 2001.

Ninan, M. M. *A Comparative Study of the Kuku Culture and the Hebrew Culture*. N.p.: CreateSpace, 2014.

Nsiku, Edouard Kitoko. "Isaiah." In *Africa Bible Commentary: A One-Volume Commentary Written by 70 African Scholars*, edited by Tokunboh Adeyemo, 835–78. Grand Rapids, MI: Zondervan, 2010.

O'Brien, Conor. *God Land: Reflections on Religion and Nationalism*. Cambridge, MA: Harvard University Press, 1988.

O'Donovan, Oliver. *The Desire of the Nations: Rediscovering the Roots of Political Theology*. New York: Cambridge University Press, 1996.

Oduha, Joseph. "South Sudan Church Leaders Organises Special Prayers for Trust Building among the Political Leaders." *Christian Times* (South Sudan), May 20, 2016.

Office for the Coordination of Humanitarian Affairs South Sudan. "South Sudan Crisis: Situation Report as of 3 February 2014." Report No. 16. OCHA, February 3, 2014. http://reliefweb.int/sites/reliefweb.int/files/resources/South%20Sudan%20crisis%20-%20situation%20update%2016_as%20of%203%20February.pdf.

Okiech, Pa'gan Amum. "Organisational Report." Presented to the 2nd National Convention of the Sudan People's Liberation Movement, 2008. Accessed 2014. http://www.splmtoday.com/docs/statements%20and%20speeches/2012%2003%20Organizational%20Report%20-%20SG%20Amum%20-%202nd%20NLC%20Meeting.pdf.

Olupona, Jacob K., and Terry Rey. Introduction to *Orisa Devotion as World Religion: The Globalization of Yoruba Religious Culture*, edited by Jacob J. Olupona and Terry Rey, 3–28. Madison: University of Wisconsin Press, 2008.

Omolo, Ouko Joachim. "Father Thomas Oliha Installed as Torit Diocese Administrator." *Jaluo dot Kom* (blog), June 8, 2013. http://blog.jaluo.com/?p=34261.

Parfitt, Tudor. *Black Jews in Africa and the Americas*. Cambridge, MA: Harvard University Press, 2013.

Parry, Helena. "From Mrs. Helena Parry, C.M.S. Nugent School, Loka, 3rd May, 1949." *Southern Sudan Mail Bag*, no. 11 (July 1949): 15–18.

Parry, J. I. "C.M.S. Nugent School, Loka." *Sudan Diocesan Review* 1, no. 4 (October 1949): 32.

Parry, J. I. "From Mr. J. I. Parry." *Southern Sudan Mail Bag*, no. 6 (December 1947): 18–20.

Parry, J. I. "From Mr. J. I. Parry, the Nugent School, C.M.S. Loka, via Juba, S. Sudan, 6th March, 1950." *Southern Sudan Mail Bag*, no. 13 (May 1950): 14–15.

Parsons, Timothy H. *Race, Resistance, and the Boy Scout Movement in British Colonial Africa*. Athens: Ohio University Press, 2004.

Paterno, Steve A. *The Rev. Fr. Saturnino Lohure: A Roman Catholic Priest Turned Rebel, the South Sudan Experience*. Baltimore, MD: PublishAmerica, 2007.

Patinkin, Jason. "In S. Sudan, Churches Struggle to Keep Role as Trusted Peacemakers." *Christian Science Monitor*, December 16, 2014.

Paul, Elhag. "Like a Leopard Can Not Change Its Spots, Machar Can Not Change." Pachodo.org, August 8, 2014. http://pachodo.org/latest-news-articles/pachodo-english-articles/9155-like-a-leopard-can-not-change-its-spots,-machar-can-not-change.

Paul, Elhag. "SPLM and Mass Media: Promoting History on Falsity." *Sudan Tribune*, September 28, 2011.

Paul, Elhag. "To Achieve Peace in South Sudan, SPLM/A Must Be Scrapped." *South Sudan News Agency* (distributed by *AllAfrica*), December 29, 2013. http://allafrica.com/stories/201312300037.html.

Peralta, Eyder. "Will South Sudan's New Peace Agreement Hold This Time?" *NPR*, November 8, 2018.

Perkins, Kenneth J. *Port Sudan: The Evolution of a Colonial City.* Boulder, CO: Westview Press, 1993.

Peterson, Derek R. *Ethnic Patriotism and the East African Revival: A History of Dissent, c. 1935-1972.* New York: Cambridge University Press, 2012.

Pinaud, Clémence. "'We Are Trained to Be Married!' Elite Formation and Ideology in the 'Girls' Battalion' of the Sudan People's Liberation Army." *Journal of Eastern African Studies* 9, no. 3 (2015): 375-93.

Pinn, Anthony B. "Cone, James Hal." In *The Dictionary of Modern American Philosophers*, edited by John R. Shook. Bristol: Continuum, 2005. http://www.oxfordreference.com/view/10.1093/acref/9780199754663.001.0001/acref-9780199754663-e-211.

Pitya, Philip Legge. "History of Western Christian Evangelism in the Sudan, 1898-1964." PhD diss., Boston University Graduate School, 1996.

Pitya, Philip Legge. "The Role of the Local Church towards the Independence of South Sudan." In *One Church from Every Tribe, Tongue and People: Symposium on the Role of the Church in the Independence of South Sudan*, edited by John Ashworth, 100-128. Nairobi: Paulines, 2012.

Poggo, Anthony. *Come Let Us Rebuild: Lessons from Nehemiah.* Edited by Tim Flatman. London: Millipede Books, 2013.

Poggo, Scopas S. *The First Sudanese Civil War: Africans, Arabs, and Israelis in the Southern Sudan, 1955-1972.* New York: Palgrave Macmillan, 2009.

Poggo, Scopas S. "Kuku Religious Experiences in the Sudan and in Exile in Uganda." In *Religion and Conflict in Sudan: Papers from an International Conference at Yale, May 1999*, edited by Yusuf Fadl Hasan and Richard Gray, 126-35. Nairobi: Paulines, 2002.

Porter, H. "Ishmaelites." In *International Standard Bible Encyclopedia*, edited by James Orr. Chicago: Hope-Severance, 1915. https://www.biblestudytools.com/dictionary/ishmaelites/.

"The Power of Ritual: The Rev. Dr. William O. Lowrey." In *Peacemakers in Action: Profiles of Religion in Conflict Resolution*, edited by David Little with the Tanenbaum Center for Interreligious Understanding, 186-214. New York: Cambridge University Press, 2007.

"President Kiir's Speech at the SPLM Retreat at Lobonok, South Sudan." PaanLuel Wël Media Ltd.—South Sudan, December 6, 2018. https://paanluelwel.com/2018/12/06/president-kiirs-speech-at-the-splm-retreat-at-lobonok-south-sudan/.

"President Museveni Calls for Unity Deal Based on Justice for the Two Sudans." State House of Uganda. July 9, 2012. http://www.statehouse.go.ug/media/news/2012/07/09/president-museveni-calls-unity-deal-based-justice-two-sudans.

"Q&A: The Impact of John Garang's Death." *New York Times*, August 2, 2005.

Radio Tamazuj. "'If You Kill People, You Are Doing Work of the Devil,' Bishop Tells Juba Congregation." *Christian Times* (South Sudan), December 12, 2016.

Report of the Commission of Enquiry into the Disturbances in the Southern Sudan during August, 1955. Khartoum: McCorquodale, 1956.

Riak, Gabriel Majok. "The Land of Sudan." *SPLM/SPLA Update*, July 22, 1996.

Rice, Xan. "South Sudan's New National Anthem." *Guardian*, July 8, 2011.

Rolandsen, Øystein H. "A False Start: Between War and Peace in the Southern Sudan, 1956–62." *Journal of African History* 52, 1 (March 2011): 105–23.

Rolandsen, Øystein H. "From Colonial Backwater to an Independent State: Reflections on the History of South Sudan." In *One Church from Every Tribe, Tongue and People: Symposium on the Role of the Church in the Independence of South Sudan*, edited by John Ashworth, 16–27. Nairobi: Paulines, 2012.

Rolandsen, Øystein H. *Guerrilla Government: Political Changes in the Southern Sudan during the 1990s.* Uppsala: Nordiska Afrikainstitutet, 2005.

Ruay, Deng D. Akol. *The Politics of Two Sudans: The South and the North, 1821–1969.* Uppsala: Nordiska Afrikainstitutet, 1994.

Rule, Sheila. "Refugees from Sudan Strain Ethiopia Camps." *New York Times*, May 1, 1988.

Ryle, John. "Peoples and Cultures of Two Sudans." In *The Sudan Handbook*, edited by John Ryle, Justin Willis, Suliman Baldo, and Jok Madut Jok, 31–42. Suffolk: Currey, 2011.

Salomon, Noah. *For Love of the Prophet: An Ethnography of Sudan's Islamic State.* Princeton, NJ: Princeton University Press, 2016.

Salomon, Noah. "Religion after the State: Secular Soteriologies at the Birth of South Sudan." *Journal of Law and Religion* 29, no. 3 (2014): 447–69.

Sandell, Liza. *English Language in Sudan: A History of Its Teachings and Politics.* London: Ithaca Press, 1982.

Sanderson, Lilian. *Education, Religion and Politics in Southern Sudan, 1899–1964.* London: Ithaca Press, 1981.

Sanderson, Lilian. "The Sudan Interior Mission and the Condominium Sudan, 1937–1955." *Journal of Religion in Africa* 8, no. 1 (January 1976): 13–40.

Sanneh, Lamin. "Preface: Religion and Conflict in Sudan." In *Religion and Conflict in Sudan: Papers from an International Conference at Yale, May 1999*, edited by Yusuf Fadl Hasan and Richard Gray, 9–12. Nairobi: Paulines, 2002.

Sanneh, Lamin. "Religion, Politics, and National Integration: A Comparative African Perspective." In *Religion and National Integration in Africa: Islam, Christianity, and Politics in the Sudan and Nigeria*, edited by John O. Hunwick, 151–66. Evanston, IL: Northwestern University Press, 1992.

Scott, Philippa. "The Sudan Peoples' Liberation Movement (SPLM) and Liberation Army (SPLA)." *Review of African Political Economy* 12, no. 33 (August 1985): 69–82.

Searcy, Kim. "The Sudanese Mahdi's Attitudes on Slavery and Emancipation." *Islamic Africa* 1, no. 1 (Spring 2010): 63–83.

"A Service of Thanksgiving in Memory of Llewellyn Henry Gwynne." *Sudan Diocesan Review* 11, no. 30 (Spring 1958): 14–17.

Sharkey, Heather J. "Christians among Muslims: The Church Missionary Society in the Northern Sudan." *Journal of African History* 43, no. 1 (March 2002): 51–75.

Sharkey, Heather J. "Jihads and Crusades in Sudan from 1881 to the Present." In *Just Wars, Holy Wars, and Jihads: Christian, Jewish, and Muslim Encounters and Exchanges*, edited by Sohail H. Hashmi, 263–82. New York: Oxford University Press, 2012.

Sharkey, Heather J. "Missionary Legacies: Muslim-Christian Encounters in Egypt and Sudan during the Colonial and Postcolonial Periods." In *Muslim-Christian Encounters in Africa*, edited by Benjamin F. Soares, 57–88. Leiden: Brill, 2006.

Sharland, Charles T. "From the Rev. C. T. Sharland, of Lainya, C.M.S. Lainya, via Juba, S. Sudan, 15/11/46." *Southern Sudan Mail Bag*, no. 3 (March 1947): 20–22.

Shea, Jim. "Second Glances." *Catholic Telegraph-Register*, June 14, 1957.

Sidahmed, Abdel [Salam]. *Politics and Islam in Contemporary Sudan*. Richmond, Surrey: Curzon, 1997.

Sidahmed, Abdel [Salam]. "The Unholy War: Jihad and the Conflict in Sudan." In *Religion and Conflict in Sudan: Papers from an International Conference at Yale, May 1999*, edited by Yusuf Fadl Hasan and Richard Gray, 83–96. Nairobi: Paulines, 2002.

Sikainga, Ahmad. *Slaves into Workers: Emancipation and Labor in Colonial Sudan*. Austin: University of Texas Press, 1996.

Simeon, James Lomole. "Allison, Oliver C." *Dictionary of African Christian Biography*, accessed May 19, 2014. https://dacb.org/stories/sudan/allison-oliver/.

Snape, Michael. *The Redcoat and Religion: The Forgotten History of the British Soldier from the Age of Marlborough to the Eve of the First World War*. London: Routledge, 2005.

Soley, Lawrence. "Heating up Clandestine Radio after the Cold War." In *Radio: The Forgotten Medium*, edited by Edward C. Pease and Everette E. Dennis, 137–45. New Brunswick, NJ: Transaction, 1995.

"South Sudanese Christians Plan 'Prophesied' Pilgrimage to Israel." *Sudan Tribune*, February 24, 2012.

"South Sudan Has Suffered Crucifixion through the War." *Vatican News*, April 18, 2019.

"South Sudan Institutions Brainstorm on Future National Anthem." *Sudan Tribune*, August 7, 2010.

"South Sudan No Longer in Famine." *BBC News*, June 21, 2017.

"South Sudan President Celebrates Good Friday with Calls to Bury Differences." *Sudan Tribune*, April 21, 2014.

"South Sudan's Army Advances on Rebels in Bentiu and Bor." *BBC News Africa*, January 10, 2014.

"South Sudan's Kiir Reiterates Call for Dialogue to End War." *Sudan Tribune*, February 7, 2017.

"South Sudan's Warring Parties Sign Ceasefire Agreement." *Sudan Tribune*, December 21, 2017.

"South Sudan's Warring Sides Accuse Each Other of Attacks, 18 Killed." *Reuters*, July 2, 2018.

"S. Sudanese MPs Extend President Kiir's Term until 2018." *Sudan Tribune*, March 24, 2015.

Stanley, Brian. "Introduction: Christianity and the End of Empire." In *Missions, Nationalism, and the End of Empire*, Studies in the History of Christian Missions, edited by Brian Stanley, 1–11. Grand Rapids, MI: Eerdmans, 2004.

Stevenson, Roland C. "Protestant Missionary Work in the Northern Sudan during the Condominium Period." In *The Condominium Remembered: Proceedings of the Durham Sudan Historical Records Conference 1982*, vol. 2, *The Transformation of the Old Order in the Sudan*, edited by Deborah Lavin, 197–202. Durham, UK: Centre for Middle Eastern and Islamic Studies, 1993.

Stewart, Katherine. "How Christian Fundamentalists Plan to Teach Genocide to Schoolchildren." *Guardian*, May 30, 2012.

Streets, Heather. *Martial Races: The Military, Race and Masculinity in British Imperial Culture, 1857–1914*. New York: Manchester University Press, 2004.

Stringham, Noel, and Jonathan Forney. "It Takes a Village to Raise a Militia: Local Politics, the Nuer White Army, and South Sudan's Civil Wars." *Journal of Modern African Studies* 55, no. 2 (June 2017): 177–99.

Sudanese Catholic Clergy: From the Beginning to 2006. Khartoum: SCBC General Secretariat, n.d.

"Sudan Referendum." *PBS Religion and Ethics Newsweekly*, January 14, 2011. http://www.pbs.org/wnet/religionandethics/2011/01/14/january-14-2011-sudan-referendum/7886/.

"Sudan's CPA Is the Bible of Marginalized People—Rebecca Garang." *Sudan Tribune*, February 1, 2007.

"Sudan's External Relations 1956–63." *Voice of Southern Sudan* 1, no. 4 (1963): 13.

"Sudan to Deport 300 Missionaries as Agitators." *New York Times*, February 28, 1964.

Suleiman, Mahmoud A. "52nd Anniversary of the Glorious October 21, 1964 Sudanese Revolution." *Sudan Tribune*, October 21, 2016. http://sudantribune.com/spip.php?article60608.

"Symposium: One Church from Every Tribe, Tongue and People—Press Statement Released on 16th October 2011." In *One Church from Every Tribe, Tongue and People: Symposium on the Role of the Church in the Independence of South Sudan*, edited by John Ashworth, 6–9. Nairobi: Paulines, 2012.

Tanenbaum Center for Interreligious Understanding. *Peacemakers in Action: Profiles of Religion in Conflict Resolution*. Edited by David Little. New York: Cambridge University Press, 2007.

TCT Correspondent. "'No More of This!' Jesus' Condemnation of Violence and the War." *Christian Times* (South Sudan), March 10, 2018.

Tesfai, Yacob. *Holy Warriors, Infidels, and Peacemakers in Africa*. New York: Palgrave Macmillan, 2010.

Thiik, Akuol Riny. "The Soldiers of the SPLA." *SPLM/SPLA Update*, June 27, 1994.

Tounsel, Christopher. "Khartoum Goliath: *SPLM/SPLA Update* and Martial Theology during the Second Sudanese Civil War." *Journal of Africana Religions* 4, no. 2 (2016): 129–53.

Tounsel, Christopher. "'Render to Caesar': Missionary Thought and the Sudanese State, 1946–1964." *Social Sciences and Missions* 31, nos. 3–4 (2018): 341–74.

Tounsel, Timeka. "#WaitingForBoaz: Expressions of Romantic Aspiration and Black Christian Femininities on Social Media." *Journal of Media and Religion* 17, nos. 3–4 (2018): 91–105.

"Transitional Executive Council Takes over in South Africa." *SPLM/SPLA Update*, December 1993.

Tryggestad, Erik. "So You Want to Attend Christian College in Africa." *Christian Chronicle*, January 19, 2015. http://www.christianchronicle.org/article/so-you-want-to-attend-christian-college-in-africa.

Tuombuk, Joseph de. "Is South Sudan Peace Process Doomed to Fail?" *Gurtong*, October 13, 2014. http://www.gurtong.net/ECM/Editorial/tabid/124/ctl/ArticleView/mid/519/articleId/15728/Is-South-Sudan-Peace-Process-Doomed-to-Fail.aspx.

Tuombuk, Joseph de. "Potential Politicization of SPLA." *Sudan Tribune*, October 25, 2009.

Tuombuk, Joseph de. "Tribalism in South Sudan: Let's Read From Matthew 7:1–5." *Gurtong*, January 20, 2015. http://www.gurtong.net/ECM/Editorial/tabid/124/ctl/ArticleView/mid/519/articleId/16058/Tribalism-In-South-Sudan-Lets-Read-From-Matthew-71-5.aspx.

Tut, Kong. "Theological Reflections on Juba Nuer Massacre of December 16–24, 2013." *Nyamilepedia*, December 28, 2014. http://www.nyamile.com/2014/12/28/theological-reflections-on-juba-nuer-massacre-of-december-16-24-2013/.

Tutu, Tia Gitta. "Who Is behind Abbass—A Reply." *Grass Curtain* 2, no. 1 (July 1971): 16–17.

United Nations Mission in the Sudan. "Independence of South Sudan." Accessed March 23, 2013. http://www.un.org/en/peacekeeping/missions/past/unmis/referendum.shtml.

United Nations Security Council. "Southern Sudan Referendum Was Timely, Fair, Peaceful, Credible, Chair of Monitoring Panel Tells Security Council." United Nations Meetings Coverage and Press Releases, January 18, 2011. http://www.un.org/press/en/2011/sc10155.doc.htm.

"UN: Muslims Ethnically Cleansed in CAR." *Al Jazeera*, January 13, 2015.

"U.S. Bans Weapons Export to South Sudan." *Sudan Tribune*, February 3, 2018.

van der Veer, Peter, and Hartmut Lehmann. Introduction to *Nation and Religion: Perspectives on Europe and Asia*, edited by Peter van der Veer and Hartmut Lehmann, 3–14. Princeton, NJ: Princeton University Press, 1999.

Voll, John O. "Imperialism, Nationalism and Missionaries: Lessons from Sudan for the Twenty-First Century." *Islam and Christian-Muslim Relations* 8, no. 1 (March 1997): 39–52.

Walshe, Peter. "The Evolution of Liberation Theology in South Africa." *Journal of Law and Religion* 5, no. 2 (1987): 299–311.

Warburg, Gabriel. "Ideological and Practical Considerations Regarding Slavery in the Mahdist State and the Anglo-Egyptian Sudan, 1881–1918." In *The Ideology of Slavery in Africa*, edited by Paul E. Lovejoy, 245–70. Beverly Hills, CA: Sage, 1981.

Ward, Kevin. "'Tukutendereza Yesu': The Balokole Revival in Uganda." *Dictionary of African Christian Biography*, accessed July 25, 2020. https://dacb.org/histories/uganda-tukutendereza-yesu/.

Ware, Rudolph T., III. *The Walking Qur'an: Islamic Education, Embodied Knowledge, and History in West Africa*. Chapel Hill: University of North Carolina Press, 2014.

Watkins, Owen Spencer. *With Kitchener's Army: Being a Chaplain's Experiences with the Nile Expedition, 1898*. London: Partridge, 1899.

Watson, Charles R. *The Sorrow and Hope of the Egyptian Sudan: A Survey of Missionary Conditions and Methods of Work in the Egyptian Sudan*. Philadelphia: Board of Foreign Missions of the United Presbyterian Church of North America, 1913.

Watts, Ian H. "From Mr. I. H. Watts, 'Nugent School,' Loka. 22nd December, 1948." *Southern Sudan Mail Bag*, no. 10 (February 1949): 4–7.

Watts, Ian H. "Mr. Ian Watts, Nugent School, Loka, Equatoria Province, Anglo-Egyptian Sudan, 3rd May, 1949." *Southern Sudan Mail Bag*, no. 11 (July 1949): 10–14.

Wawa, Yosa. "Background to the Southern Sudan." In *The Southern Sudanese Pursuits of Self-Determination: Documents in Political History*, 1–21. Kampala: Marianum Press, 2005.

Wawa, Yosa. *Southern Sudanese Pursuits of Self-Determination: Documents in Political History*. Kampala: Marianum Press, 2005.

Weanzana, Nupanga. "1 and 2 Chronicles." In *Africa Bible Commentary: A One-Volume Commentary Written by 70 African Scholars*, edited by Tokunboh Adeyemo, 467–531. Grand Rapids, MI: Zondervan, 2010.

Weanzana, Nupanga, Samuel Ngewa, Tewoldemedhin Habtu, and Zamani Kafang. "Psalms." In *Africa Bible Commentary: A One-Volume Commentary Written by 70 African Scholars*, edited by Tokunboh Adeyemo, 605–772. Grand Rapids, MI: Zondervan, 2010.

Wheeler, Andrew. "Christianity in Sudan." *Dictionary of African Christian Biography*, accessed April 11, 2019. https://dacb.org/histories/sudan-christianity/.

Wheeler, Andrew. "Gateway to the Heart of Africa: Sudan's Missionary Story." In *Gateway to the Heart of Africa: Missionary Pioneers in Sudan*, edited by Francesco Pierli, Maria Teresa Ratti, and Andrew C. Wheeler, 10–25. Nairobi: Paulines, 1999.

Wheeler, Andrew. "Richard Jones and the Sudan Revival of 1938." *Anglican and Episcopal History* 71, no. 2 (2002): 168–86.

Williams, Delores S. "Womanist Theology: Black Women's Voices." In *The Womanist Reader*, edited by Layli Phillips, 117–25. New York: Routledge, 2006.

Wilson, Salim C. [Hatashil Masha Kathish]. *I Was a Slave*. London: Stanley, Paul, ca. 1939.

Wöndu, Steven. *From Bush to Bush: Journey to Liberty in South Sudan*. Nairobi: Kenway, 2011.

Wöndu, Steven. "The Knights of Lucifer." *SPLM/SPLA Update*, July 17, 1995.

Woodward, Peter. *Condominium and Sudanese Nationalism*. London: Rex Collins, 1979.

Woodward, Peter. "Religion and Politics in the Southern Sudan: The Ugandan Dimension." In *Religion and Conflict in Sudan: Papers from an International Conference at Yale, May 1999*, edited by Yusuf Fadl Hasan and Richard Gray, 169–79. Nairobi: Paulines, 2002.

Woodward, Peter. "The South in Sudanese Politics, 1946–56." *Middle Eastern Studies* 16, no. 3 (October 1980): 178–92.

Yangu, Alexis Mbali. *The Nile Turns Red*. Edited by A. G. Mondini. New York: Pageant, 1966.

Yoh, John G. Nyuot. "The Historical Origins of the Sudanese Civil Wars: The Politics of Gunboat Diplomacy." Presented at the South Africa Human Rights Commission, Johannesburg, May 25, 2001.

Zink, Jesse A. *Christianity and Catastrophe in South Sudan: Civil War, Migration, and the Rise of Dinka Anglicanism*. Waco, TX: Baylor University Press, 2017.

Zion, Kwarnyikiir Abdelilah. "The Military Boots." *SPLM/SPLA Update*, March 13, 1995.

Index

biblical narratives (*continued*)
  resurrection, 126; Sodom, 101–2; unity
  and, 100; use of, 142–43. *See also* Israel,
  biblical
bin Laden, Osama, 102
black liberation theology, 135–36
blackness, 4
black theology, 8
Bong, Ngundeng, 74, 86, 106
Bor Massacre, 123
Boy Scouts, 31–32
British and Foreign Bible Society, 27
Brown, W. B. E., 53
Buay, Gordon, 118, 141–43
Butler, Judith, 19

Carey, George, 93
Catholic Church, 73–74, 86; missions,
  27, 28, 33–37, 40, 49
Chang, Kong, 98
Chapman-Andrews, E., 65
chosenness, 17, 76. *See also* Israel, biblical
Christian schools. *See* Nugent School;
  schools
Christian Solidarity International (CSI),
  94–95
Christian unity, 40–41, 96, 100, 126–27,
  130–33
Churchill, Winston, 24
Church Missionary Society (CMS), 24–25,
  28–29, 35, 73. *See also* Nugent School
civil wars: First Sudanese Civil War,
  67–87; Second Sudanese Civil War,
  88–111; South Sudan civil war, 115–33
clubs, 75
Collins, Robert O., 14, 33, 58, 72
Comprehensive Peace Agreement (CPA),
  110–11, 115–16, 120–21
Condominium agreement (1899), 28
condominium rule, 19, 46–47
Cone, James, 7
"Controversy over the Belanda, The"
  (*Messenger*), 36–37
Cosner, Faustin, 49
Cotran, Tawfiq, 64
Cromer, Earl of (Evelyn Baring), 24, 59

Crucifixion analogy, 102
Cush (kingdom), 2–3, 105–10, 117–19, 141

Daau, John, 104, 128
Dak, James Gatdet, 131
Danforth, John, 97
Dau, Isaiah, 129
David and Goliath, 88–90, 98–99
Decker, Alicia, 19–20
Deng, Barnaba, 78, 84
Deng, Daniel, 111, 128, 130–31, 133
Deng, Francis, 6, 7–8, 16, 25, 33, 92, 96
Deng, George, 117
Deng, J. M., 77
Deng, Rodolfo, 84
Deng, Santino, 72–73
Deng, William, 71, 72–73
Department of Religious Affairs (DRA), 69
de Saram, Brian, 35–36, 39–40
diaspora, Sudanese, 97–98
dictionaries, 37
Diing, Ezekiel, 111
Dinka: Agara Dinka revolt, 27; Cush
  and, 108; Equatorial Corps and, 49,
  58; Islam and, 27–28; Koc Roor, 71;
  missionaries and, 33–34, 92; Nilotics,
  26–28, 48; and Nuer, 38, 40, 93–94,
  114–15, 122–23, 132; and religion, 33–34,
  73, 75; slavery and, 58–59; SPLA and,
  106, 108; translation and, 37. *See also*
  ethnicity; Nugent School
Doggale, Paolino, 21, 70, 80, 83, 86
Driberg, Jack H., 49
Dronyi, Sosthenes, 81–82
Dud, Ireneo, 73, 77–78
Dunn, John, 58–59
Dwatuka, Gabriel, 56

Earl, G. F., 38
education. *See* Nugent School; schools
English language, 29, 34–35, 47, 49
Episcopal Church of the Sudan (ECS),
  74, 86
Equatorial Corps, 46–51. *See also* Torit
  Mutiny
Equiano, Olaudah, 108

Ethiopia, 92–93
ethnicity: Christianity and, 40–41, 96, 100, 126–27, 130–33; and conflict, 37–41, 42–43; Equatorial Corps and, 48–49; God and, 18, 126, 136, 140; Mahdist War and, 27–28; Nilotics in pre-Mahdi Sudan, 26–27; Nugent School and, 34–37, 42; race-religion-politics interplay and, 13; and southern unity, 9–11; Torit Mutiny and, 57–58
Evans-Pritchard, Edward, 15, 75, 155n19

Fadlalla, Amal, 8
famine, 123–24
Fanon, Frantz, 141
Farquhar, Marian, 56–57
Feierman, Steven, 5, 152n18
Ferrara, Domenico, 78, 80
First Sudanese Civil War, 67–87
Fuli, Adelino, 83
Fuze, Magema, 108

Gai, Taban Deng, 124
Gairdner, W. H. T., 24
Garang, John, 3, 76, 90, 93, 98, 99, 103, 107–12, 142
Garang, Rebecca, 116, 122
Gatatek, Wutnyang, 123
Gatjang, Jickson, 122
Gatkuoth Gual, Peter, 86
Ga'le, Fuli Boki Tombe, 80–81
Gemaa, Ismal, 54–55
gender, 18–20, 31–33, 43
Geyer, Franz, 46
Gibia, Roba, 116
Glassman, Jonathon, 5, 55
God: Dinka *Nhialic* translated as, 33; ethnicities as gifts from, 18, 126, 136, 140; First Sudanese Civil War and, 79–81, 83–85
Goliath, 88–90, 98–99
Gordon, Charles, 24, 46, 59
Gordon, David M., 13–14
Gordon Memorial Mission, 24–25, 29. *See also* Church Missionary Society; Nugent School

Graduates General Congress, 51, 52
Grass Curtain, 77
Gray, Richard, 8, 14, 16
Gregory XVI (pope), 27
Guarak, Mawut, 116–17
Gwynne, Llewellyn, 23–25, 129, 133

Haley, Nikki, 124–25
Hickson, A. G., 35, 36

Igga, James Wani, 128
imagined community, 21, 69, 110, 154n74
Islam, 26; Islamization policies, 69–71; "Islam noir," 9; and martyrdom, 90; military and, 46–47; mission efforts to forestall, 30, 32; and nationalism, 4–5; respect for, 104, 136–37; Sharia law, 91, 92, 110–11; SPLM/A and, 104–5; Torit Mutiny and, 55
Ismail, Khedive, 59
Israel, biblical, 67–68, 79–81, 108–9
Izale, Benjamin, 100

Jaden, Aggrey, 41, 72–73, 101
Jaden, Latio Lo, 100–102, 104
James, Wendy, 100, 109
Johnson, Douglas, 8, 27, 48–49, 75, 106, 155n19, 169n33
Johnson, Hilde, 125
Jok, Jok Madut, 2, 3, 9–10
Joseph, Athian, 83

Kairos Document, 8
Khalil, Abdallah, 69
"Khartoum by Night" (Jaden), 101–2
Khartoum Declaration of Agreement, 125
Khoryoam, Deng Riak, 118
Kiggen, J., 37
Kiir, Salva, 3, 5–6, 105, 111, 114–16, 119–34, 135
Kita, Juliano, 79
Kitchener, Herbert, 24, 59, 101
Koc Roor, 71
Kony, Joseph, 137–38
Kueth, James Mut, 106
Kuku, 81–84, 108–9
Kule, Felix, 83

Northcote, C. S., 47
North-South binary, 8–11
Nsiku, Edouard, 109–10
Nuer: Ngundeng Bong, 74, 86, 106; church, 73, 74; Dinka and, 38, 40, 93–94, 114–15, 122–23, 132; Equatorial Corps and, 49, 58; fighting among, 107; Juba Nuer Massacre, 131; missionaries and, 56, 74, 91–92; Nilotics, 26–28, 48; SPLA and, 106; SSDF and, 116; translation and, 37. *See also* ethnicity; Nugent School
Nuer-English Dictionary (Kiggen), 37
Nugent, Sophia, 29
Nugent School: alumni, 41; Boys' Brigade, Crusader Bible class, and Boy Scouts, 31–32; and Christianity, 34–37, 42; and English language, 29–30, 34; and ethnic conflict, 37–38, 40–41, 42–43; gender and, 31–32, 43; and Islam, 32; Maltese cross and, 30–31; opening of, 25, 29; and unity, 35–36
Nyigilo, Ibrahim, 76–77

Obote, Milton, 77, 86
Oboyo, Saturlino, 53
O'Brien, Conor, 163n4
October Revolution, 72, 85
O'Donovan, Oliver, 154n64
Oduho, Joseph, 71
Ogwana, Airo, 55
Omdurman, 24

Pan-Africanism, 1, 71, 106–7
Parfitt, Tudor, 108
Parry, Helena, 31
Parry, John I., 31, 37–38, 40, 136
Parsons, Timothy, 31–32, 48
parties, political: Ashiqqa, 51; Khatimiya People's Democratic Party (PDP), 69; Liberal, 52–53, 69; National Union Party (NUP), 52; Umma, 51, 69. *See also* Sudan People's Liberation Movement/Army (SPLM/SPLA)
Paterno, Steve, 9–10
Patinkin, Jason, 127–28

Paul VI (pope), 78, 84–85
Paul, Elhag, 97, 108, 131–32
Poggo, Anthony, 142
Poggo, Scopas, 57, 60
political theology: defined, 154n64; evolution, 115; First Civil War and, 68; implications, 137–40; in post-CPA period, 133–34; Second Civil War and, 90, 109; understandings of, 42–43
Popular Defense Force (PDF), 90
Port Sudan, 62–63
prisons, 61–63
prophets, 74–75, 86, 106

Quo Vadis (film), 44–45

race: black liberation theology, 135–36; First Sudanese Civil War and, 76–79; and identity, 4, 10, 12; martial race ideology, 49; religion and, 11–13; Torit Mutiny and, 54. *See also* ethnicity
radio stations, 93, 121, 128
Rankin, Dorothy, 57, 79–80
Rannat, Abu, 55
refugees: from civil war, 125; evacuation of Ethiopian camps, 92–93; Exodus narrative and, 100; from First Sudanese Civil War, 75–76; Lost Boys, 97–98; number of, 169n33
Regional Self-Government Act, 91
Revitalized Agreement on the Resolution of the Conflict in South Sudan, 125
Riak, Gabriel, 103
Rolandsen, Øystein H., 15, 151n4
Rumbek, 63
Rume, Marko, 52–53
Rwanda, 138

Said, Mehmed, 63
Samaritan's Purse, 128–29
Sanneh, Lamin, 4, 16, 17, 33
schools: Catholic, 33, 34; and Christian names, 35; CMS and, 28–29; and ethnic conflict, 37–41; gender and, 31–33; language in, 33–35; nationalization of, 70–71. *See also* Nugent School

Scroggins, Deborah, 106
Sebit, Jacob, 62–63
Second Sudanese Civil War, 88–111, 115–16, 120–21. *See also* Sudan People's Liberation Movement/Army (SPLM/SPLA)
Selassie, Haile, 85
Shaw, Archibald, 24–25, 46–47, 50
Sierra, Sister, 121
Siri, Jerome, 80, 81
slavery: Exodus and, 99; First Sudanese Civil War and, 76–77; rhetoric of, 2; "slave redemptions," 94–95; Torit Mutiny and, 58–63; trade, 58–59, 63
Smith, Mike, 120
Smith, William Alexander, 31
songs, 81–84, 106; national anthem, 117–18
"South" (term), 11
South Africa, 6–7
Southern Sudan Christian Association, 76–77, 165n36
Southern Sudan Liberation Movement, 85
South Sudan: Christians in, 126–27; civil war, 115–33; independence referendum (2011), 2, 118–19; national anthem, 117–18
South Sudan Council of Churches, 120–21, 128–29
South Sudan Defence Forces (SSDF), 116
SPLM/A in Opposition (SPLA-IO), 122
SPLM/SPLA. *See* Sudan People's Liberation Movement/Army (SPLM/SPLA)
SPLM/SPLA Update: on Cush, 105–7; on David and Goliath, 98–99; on Exodus, 99–100; as global forum, 96–97; on Islam, 104; Lost Boys stories, 97–98; martial theology of, 98–109; on NIF and Arabs, 100–103
Suakin, 61–62
Sudan: history of, 26–28; independence, 1, 52, 63–64; and South Africa, 6–7
Sudan African National Union (SANU), 71–73, 76
Sudan Council of Churches, 85, 86, 93, 111
Sudan Defence Force, 48, 64

Sudanese Christian Association in East Africa (SCAEA), 76–77, 165n36
Sudanese in Diaspora (SID), 98
"The Sudan Laugh" (Abuk), 107
Sudan People's Liberation Movement/Army (SPLM/SPLA): Christian language and, 90; and church, 92; and Cush, 105–10; Dinka-Nuer conflict within, 93–94; Garang and, 3; international activism and, 94–98; Mayardit and, 3; Muslims in, 104–5; Mengistu and, 91–92; NIF and, 91; Radio SPLA, 93; SSDF and, 116; women and, 102–3. *See also* South Sudan, civil war
Sunday Protests, 70–71

Taban, Joseph, 16, 139–40
Tafeng, Emedio, 61, 84–85
Taha, ʿAli Osman Muhammad, 110–11
Telar, Moses, 128–29
te Riele, Herman, 78
Tombe, Enoch, 127, 132–33
Tongun, Daniel, 52–53, 65
Torit Mutiny, 45–46, 53–66
Tounsel, Timeka, 139, 174n6
translation, 33–34, 37
Trump, Donald, 138
Tuombuk, Joseph de, 131–32
Turabi, Hasan al-, 90, 92
Tut, Kong, 131
Tutu, Desmond, 6–7

Uganda, 48–49, 73, 75, 78, 80–83, 101, 114, 124–25, 137–38
UN Security Council, 123–25

van der Veer, Peter, 154n60
vernacular languages, 34–37

Wako, Gabriel Zubeir, 126
Watkins, Owen S., 101
Watts, Ian, 32, 38, 41
Weanzana, Nupanga, 110
Wheeler, Andrew, 76, 86, 101–2
White-Hammond, Gloria, 95